Govind Ballabh Pant

Govind Ballabh Pant

Series Editor
Dr. M.H. Syed

Editor
R.K. Singh **P.K. Choudhry**

Himalaya Books Pvt. Ltd.

'Ramdoot', Dr. Bhalerao Marg, Girgaon, Mumbai - 400 004
Tel : (022) 23863863, Fax : (022) 23877178
Email : himpub@vsnl.com

First Edition : 2011

Published by : H.B.P.L.
"Pooja Apartments", 4-B, Murari Lal Street, Ansari Road,
Darya Ganj, New Delhi-110 002
Phones : 23270392, 23278631 Reliance : 30180392 to 396
Fax : 011-23256286 Email : hphdel@vsnl.com

Sole Distributers : HIMALAYA PUBLISHING HOUSE PVT. LTD.

Branch Offices

Mumbai : "Ramdoot", Dr. Bhalerao Marg, Girgaon, Mumbai-400 004.
Phones : 23860170/23863863 Fax : 022-23877178
Email : himpub@vsnl.com
Website : www.himpub.com

Nagpur : Kundanlal Chandak Industrial Estate, Ghat Road, **Nagpur 440-018.**
Phone: 2738731, 3296733 Telefax : 0712-2721215

Bengaluru : No. 16/1 (Old 12/1), 1st Floor, Next to Hotel Highlands,
Madhava Nagar, Race Course Road, **Bengaluru - 560 001.**
Phone : 22281541, 22385461, Telefax: 080-22286611

Hyderabad : No. 3-4-184, Lingampally, Besides Raghavendra Swamy Matham,
Kachiguda, **Hyderabad - 500 027.** Phone: 040-27560041,
27550139, Mobile:- 09848130433 Telefax: 040-27560041

Chennai : No. 85/50, Bazullah Road, T. Nagar, **Chennai - 600 017.**
Phone: 044-28344020, 32463737, 42124860

Pune : No. 527, "Laksha" Apartment, First Floor, Mehunpura,
Shaniwarpeth, (Near Prabhat Theatre), **Pune - 411 030.**
Phone: 020-24496323/24496333/32326733

Lucknow : Jai Baba Bhawan, Near Dr. Sanjiv Awasthi, Church Road,
Kurshi Road, Aliganj, **Lucknow - 226 024.**
Phone: 9305302158, 9415349385

Ahmedabad : No. 114, "SHAIL", 1st Floor, Opp. Madhu Sudan House, C.G.Road,
Navrang Pura, **Ahmedabad – 380 009.**
Phone: 079-26560126, Mobiles: 09327324149,09314679413

Ernakulam : No. 39/104 A, Lakshmi Apartment, Karikkamuri Cross Rd.,
Ernakulam, **Cochin – 682011**, Kerala.
Phone: 0484-2378012, 2378016, Mob.: 09344199799

Bhubaneswar : 5 Station Square, **Bhubaneswar (Orissa) - 751 001.**
Mobile: 9861046007, E-mail:-orissa@himpub.com

Indore : Kesardeep Avenue Extension, 73, Narayan Bagh, Flat No. 302,
IIIrd Floor, Near Humpty Dumpty School, Narayan Bagh,
Indore (M.P.) 452 007 Mobile: 09301386468

Kolkata : 108/4, Beliaghata, Main Road, Near ID Hospital, Opp. SBI Bank
Kolkata - 700 010. Mobile: 09910440956

Printed at : Shri Krishna offset Press Delhi-93

Preface

Biography, is now a form of literature, very much in vogue. In fact, biography is a description or account of someone's life and the times, which is usually published in the form of a book. A biography is more than a mention of personal facts (life, education, work, relationships and death), it also portrays the subject's experience of events. Technically speaking, a work is biographical, if it covers, all of a person's life. Biography writing has a long history. A biography is real. Ancient Greeks developed the biographical tradition, which we have inherited, although until the 5th century AD, when the word 'biographia' first appeared, in Damascius' "Life of Isodorus," biographical pieces were called simply "lives". It is quite likely that the Greeks were drawing on a pre-existing eastern tradition. Certainly Herodotus' "Histories" contains more detailed biographical information on Persian kings and subjects. The earliest surviving pieces, which we would identify as biographical are Isocrates' "Life of Evagoras" and Xenophon's "Life of Agesilaos," both from the fifth century BC. "Parallel Lives" by Plutarch, a Greek writing under the Roman empire, is a series of short biographies of eminent men.

The Golden Age of English biography emerged in late eighteenth century, the century in which the terms "biography" and "autobiography" entered English lexicon. The classic works of the period were Samuel Johnson's "Critical Lives of the Poets" and James Boswell's "Massive Life of Johnson". Generally American biography followed English model. By World War I, cheap hardcover reprints had become popular. The decade of the 1920s witnessed a biographical 'boom'. Later, biographical writings developed a lot and today biographies are written and compiled in the finest form of the genre. In India too, biography, as a form of literature has been evolved, cultivated and polished over the years. Here is an effort to promote this tradition further.

This series of biographies of great men, great women and celebrities in all walks of life is an adventurous academic endeavour, in its own right. A team of researchers and compilers has worked for a good period of time to accomplish the project. For this purpose, hundreds of books by eminent authors and editors have been consulted and referred to. We have benefited from various works, liberally, in order to illustrate and enrich this effort of ours. Present book is devoted to the great personality of Govind Ballabh Pant.

Govind Ballabh Pant was a great freedom fighter, an important political leader from Uttar Pradesh and a forerunner in the movement to establish Hindi as the national language of India. He began his career, as a lawyer in Kashipur (now in Uttarakhand). In 1921, he entered politics and was elected to the Legislative Assembly of the United Provinces. He was arrested and imprisoned for several times. In 1935, Pant joined the new Legislative Council, as a member. After independence in 1947, Pant became Chief Minister of Uttar Pradesh. Among his achievements in that position, was the abolition of the zamindari system. He was called to join as Union Home Minister, after Patel's death. In 1957, he was awarded the Bharat Ratna.

This is a compact and comprehensive account of the above mentioned great life, which is bound to attract the attention of scholars, researchers, students and the general readers, alike. Let's hope this humble effort would receive a warm welcome and due applause.

— ***Editors***

Contents

1

An Illustrious Life

The Backdrop

All of you know that the Himalayan mountains extend from Jammu and Kashmir in the northwest to Arunachal Pradesh in the northeast of India. From time immemorial these majestic mountains have stood in silent grandeur guarding the northern frontiers of India. If you look at the map of India you will notice that these mountains stretch from northwest to northeast forming a semicircle. That is why an imaginative poet has described the Himalayas as a beautiful crown worn by Mother India.

'Himalaya' literally means the abode of snow; but many legends are current in Indian mythology about the sacredness and greatness of these mountains.

The sacred Ganga originates in this abode of snow and a number of holy shrines and temples have sprung up on its route since remote antiquity. Surely you have heard of Gangotri and Badrinath temples situated in the mid-Himalayan ranges in Uttar Pradesh.

People from distant corners of India from Kanyakumari to Gujarat, from Orissa to Maharashtra and from Bengal to Jammu and Kashmir, visit these temples and places of pilgrimage.

The Home State

The State which is now called Uttar Pradesh is geographically the heart of India. It is one of the ingredient states of the Indian Republic and has always occupied an important place in the history of the country. It has been the cradle of religious, cultural, historical and political movements and represents the best synthesis of Hindu and Muslim cultures. Its language today is the language of the Republic. The two provinces of Agra and Oudh were combined in 1877 and twenty-five years later the combined area became known as the United Provinces.

To the north are lofty Himalayas covered with eternal snow. Their loftiest peaks can be seen from a great distance; Mt. Everest 29,002 ft, Nanga Parvat 26,000 ft, Nanda Devi 25,000 and Dhaulagiri 26,000 ft. They abound in magnificent sceneries and one is simply charmed by the picturesque beauty. One great English civilian who was employed in Kumaon for ten years in earlier part of his life and spent many summers in the higher regions of the Himalays wrote:

> "I have seen much of European mountains, but in stupendous sublimity, combined with magnificent and luxuriant beauty, I have seen nothing that can be compared with the Himalays."

The Kumaon Division which is situated in the north in the Himalayan tract included three districts of Almora, Nainital and Garhwal with an area of more than 12,000 square miles. Its whole surface is covered by mountains, which rise with strange suddenness. In one of its valleys lies the most beautiful lake of India around which the Queen of hill stations, the city of Nainital, is situated.

In the opening years of the 19th century the British Government gained the most valuable portion comprising the present Kumaon Division under its control by the treaty of Sigauli which closed the Nepal War in 1815.

In early times Kumaon was divided into small principalities. The first dynasty to achieve consolidated dominion over Kumaon was the Chand dynasty. The traditional founder of this dominion was Som Chand of Jhunsi, on the Ganges near Allahabad, who in about the 7th century married the daughter of Katyuri Raja, then holding sway in the interior of Kumaon. Champawat in Almora district and the land in the Tarai and Bhabar in Nairn Tal district were given as the lady's dowry. Champawat was thus the nucleus from which the Chand Dominion expanded over the whole of Kumaon.

Pants originally belong to Maharashtra and they were Brahmins of high class. The ancestors of Pandit Pant— Jai Dev Pant of Bhardwaj Gitra, during the reign of Chand Kings in the 10th century, came to north for a pilgrimage to Badrinath. He was accompanied by his sister's husband, Dinker Rao Pant and one Surya Dixit. They visited the holy places, and were so much attracted by the beautiful sights, bracing climate and the pretty panorama of the snow clad mountains that they abandoned the idea of returning.

They visited the court of the then ruler of Gangoli, who honoured them and asked them to stay in his court. They thus settled there, and since then twenty five generations have passed. Pants are now classed in four sects after the names of four brothers who received recognition in the courts of Kumaon rulers. The descendants of the just three Pant families are strictly vegetarians. Pants though do not eat meat, but intermarry with Tiwaris, Joshis, Pandeys and Bhatts. Their women irrespective of their gotra do not cat meat. Their daughters may, if they like, eat meat after their marriages in the families of their husbands. Pants produced many notable scholars, poets and physicians.

In the year 1887 in the wings of the snow covered mountains of the Himalays in the Almora district on September 10, Anant Chaudas, in a small village in a far remote northern corner— called by the name Khoot in the valley of Shayahidevi Hill in humble surroundings saw the birth of this dynamic personality who was to rule the hearts of millions and was to play such a great part in the history of his country.

The year 1887 marked the beginning of an epoch in the history of modern India. The whole world stood at the verge of a new era. It was the year of the first Jubilee of Queen Victoria's rule.

It saw the rise of new nationalism in India and new Trade Unionism in England. The Indian National Congress was only a baby of two years. Gandhiji had passed his Matriculation Examination. Gladstone, Cobden and Bright were breathing a new spirit of liberalism in British politics. The thinkers like Mill, Spencer and Carlyle were revolutionising society with new theories of social reconstruction. In this year two great institutions were established which had profound association with the future life of Pandit Pant; first the foundation of the Allahabad University from which he graduated and other the establishment of the U.P. Legislative Council. The latter was the scene of his laurels, of which he was the leader for more than 35 years, first in opposition and afterwards on the Treasury benches. It was the arena of his joys, of his triumphs, of his great speeches in memorable debates.

Conditions around Birth

At the dawn of the 20th century, India was struggling with new ideas, new hopes, new aspirations and new ambitions. This was the period of national Renaissance. Lord Curzon was then the Governor-General. He was a great reformer. He was also a great imperialist. In his time he had launched the biggest reforms of the century. He laid the foundation of the nation building departments for improving the lot of the toiling masses and increasing the material prosperity of the country. He arrived in India with a programme of twelve reforms.

In his first budget speech in 1899 he made a mention of twelve subjects of his original programme which he doubled afterwards. All our reforms originated in his days and they are imperishable monument of his genius, ability and imagination. For generations land revenue policy was the subject of bitter controversy. The Government was charged with taking an undue share of the produce of the soil. R. C. Putt, whose works: "The Economic History of India" under early British rule and Victorian age- had stirred the young minds, wrote a series of open letters. Lord Curzon enunciated the Government's policy in his famous resolution of 1902. He appointed various committees and commissions for improvement in agriculture, cooperation, irrigation and university education. He realised the extent of the evil of the agriculturists indebtedness, which he had characterised as "a canker eating into the vitals of the national life." To give them relief he enacted legislation and started cooperative credit societies and also created agricultural banks. He established an Imperial Agriculture Department. He founded the Agriculture Institute at Pusa for agricultural education and research. He secured a donation of £40,000 from a generous American friend.

Legislation was enacted to facilitate the reconstruction of the universities. Police was overhauled. Commerce and Industry Departments were created. India was flooded by bounty fed beet sugar from the continent while its great sugar cane languished.

Much was done in his time. "No Viceroy has ever played a part larger than the part played by Lord Curzon" wrote Lovett in his History of Indian Nationalist Movement. It was an irony of history that a man of such tremendous intellect, great energy and profound vision should be a tragic figure in history. The partition of Bengal so much agitated the minds of the people and gave a great flip to Indian Nationalism. He did not follow the advice which he gave. "The first temptation that you should avoid," he told the graduates of the University of Calcutta in February, 1902, "is that of letting words be your masters instead of being masters of your words." But the knowledge of the existence of a particular pitfall is not always sufficient to prevent a man from stumbling into it. He himself fell down when he attacked the ethics of the East and wounded the feelings of the people by his uncalled for sweeping indictment.

The chief danger of which Curzon warned his young audience was a temptation to minimise the importance of adhering rigidly, in all the varied circumstances of life, to truth. There were many guises in which this particular temptation presented itself. Flattery was one, vituperation was another. Flattery was only too often a deliberate attempt to deceive—to get something out of some one else by playing upon the commonest foible of human nature. But it seemed to him that in India the danger of the opposite extreme was greater still. He exhorted. "Let those who were now going further from the portals of the university be on their guard against these dangers. Do not exaggerate; do not flatter; do not slander; do not impute; but turn naturally to truth as the magnets to the pole."

Curzon was enunciating a great truth which he wanted to advise his young friends. All would have been well if he would have stopped there. He continued and laid considerable emphasis on the fact that the highest ideal of truth was to a large extent a western conception. He said: "But undoubtedly truth took a high place in the moral codes of the west before it had been similarly honoured in the East."

This gave rise to a storm of denunciation. In the next day's edition an enterprising subeditor of the Amrita Bazar Patrika turned the tables by publishing the following extract from Lord Curzon's book 'Problems of the Far East':

> "Before proceeding the royal audience I enjoyed an interview with the President of the Korean Foreign office
>
> "I remember some of his questions and answers.
>
> "Having been particularly warned not to admit to him that I was only thirty-three years old, an age to which no respect attaches in Korea, when he put to me the straight question, 'How old are you?' I unhesitatingly replied, 'Forty'.
>
> "Dear me,' he said 'you look very young for that. How do you account for it.?'
>
> "By the fact,' I replied, 'that I have been travelling for a month in the superb climate of His Majesty's Dominions.'
>
> "Finally he said to me, 'I presume you are a near relative of Her Majesty the Queen of England.'
>
> "No", I replied 'I am not.'
>
> "But observing the look of disgust that passed over his countenance, I was fain to add, 'I am, however, as yet an unmarried man with which unscrupulous suggestion I completely regained the old gentleman's favour."

This caused great sensation, and this self-admission condemned Lord Curzon.

This passage was omitted from the later editions of the book. Lord Curzon had not the slightest intention to insult the Indian people. The whole incident was most unfortunate. He said it at a time, and his indiscretion condemned him when the atmosphere of hostility was fostered against him in India and England.

Four months later with echoes of the clamour still ringing in his cars he gave vent to his feelings of astonishment in a letter to the Secretary of State for India:

> "My convocation address to Bengali students was travestied as an attack upon the character and scriptures of the entire nation,
> A more unscrupulous and mendacious agitation it is impossible to conceive."

Such were the times and such were the feelings which agitated the minds of students. Henry George's 'Progress and Poverty' made a tremendous impression in USA and Britain. No book ever written on the social problems made so many converts. Economic facts and theories have never been presented in such an attractive way. The author was not a socialist but his book led many to socialism. Student Pant quoted from this book while speaking in debates. He felt that so long as the social system was based upon exploitation, the mass of the people remained poor. Poverty according to him was the greatest social evil. To eradicate was the greatest problem.

Family Background

The ancestors of Govind Ballabh Pant came from Maharashtra nearly a thousand years ago on pilgrimage to these holy places, and enchanted by their beauty decided to settle down on the Himalayan foothills, in the Kumaon hills in Uttar Pradesh.

When the British ruled over these hilly regions in the nineteenth century, a number of hill-stations, as they were called, were developed. That is how the townships of Shimla in Himachal Pradesh, Nainital in Uttar Pradesh, Darjeeling in West Bengal,

Ootacamund in the South, Mahabaleshwar in Maharashtra, Panchmarhi in Madhya Pradesh, to mention a few of them, were established by the British. As you know, the British came from a very cold climate and could not bear the summer heat of India and hence they spent nearly five to six months in a year in these towns, which served as summer capitals of respective provinces.

In Uttar Pradesh, in the Kumaon hills, are situated Nainital, Almora and Kashipur, which are well-known hill-stations. The beautiful landscape of the Kumaon hills enchanted every visitor. It is sheer joy to breathe the cool, fresh air and listen to the rustling sound of the wind blowing across the deep valleys and lush green forests of the mountains. Equally captivating is the music of gurgling spring waters flowing down from the mountain ranges towards the plains. The people of the hills therefore love nature. They love music and dance too, which are essential parts of their social life. Govind Ballabh Pant was also very fond of music.

The joy of living in the land of beauty, however, was marred by the harshness of the realities of life. To eke out a living in these regions was not easy. Unlike in the plains, only the hill slopes near the rivers and springs are fit for cultivation and crops are produced after a good deal of labour. You know, in the Gangetic basin of Uttar Pradesh crops are produced in plenty and with much less labour. People in the hills were not very rich. Agriculture, rearing of cattle like sheep, goats and milch cows were their principal occupations. Rice, jawar, bajra, vegetables and occasionally, some wheat were grown. Coarse woollen clothes were manufactured along with some handicrafts. The economy of the towns was mostly dependent on the population which came on pilgrimage or visits to these hill-stations and the goods of everyday needs were transported to the hills from the plains.

In the nineteenth century, as the British rule penetrated into these areas, roads were constructed, linking up several towns. Bungalows for the British were built. Schools run by Christian missions were started and courts and police establishments were set up for administration, and the economy began to flourish. But the people of the hills, by and large, remained poor, their demands were few and they led a simple rural life. Only the landed gentry and the merchant class thrived along with the administrators.

As for the ancestors of Govind Ballabh Pant, the story was different. Most of them were able and well-educated according to the standards of those days and enjoyed the patronage of the rulers of the land. In the nineteenth century, when the British ruled over the Kumaon hills, Govind Ballabh Pant's father, Manorath Pant and maternal grandfather, Badri Dutt Joshi, were men of means and held positions of importance in the British administration of Kumaon.

Badri Dutt Joshi, maternal grandfather of Govind Ballabh Pant, was a Sadr Amin and a great confidant of Sir Henry Ramsay, Commissioner of Kumaon. Joshi was a wealthy man and lived in style and enjoyed considerable power in the area. Pant's father was also appointed to a fairly good position in the Almora court, who later rose to be a Revenue Collector, in Kumaon. When he was transferred to Kashipur from Almora, he left behind his wife and the child (Govind) to be looked after by the joint household of Joshi.

Birth and Early Life

Govind Ballabh Pant was born at Almora, on Sep. 10, 1887. Govind Ballabh was a bright child and learnt his alphabet at home. Till the age of ten, he received education from private tutors, under the care of his maternal grandfather. He was deeply interested in his studies, and through his intelligence, he acquired sufficient mastery in mathematics. In 1897, he joined the Primary School of Ramsay College, Almora. In all his class examinations he did very well, and passed with credits. It is said that the mathematics teacher of his school was greatly impressed by him and whenever the teacher was unable to solve a problem, Govind was called upon to solve it, and however difficult the sum might have been, he always succeeded in his effort.

Govind Ballabh did not play many games himself, but was fond of sports. He would watch others play, and at times, he was asked to act as a referee by his schoolmates. It shows that his friends had faith in his judgement, sense of fairplay and impartiality. Govind loved walking and took to horse riding. In addition, he had a passion for music, which he retained even when he was grown up and studied in the college. He records in his diary, which he maintained while he was a student at Allahabad University, that every morning he used to practise music at least for half an hour.

He took part in debates in the school and formed a debating society at Ramsay College. Govind, along with a few friends, founded a secret society called Happy Club, where the members discussed politics of the day. The Happy Club was not a revolutionary society, but during those days political discussions were not encouraged by schools and colleges run by the British. Later, when he grew older, he participated in debates held at Almora Akhbar Building. He was a good debater. In the college, he excelled in this skill and was known for his eloquence and oratory full of persuasive arguments.

In 1899, Badri Dutt Joshi died, which was a great shock to the family and specially to Govind Ballabh Pant, who was deeply attached to him, and who had been his mentor and a source of inspiration. With the death of Joshi, the family fortunes also dwindled to an extent.

Occasionally, during these quiet days, some distinguished persons visited Almora and addressed public meetings. Among them were Swami Vivekananda, Motilal Nehru, Dr. Bhagwan Das and Annie Besant.

You have, no doubt, heard the names of these great leaders. Swami Vivekananda was a great religious preacher who attended the Conference of World Religions in America in 1893. There he delivered speeches on the philosophical basis of Hinduism and greatness of Indian culture. The people of the West, who listened to him with great interest, were thrilled and began appreciating Indian culture. Swami Vivekananda was considered as the greatest exponent of Indian religious and philosophical texts. He instilled in Indians a sense of pride in the greatness of India and its culture.

Annie Besant was an Irish woman who joined the Theosophical Society in India and was deeply interested in Indian philosophy, religion and culture. She rose to become an important leader of the Indian National Congress, which demanded freedom for India. She started the Home Rule League, demanding self-government for the Indian people. Motilal Nehru was an eminent leader of the

Indian National Congress, a friend of Annie Besant, Mahatma Gandhi and other great men of his times, and a renowned lawyer. He was father of Jawaharlal Nehru. Dr. Bhagwan Das was a learned man and a philosopher. He lived in Benaras.

These great leaders inspired the young by their learning, wisdom, idealism, sincerity of purpose and patriotism. Govind was deeply moved by listening to them. He read on a wide range of subjects as a student in Almora. He also read through newspapers with care and discussed topics of interest with his friends. In 1905, he passed the Intermediate examination from Ramsay College, standing 20th in Kumaon, earning a scholarship of Rs. 20 per month. He would have done better in the examination had he not suffered from a heart attack in 1904, at the young age of seventeen.

Childhood

Since, the father of the child, Pandit Manorath Pant, was in government service in Garhwal district and therefore, was away from his home village. Shortly after the mother moved with the little child and her elder daughter to her maternal village Chakata, near Bhimtal, nine miles from Nainital. His four years were spent in this village, noted for its beauty and sceneries, surrounded by lakes like Naukachiyatal—"the lake of nine corners".

At the age of four he came to Almora to live with his maternal grandfather, Rai Bahadur Badri Dutt Joshi who was Judicial Officer of Kumaon. His father was still in Garhwal, and it was not possible for him to take the family there. He came to Almora often. His maternal grandfather looked after his elementary education.

Schooling

Young Govind showed considerable aptitude for studies at school. He passed his Middle examination in the first division. He also secured a first division in the Matriculation Examination. In his English paper there was a question — "What is a maiden speech?". The boy then little knew that he would often make and hear the maiden speeches. He remembered the some ingenious answers given by the students who answered a maiden speech as "a female speech," "a speech made by a maid," "a well made speech," "a speech in chaste language," and "a speech as one requiring a great deal of consider.

Secondary Education

He passed his Intermediate examination in 1905 from the Ramsay College, Almora. This college which has done immense service for the cause of education in the far off hill districts of U.P. was commenced in 1850 by the Rev. J. H. Budden on behalf of the London Missionary Society. In 1871, the handsome building in which it is housed was opened. Rev. E. S. Oakley was its principal and professor of English and many of us read his English text books in our school days. Rathee was the teacher in Mathematics. Pant secured a scholarship in the Intermediate examination and his people decided to send him to Allahabad. In the Intermediate class he was known as Govind Ballabh Maharashtra.

Higher Education

After passing the Intermediate examination, he went to Allahabad and joined Muir College. In the B.A. course he took mathematics, politics and English literature. Professor Cox, who taught mathematics, was attracted by him for his gifts in mathematics.

Allahabad University was one of the finest universities in India. There were only five universities in India then. They were: Calcutta, Bombay, Madras, Punjab and Allahabad. Besides, Allahabad was the capital of Uttar Pradesh. It had a High Court and the legal profession was greatly valued. Eminent lawyers were members of the Allahabad Bar; among whom were Madan Mohan Malaviya, Motilal Nehru, Tej Bahadur Sapru, Sunderlal and a large number of public figures. All of them took part in the Indian struggle for freedom. Govind Ballabh Pant took full advantage of this great opportunity of being a student in Allahabad. He studied hard, but also took part in all kinds of university campus activities.

Allahabad was also a centre of political activity. In 1905, Lord Curzon, the Viceroy of India, partitioned Bengal in two parts on communal lines. East Bengal had a Muslim majority, whereas in West Bengal, Hindus were in majority. The partition of Bengal was considered by Indian people as a deliberate attempt on the part of the British government to destroy the unity of Indian people. Partition of Bengal was opposed by the entire nation. Numerous protest meetings, processions and demonstrations, were held in Calcutta and different towns of Bengal. Rakhi was exchanged between Hindus and Muslims as a bond of brotherhood and as a symbol of national unity. The song, *Bande Mataram,* which was prohibited by the government, was sung in every part of the country defying the government orders. People greeted each other with *Bande Mataram.* A beginning in Swadeshi movement was made in Bengal, when British goods were boycotted for the first time.

There was a lot of excitement in Allahabad and Govind Ballabh as a boy of eighteen was deeply influenced by these events. The annual session of the Indian National Congress was held at Benaras in December 1905. Gopal Krishna Gokhale, a member of the Central Legislative Council, was one *of* the most eminent leaders of the time, who presided over the Congress. Govind Ballabh attended the Congress session and served as a volunteer, in spite of his weak Constitution. In 1907, Gokhale visited Allahabad again. A public meeting was held with Motilal Nehru in the chair. The entire community of students of Allahabad University attended the meeting. Govind Ballabh was one of them.

The same year, when the Kumbha Mela was held at Allahabad, he again volunteered for social service. The Congress used to organise such service to help millions of pilgrims who gathered for bathing in the *sangam* of the Ganga, Yamuna and Saraswati rivers. In the evenings, taking advantage of such large gathering of people, the Congress held meetings, and speeches were delivered, exhorting the people to unite against the British rule and fight for freedom. Govind Ballabh made a fiery speech at one of these gatherings and as a result, Principal Jennings of Muir College, issued orders debarring him from taking the examination. Principal Jennings was an Englishman who did not sympathise with Indian aspirations. This upset Govind Ballabh's preparation for his B.A. examination. His mathematics teacher, Prof. Cox, who was fond of him, intervened and appealed to the Principal to show leniency towards Govind Ballabh and he was finally allowed to appear in the examination. He passed his B.A. examination in the second division.

Soon after, he joined the Law College, which was a part of Muir College itself. Eminent lawyers like Tej Bahadur Sapru and Mohan Lal Nehru were professors of law. Govind Ballabh was a brilliant student of law and stood first in the law examination in 1909, winning the Lumsden Gold Medal of Allahabad University.

During these formative years, he emerged as an all-rounder. He listened to the great leaders of Indian National Congress. He wrote in his diary about their visits to Allahabad University, and noted the names of Lala Lajpat Rai, Surendranath Banerji, Rash Bihari Ghosh, and that he saw Gokhale from close quarters. Madan Mohan Malaviya was another great leader. He founded Banaras Hindu University and started journals and newspapers for political awakening. Thus, Govind Ballabh's training in politics began, while he was still in the college.

He also read widely. In addition to his subject of study, which was Law, he was attracted by the writings of great authors like Tolstoy, Maxim Gorky, Bacon, Emerson, James Mill and John Stuart Mill and other men of literature and science. At the same time, he did not forget reading through the *Rig Veda, Quran* and *Bible,* specially the Sermon on the Mount. He took pride in being an Indian and believed in the composite culture of India.

As has been said, Govind Ballabh maintained a diary, in which he recorded his thoughts and feelings everyday. Only a few diaries of his student days are available. It is interesting to read a page from his diary of February 1908, in which he made the following resolutions: I shall learn at least 15 new notes of music. I shall practise truth and gentlemanliness. I shall write loving letters—to dear ones. I shall not smoke from today.

He wrote about the books which he read, the lessons which he must complete, and many more matters of personal nature, including that he must take more care of his health.

It is obvious from the above story that Govind Ballabh had grown as a young man full of idealism and patriotism. His love for the motherland and the society which he decided to serve became deeper and deeper as he grew older. He was a handsome youth, six feet tall, with large eyes and a serene face. With his pleasing manners, he won everybody's friendship. He seldom offended any of his friends in the school or college. He was a young man of great courage.

His life as a young man was rather sad. Yet, he faced life with great courage and strength of will. In spite of socioreligious reform movements and impact of Western ideas, Indian society in the nineteenth century continued to be orthodox in its attitude to social problems. Practices like child marriage were prevalent and children often at the age of ten or twelve were married. Govind Ballabh was married in 1899 at the age of twelve. In 1908, when he was about 21 years old and still studying at the college, Govind Ballabh became the father of a son. Within a few months, however, the child died and soon after his wife also expired.

These happenings were normal in those days. There were not many hospitals or qualified doctors. In small towns and hilly areas, the condition was even worse. The British government in India, being a foreign government, was interested in the collection of revenue and maintenance of law and order. It was not a welfare-oriented state. Disease, epidemic and famines ravaged many parts of India from time to time and millions of people died of cholera, smallpox, plague, malaria and influenza. Floods and droughts also took their heavy tolls. It is, therefore, no wonder that mortality among children and women was very high. In India today, the conditions are different. We are a modern nation. Application of science in agriculture and industry has brought prosperity to people. Medical facilities have reached literally every home. Education has transformed the people's attitudes to life. But the story of the Indian society of the last century was depressing.

Govind Ballabh was persuaded to marry again in 1912. In 1914, his wife gave birth to a son, but both of them died within a few months. You will notice, that there was so much unhappiness in the life of young Govind Ballabh Pant. His father died of cholera in 1913 at the age of 46. His sister became a widow at a young age. In a few years he lost his mother also. Before her death, she persuaded Govind Ballabh to marry again. He remarried in 1916. Fortunately, from this marriage, three children were born; one of them Krishna Chandra Pant, was a Cabinet Minister at the Centre. Govind Ballabh had suffered from a heart attack in 1904 when he was just a boy of 17. Although he recovered from the attack, he continued to complain of chest pain. In 1909, he fell from a horse. This caused him a serious injury, and the pain in the back never left him. In 1928, during the Simon Commission demonstration at Lucknow, he received lathi blows on the nape of his neck, and the back and shoulders. As a result, he suffered from pain in the neck and the back throughout his life. He narrowly escaped direct lathi blows on his head. If he had received one, he might have met with the same fate which awaited Lala Lajpat Rai. Lala Lajpat Rai died in 1928 as a result of lathi blows received during the Simon Commission agitation at Lahore. In spite of these mishaps, personal bereavements and sufferings, Govind Ballabh remained a cheerful man, maintaining a robust sense of humour and continued to perform his duties as a student with a sense of dedication. Indeed, these adversities made him a braver man and he pledged himself to serve his motherland with greater determination and devotion.

India is one country. The apparent variety in its culture, and diversity in its customs have always been beautifully and organically linked together. This bond of oneness has to be strengthened and developed.

Allahabad University Days

> "Allahabad has always held a position of unsurpassed eminence in the annals of our country. Several of our foremost leaders were born here. Jawaharlal Nehru, the idol of the people, who is steering the ship of State with consummate skill against many opposing forces also has his home in Allahabad. Allahabad has seen the synthesis of the culture of India from the days the Aryans settled here. Prayag, 'the place of sacrifice,' has fully maintained its traditions by its varied and great sacrifices on the altar of freedom. Here we have

> a number of great relics, full of archaeological interest and importance. Just close to us is the Bharadwaj Ashram, the hermitage where thousands of years ago Rishi Bharadwaj entertained Ram and Lakshman. There within the fort founded by Akbar on the banks of the Ganges and the Jamuna stands the pillar of Ashoka. And not far from it one sees what is known as the Proclamation Pillar. These monuments remind us of the various epochs of India's history and embrace within their compass the myriad events and happenings of several centuries."

In the year 1905 when Pt. Pant was nearly eighteen years of age, he went to join Muir Central College of Allahabad for further studies. The College was one of the premier constituent colleges of the Allahabad University. It was founded in 1870-71 by Sir William Muir, built in a modified saracenic style. Jennings was the Principal of the College who continued upto 1913. Pant had Mathematics and Politics with English as his subjects. Randle and A.C. Mukerji were his teachers in English and Homersham Cox and Umesh Chand Ghosh in Mathematics. Cox who died in 1918 was not only a mathematician of very exceptional capacity but also brought an incisive mind to bear on all questions affecting the University. The teachers were of high character and influenced students greatly.

Student Pant got a room in the Macdonell Hindu Boarding House. It was then built by the efforts of Pt. Madan Mohan Malaviya. He took great interest in the welfare of the inmates of the hostel. Now this Hostel is named after Malaviyaji and has been converted into a Tutorial University College, the opening ceremony of which was performed by Pt. Pant in 1949. The students had the opportunity to meet Malaviyaji at his house. He used to come to the Hostel very frequently. Thus the students were influenced and inspired by his lofty idealism, his highly critical and cultivated mind, by his noble example and precept.

Forty years later at the death of Malaviyaji, speaking in U. P. Assembly Pt. Pant with tears in his eyes in a reminiscent mood paid the following respectful tribute:

"It is difficult for me to pay my humble tribute to the memory of the late Pandit Madan Mohan Malaviya, one of the greatest of men ever born and one at whose feet I received my first lesson in public life. He was one about whom one could say that the elements combined to invest him with a perfect personality. In him were combined all those virtues which go to make a man a gentleman and a great man. He devoted more than sixty years of his active life to the service of the people of this country. Every minute of his existence was dedicated to the betterment of the lot of the people of India as a whole. He combined in himself gentleness with firmness. He was pure in thought, pure in mind, pure in character, pure inaction and pure in behaviour. If there was anyone about whom one could say that he never consciously did anything wrong, it was, I believe, revered Pandit Malaviya. He represented and embodied in himself the ancient culture of this land in all its richness and all its varieties. Though orthodox in his views, he was never sectarian nor narrow minded. He possessed the most liberal outlook and overflowed with that milk of human kindness and sympathy which one rarely finds in human nature. He was a doughty fighter in the cause of *Swaraj* and independence. There was no good cause which did not receive his loving assistance and sympathy. Where he did not work himself actively he placed those who wanted to work in a good cause. Neither the young nor the old had ever any dread of that great man and they all approached him. Even the students of schools and colleges approached him as one would have approached one's own father and they never met at his hands anything except affection and kindliness. He was a great orator and his silver tongue oratory was the byword not only in our land but also in countries outside. He was of the sweetest of men endowed with that reasonableness and regard for other men's point of view which marked a cultured

> man from a fanatic. He had that profound faith in the destinies of our country which ever made him a robust optimist even in the midst of dense gloom. He devoted his talents exclusively to the service of others; his activities were not confined to the political field alone. His name will ever be enshrined in the history of this country as one of the most distinguished architects of modern India. He built up many institutions but one which claimed most of his attention in the latter part of his life is the Banaras Hindu University which will be a monument of his energy, his zeal, his patriotism, his constructive genius and the influence which he commanded over all sections of the people in this country. I find it difficult to say more about him. In fact I had to exercise a great degree of restraint on myself in order to be able even to utter these few words. His soul will ever be there to inspire us and with his blessings we will soon achieve the goal for which he worked, for which he lived and for which he died."

The minds of the people were agitated on the Bengal partition issue. Seventh August 1905 was observed for boycott of foreign goods and the students at Allahabad had taken enthusiastic interest in it. The 21st session of the Indian National Congress was held at Banaras in December 1905 under the presidentship of Gopal Krishna Gokhale. Student Pant went to Banaras to attend the Congress session as a volunteer. This was the first occasion of his life to witness such a political gathering, and it influenced his young mind. The feelings of that time were aptly mirrored in the introduction to the proceedings of the Banaras Congress Session published then. It said "India was declared to be distracted, discontented, despondent, the victim of many misfortunes, political and others."

Gokhale came *to* Allahabad in February 1907 when Pant was in the B. A. final class. He addressed a public meeting which was presided by Pt. Motilal Nehru. Gokhale spoke for more than an hour on the work that lay before them. The speech had a profound effect on Pant. He mentioned it twenty years after in his address at the U.P. Political Conference in 1927. In his speech Gokhale had advised that the service of the motherland should become a great and overmastering a passion and that young men should give up all thought of personal advancement and devote themselves in the spirit of sacrifice to the service of the motherland. Pant decided to carve out an independent profession for himself. The wish of his elders was that he should become a deputy collector but he pressed to be a lawyer. He began public speaking outside the princints of the University. He made speeches at the Kumbh Mela. The university authorities took a serious view and disallowed him to take the examination. He thought that a year was lost but due to the intervention of prominent persons he was permitted at the last moment.

He joined the LL.B. class in 1907. The Law Department of the Muir Central College was converted into the School of Law of the Allahabad University, and his was the first batch. Prof. R. K. Sorabji was its principal. Dr. M. L. Agrawal, afterwards an authority on U.P. Tenancy Law, Mohanlal Nehru were the teachers. Sir Tej Bahadur Sapru was also on the teaching staff for some time. He stood first in Law final examination and was awarded Lumsden Gold Medal.

He took a leading part in the debates. He spoke without a trace of nervousness and in a convincing manner with apt quotations. He quoted from memory.

The study of mathematics made him an exact man. It gave him a good mental training for his later life. He swayed the young audiences—as he has clone afterwards— to his point of view. He participated in a debate expressing the view that India's financial condition had deteriorated under the British rule. Prof. Sorabji while addressing the gathering in the course of his concluding observations, complementing student Pant on his magnificent performance, remarked that one day Pant would be the Premier of India. This was said 45 years ago when no one could visualise that one day India would attain that status. How true proved the prophecy of Prof. Sorabji, made at a time when the horizon of Indian political scene was so hazy.

This was a happy period of his life. The Allahabad years were among the richest. He while inaugurating the Allahabad University

Law Society in November 1949 recalled some events that took place nearly 40 years ago. He pointed out that when he was a student of law, the Law College had no building of its own. Law classes used to meet in one of the quarters of the Muir Central College. They had also no hostel of their own, but used to live in a house on the Katra Road which had been converted into a hostel now. He said that they lived in hard times; but the circumstances in which they worked had at least one merit. They had to be hardy and they had an atmosphere of a public school. He added:

> "I wonder if any other institution has ever enjoyed that spirit of comradeship, mutual trust and the *espirit de corps* which was our good luck to enjoy in those days. We realised that man lived not by bread alone. Those were pleasant days and in universities then they enjoyed that vivacity, that vitality, that vigour which perhaps one did not enjoy at least to the same degree today. We worked with labour and with faith and we enjoyed life in a wholesome manner— in a manner which tended to help us and which enabled us to help others then and possibly later. The College in which we had our education does not exist anywhere in brick and mortar today. I am not sure if the environment;, the spirit and the atmosphere, which we had then, are now really permeating the precincts of the Law College."
>
> "If I were asked," continue Pandit Pant, "which were the best moments of my life, I would say that barring the time I spent in prison, the most useful and constructive part of my life was in the Law College."

A mention may be made of Pant's contemporaries at the Allahabad University College. Sri Purushottam Das Tandon who had graduated in 1904 was in the College for M.A. Dr. Kailash Nath Katju, who was senior to him by one year, later, Chief Minister of Madhya Pradesh, was the Minister of Justice in his first Cabinet in 1937 and also in the second Cabinet in 1946. Har Govind Pant who afterwards became the Deputy Speaker of U.P.

Assembly and died of food poisoning in 1957 when he was M.P. was all along with him. So was Acharya Narendra Dev and Fazl Ali.

Student Pant was a voracious reader. His speed of reading was high and he thoroughly grasped the subject. Bankim Chandra Chatterji's famous novel 'Ananda Math' (Monastery of *Joy)* created a great impression on him. Though written many years previously then became the most widely read book and several translations of it appeared in English and other Indian languages. The famous song 'Bande Matram' in this book became so popular that it came to occupy the place of a national anthem and many sacrificed their lives for it. In July 1952, Pandit Pant was in Dehradun for a holiday when he saw the film based on the novel 'Ananda Math' and was taken to those old days when it inspired him.

To create a patriotic sentiment among the younger generation Joseph Mazzini was put as the ideal of the Indian patriots. His writings were read with great interest. He was the symbol of the downtrodden races, who exhibited in his own life; and character an example of heroic self-sacrifice, of noble self-endurance, of burning love for mankind and of steadfast hatred for tyranny.

He devoted much of his time in reading outside books. He had read the works of Digby, Dadabhai, Ramesh Chand Dutt, Ranade, Spencer and Mill. He liked the novels of Dickens, Thackeray, Scott and Marie Corelli. Mill's works like 'Liberty' and 'Subjection of Women' had effect on his views. He once quoted Mill in the course of a debate: "The Government of a people by itself has a meaning and a reality; but such a thing as government of one people by another people does not, and cannot, exist. One people may keep another for its own use, a place to make money in a human cattle farm to be worked for the profits of its own inhabitants."

Mill's essay on Liberty was a manifesto against despotism of all kinds and was one of the most eloquent and persuasive arguments ever written for social and political freedom. His whole outlook was guided by this noble essay.

In 1947 the Diamond Jubilee of the Allahabad University was celebrated with great enthusiasm.

The degree of Doctor of Laws, *honoris causa* was conferred on Pandit Pant. The following citation was read by the Dean of the Faculty of Law:

> "I present to you the Hon'ble Pandit Govind Ballabh Pant, a distinguished graduate of the University. He has been a foremost figure in the country's public life. He was the first Premier of the United Provinces and successfully demonstrated that skill in debate can be combined with skill in administration. He is firm without obstinacy, and gentle without being weak. He is held in high regard even by those who differ from him for his uprightness, for his unrivalled mastery over the intricacies of Indian finance and for his leadership."

On January 28, 1949, at the Special Convocation of the Lucknow University Pandit Pant was lustily cheered by the young audience when he was presented to take the degree of Doctor of Laws. The cheers were the loudest; and it was an indication that in how great esteem he was held by the people and the youth of the country. H.E. Shrimati Sarojni Naidu, Chancellor of the University, who presided, and it was her last public appearance, speaking of Pandit Pant said that she was reluctant to pay any compliments "for if I begin praising my Premier, it will be offering bribes." She described him as the living symbol of vigilance, and added that "he is the jewel among the Premiers."

Pandit Pant was described in the citation thus:

> "His independent spirit could not remain restrained within the narrow confines of success at the bar, and the call of the service and sacrifice for the motherland found him in the forefront of the battle for freedom. The battle is won, but the triumph has brought him no rest. He bears unwearied on his massive shoulders the burden of the biggest province which is grateful to him for his exclusive devotion to it. He is a high-ranking statesman, a great financial expert, and is unrivalled as a parliamentarian. Calm in the midst of

> severest trials, he is one of the ablest administrators, the country has produced and is highly recognised as one of the foremost sons of modern India. This province is justly proud of a great man of his stature and in honouring him, the University is honouring one whose personality, life and achievements will inspire generations to come."

On December 2, 1918, only a month before Lucknow University Special Convocation, Banaras Hindu University held a Special Convocation and the degree of Doctor of Laws, *honoris causa* was conferred on Pandit Pant. The citation mentioned:

> "One who has long compelled the admiration of critical assemblies, he has won the respect even of those who differ from him. He hold the supreme position in this province alike in administration and in the affections of the people. A fine speaker, and a skilled debater, he is also a mister of finance, not disdaining the use of decimals and even vulgar fractions. He is the first servant of the State in action faithful and in honour clear."

On February 27, 1950, Aligarh Muslim University in its convocation conferred the Degree of Doctor of Laws on Pandit Pant and Agra University conferred the degree of Doctor of Laws *honoris causa* on him at its Silver Jubilee Convocation on December 6, 1952.

Pandit Pant did not appreciate when he was addressed as Doctor. When a speaker referred to him as Dr. Pant, he very humorously remarked: "I have been all along a patient. I have no physical strength to bear the burden of a doctor." He never allowed it to be written before his name.

Career in Law

> "Lawyers have occupied a conspicuous place in our public life. In fact with the advent of democracy, lawyers came to dominate over the political life of our country. Even before democracy took birth, lawyers

> took a prominent part in the struggle for democracy. Law is after all the foundation of civilized life," said—Pandit Govind Ballabh Pant, inaugurating the 2nd U.P. Lawyers Conference in 1946 at Lucknow.

Pandit Pant topped at his law examination at the Allahabad University and decided to adopt law as his profession. He viewed law as a noble profession, and bar offered a career which would enable him to enter public life. He looked upon the bar as a source of leadership where he could maintain his independence. A great attraction was that it was a road to public service. He was full of enthusiasm for public work. He had all the qualities that we associate with youth—ardour, earnestness, capacity for hard work, determination to succeed, and confidence. Law fascinated him. His people at home wanted him to go to the government service. When he was a student of B.A. class he had decided that he would adopt an independent profession and he chose law. He made his choice,— a right choice. He was fully equipped for a Lawyer's profession. He had eloquence. He had knowledge of human nature and of law. He knew that there was no short cut to success at the bar. Law was an exacting profession. A steady practice could only be developed by energy and ability.

> "The first years at the bar are of great importance", as he once mentioned to young lawyers. "It is a test to them, to their energy, to their patience, and to their intellect. Then methods are developed, technique acquired and right habits were formed which stood them in life and which were a source of their success in other walks of life."

He had full confidence in himself. In course of time he became the most adroit and successful advocate. He came to the forefront by dint of merit. He was a lawyer of a very high calibre. It can be said of him that he was equalled by few and was surpassed by almost none. He was the greatest lawyer who ever set foot in Kumaon courts. His career at the bar was one of almost unclouded brilliance, who had marvellous industry and matchless knowledge of details, who observed and inculcated higher professional standards. He felt that a man's livelihood should not be the whole of a man's business. He earned a lot and spent a lot. He never kept any personal account. He had a charitable heart and helped the helpless. He had qualities which pointed to a potential success as a leader at the bar—sound judgement, absolute integrity, dauntless courage and a desire to serve. As a lawyer he soon built a lucrative practice and his success at the bar was very rapid. He possessed the greatest analytical intellect. His learning and forensic skill were proverbial.

Throughout his career it was his practice to put his several hours work on his briefs. He must have complete command of every detail in the most complicated cases. He would study with punctilious care all the case law on every aspect of his brief. He would understand the weakness of his opponent's case, attack it and finish him. He was thorough and always straightforward. He was always scrupulously fair, just and generous to his opponents. Nothing is so ingratiating as good manners to disarm antagonism and enlist sympathy. He never yielded on essentials. He acted in his life on the words of a distinguished British Lord Chancellor Eldon who said to succeed as a lawyer one must work like a horse, and live like a hermit. This was the secret of his phenomenal success.

The qualities which he inculcated as a lawyer were the foundation of his success which he achieved in wider fields and the strength which enabled him to bear the heavier responsibilities with distinction. To be a good statesman and administrator, one must be a good lawyer. Life in the law courts inculcates a deep sense of realism, and a constant witnessing of the intricate working of human mind and emotions. Lawyer's profession makes capable of grasping the real problem. The real foundation of his life was laid in the law courts where he acquired the great virtues of life. It enabled him to acquire the capacity of departmentalising his mind—the ability to turn his attention completely to the matter in hand to the exclusion of other preoccupations, which enabled him to carry the weight of varied interests. That has stood him in his parliamentary career and in administrative field.

Law was a practical business. He had the power to discern—the shape of things to come. He was never taken by surprise or at a loss to counter any move of his opponents. Surely he is the man who can sec the coming events. He had clarity and insight, summed them up and presented to the courts in words which arrested their attention and left a clear impression. He was a powerful and effective cross examiner. He had immense patience. He would never be tired, nor tire the court; but of course tire the witness. Cross examination does not mean examining crossly. He used to arrest the attention of the court in the first sentence. Manner and matter were two things which were important to the advocate. It is the art of persuasion which we call advocacy. His manner was cool and collected. He was meticulously polite. He was courteous without being obsequious. His most deadly cross examination was invariably the most courteous. If he had a number of points in his favour, he would bring out the best one early. If he would have to attack, he would attack the weakest point first. If he had a useful admission, he would keep it in cold storage—and at the right moment he would flung it at the opponent and would finish him.

The surest way to success, according to him, was to act at all times to the highest standards of professional integrity. In law, as in business, 'honesty is the best policy'. Simplicity, sincerity and moderation were the traits which he got by the profession of law. He learnt work was the sum and substance of life. Referring to the task of lawyers, once speaking to the law students, he recalled the advice given by Dr. Johnson which he read as a student in the then popular book—'Boswell's Johnson':

"Sir, a lawyer has no business with the justice or injustice of the cause which he undertakes.

He said that the law was based on reason and reason was law. He referred to a saying by one of the greatest English lawyers—Chief Justice Coke—who wrote at the beginning of the 17th century:

> "The reason of the law is the life of law, for tho' a man can tell the law, yet if he knows not the reason thereof, he shall soon forget his superficial knowledge, but when he findeth the right reason of the law and so bring it to his natural reason that he comprehendeth it as his own, this will not only serve him for the understanding of the particular case but of many others."

He gained an immense local reputation. He soon made a great name for himself in the law courts. The first few years he practised in Kashipur where he was also a member of the Municipal Board. He had many interests outside his profession. He was associated with the establishment of a high school which has now become an Intermediate College. He with Badri Dutt Pandey started Kumaon Parishad to study the problems of Kumaon, and also started a weekly paper 'Shakti'. He carried agitation to abolish Kuli Begar. The government officials used to force any villager to work for them as coolie without any payment.

He was so much charmed by Nainital that he established his legal practice at Nainital. Only exigencies of an ever growing public life brought him in contact with plains. He always resisted the temptation of going to the High Court. Then the Allahabad Bar was one of the strangest Bars in India. It commanded the greatest prestige in the public estimation. Sir Sunder Lal, Pt. Motilal, Pt. Madan Mohan Malaviya, Jogendranath Chaudhary held the leadership of the profession.

His outstanding success in legal profession furnished a good criterion of his great merit. A distinguished lawyer who afterwards became the judge of the Allahabad High Court, was with him in some important case in 1916-17 said that every one was impressed by his well marshalled arguments, thoroughness and transparent honesty.

Soon after obtaining the degree in law from Allahabad University, Govind Ballabh began practising law in Almora. Within a very short time, he was recognised as a most competent lawyer. His earnings increased every month. Within a few years he started earning about Rs. 1000/- per month, which was then considered a big sum. During his student days, he had been an intelligent debater and was gifted with a strong memory. These qualities helped him in his profession. He did his home work thoroughly, mastering every point of law before going to the court. His presentation of the case, marshalling of facts and figures, his logical and persuasive arguments were superb. He won many cases.

Govind Ballabh was also a man of convictions. While practising law, he saw to it that he did not take up false cases. It is said that once, after winning a case on behalf of his client, he came to know that the whole case was fabricated by the client. He returned the entire amount of fee which he had charged.

While arguing a case at the Almora court, Govind Ballabh came in conflict with the English magistrate. He told the magistrate that he would not enter his court again, and began his practice at Kashipur. Once he went to the court at Kashipur wearing khadi *kurta* and *pyjama* and a khadi cap. The English judge asked Govind Ballabh to change his dress but he told him that he would rather leave the court.

In another incident, an Englishman pushed aside the chair on which Govind Ballabh was sitting, taking tea, because Pant did not get up to greet the Englishman. He asked the Englishman to apologise for his insulting behaviour, otherwise he would have to do so in the court of law. Govind Ballabh Pant told him that the entire crowd will be his witness. The Englishman, when he came to know that he was talking to Govind Ballabh Pant, apologised and left.

These incidents showed the kind of man he was: fearless, upright and principled. He went round from one place to another on horseback and soon became popular with the people because of his honesty, hard work and patriotic fervour.

Zenith, as a Lawyer

As a lawyer he was at the zenith in the Kakori Conspiracy case, which was the first of the biggest political conspiracy cases of Northern India in which the prosecution was represented by the late J.N. Mulla, the leading and distinguished lawyer of Oudh. Pantji led the defence. He was assisted by Mohanlal Saksena, Chandra Bhan Gupta, who became a minister in his second Cabinet in U.P. and who used to wear turban as a lawyer. Out of 28 persons sent no for trial 21 were committed to the Court of Sessions in April 1926. They were charged with conspiracy to deprive the King-Emperor of the sovereignty of British India; and conspiracy to commit dacoities in order to collect funds for that end. These 21 persons were tried by Sessions Judge Hamilton, specially appointed. The recording of evidence took more than eight months.

It was on the basis of this evidence that he attacked the flimsiness of the evidence produced by the prosecution. The skill, ability and exemplary patience which he displayed deserved the highest praise.

Ram Prasad Bismil, Rajendranath Laheri and Raushan Singh were sentenced to death, Sachindra Nath Sanyal to transportation for life and only two were acquitted. During the course of the trial two of the absconders Ashfaqullah and Sachindra Nath Bakshi were apprehended. They were tried in a supplementary case and Ashfaqullah was sentenced to death and Bakshi to transportation for life. Of the absconders only Chandra Sheikher Azad alias 'Quicksilver" who was shot dead in Alfred Park, Allahabad after six years remained untraced.

Damoder Swroop Seth was taken seriously ill and could not be tried on account of his illness. He was an old revolutionary and co-accused of Sachindra Nath Sanyal in the Banaras Conspiracy case. In the Rowlett Committee Report he was described as a teacher. His condition in jail became so serious that it was not considered desirable to proceed with the case against him. He was released on bail as there remained no hope of his survival. His friends and relations deserted him. He was brought from jail in a precarious condition by the late Satish Kumar Capoor of Bareilly to the residence of Pt. Dwarka Prasad in Bareilly. Afterwards Sethji became a prominent Congress Leader.

The affairs which gave rise to the case was a dacoity in a running train on the evening of the 9th August, 1925 near Alamnagar Station between Kakori and Lucknow. The train was stopped by pulling the communication cord of the alarm signal in a second class compartment. After the train had stopped a number of persons collected at the brake van overpowered the guard. While some of the men were breaking open the safe, others posted themselves on each side of the train. Cries were raised that their object was not to injure private persons but to take 'Sarkari property'. In about half an hour the safe was opened and the contents were taken away. The train then proceeded on its way to Lucknow.

R.A. Horton, Superintendent of Police of the C.I.D. was deputed to investigate this occurrence. The dacoity seemed to be of an unusual kind and it was thought that it had been committed by an organised gang of educated men. Several other dacoities took place in U.P. during the previous year. The police could not trace the miscreants for such a long time. Horton suspected that it was the work of the revolutionaries. He turned his attention to the actions of certain suspects.

His attention was attracted to Shahjahanpur as he had heard that some of the notes stolen in the Kakori train dacoity had been traced there. Suspicion fell on Ram Prasad. Indu Bhushan Mitra, a student in the local Government High School was suspected of being his post-office. He was only 14 years of age and his father was the Medical Officer of the Health. Idris Ahmad was the head master of the School. He was afterwards our head master in Bareilly Horton arranged with the Head Master that he should open letters addressed to Indu Bhushan, take copies of the contents, reclose them and deliver to Indu Bhushan and inform the police of what the letters contained.

Through the letters of Ram Prasad, which passed through his postbox, Indu Bhushan, Horton surmised that a meeting of the leaders of the revolutionary party would take place on the premises of the Vaish Orphanage in Meerut on September 13, 1925. Vishnu Saran Dublish, now M. P. from Meerut was the Superintendent of the Orphanage. One of the letters written by Dublish to Ram Prasad which was intercepted was as follows:

> Vaish Orphanage, Meerut Dated 9th Sept. 1925. My dear brother,
>
> "Everything is all right. All arrangements about the Executive Committee of the Orphanage are complete. The Updeshak at Lahore had promised to attend the function. You are requested to intimate to your friends to put up in various Dharamshalas. Jain Dharmshala is in the way *to* the railway Station. Dharam Das Dharamshala is just near the clock tower.
>
> The place of the function has been after due deliberation fixed at my own place".
>
> Yours Supt. V. O.

Watchers became busy at Meerut. They remained outside the main gate of the Orphanage. Nothing was observed during the day until shortly before sunset when eight men came out of the residential quarters of Dublish. Among them were Damoder Swroop Seth, Ram Prasad and Rajendra Nath Laheri. There was a piece of paper which was recovered from Jogesh Chatterji at the time of his arrest in Calcutta, which was a record of the proceedings of a meeting held in October 1924 of the provincial Council that disclosed that efficient representatives were acting as district organisers all over U.P.

It was believed by the police that a revolutionary organisation had been created in the U.P. Horton connected this knowledge with the other facts and felt convinced that the dacoity was the act of revolutionaries in which the educated youths were involved. Horton issued warrants of arrests which were executed on 20th September, 1925, against Damoder Swroop Seth and two dozen other young men.

2

Rise in Politics

Pt. Pant did not confine closely to the legal work but he attempted to unite it with a political career. He had busy professional life; but still he could find time to devote to other activities.

In August 1914, the war broke out. The Foreigners Ordinance and the Ingress into India Ordinance were passed immediately. The Defence of India Act and Rules came into force early in 1915. The Regulation III of 1818 was also put into operation.

In March 1916 Sir Ibrahim Rahmatullah moved a resolution in the Imperial Legislative Council urging the appointment of a committee to consider and report what measures should be adopted for the growth and development of industries in India. Sir William Clark who was then Member for Commerce and Industry accepted the Resolution on behalf of the Government. He announced that he had taken stops to constitute not a committee, but a more important body, a Commission. The Indian Industrial Commission was appointed in May 1916 under the presidentship of Sir T. H. Holland. Pandit Madan Mohan Malaviya, Sir R.N. Mookerji of the Martin & Co., Sir Dorabji Jamsetji Tata, the Rt. Hon'ble Sir Horace Curzon Plunkett were some of its members. The Report was published in 1918 and sketched the lines of economic development along which India moved since she first came in contact with western traders. Pandit Malaviya appended a separate note which was a treatise on the industrial development—past, present and future. It became a theme for nationalist speakers and writers to condemn the Government. Early in the year 1916 Lord Harding left India. He was succeeded by Lord Chelmsford. The War had entered into a crucial stage. Tilak was released from prison.

Entry into Politics

Before Mahatma Gandhi stormed the political scene as a national leader, Govind Ballabh Pant started taking part in the political affairs of hilly regions. In 1916, he set up Kumaon Parishad, which was a political organisation of the hill people. The main objective was to spread political awakening among them and solve the problems of Kumaon. He attended the Congress session held at Lucknow in 1916, where the Indian National Congress as well as the Muslim League held joint session. He represented Kumaon. He met Gandhiji for the first time there and was deeply influenced by him. Other leaders whom he met at Lucknow were Sarojini Naidu, Annie Besant and Bal Gangadhar Tilak. Sarojini Naidu was a poetess and a great leader of the Congress. Tilak was the fiery leader of Maharashtra who had given the famous slogan to the Indian people: "Swaraj is my birth right and I shall have it".

In 1917, he persuaded Annie Besant to preside over the Kumaon Parishad. Within a year Gandhiji launched Satyagraha against the Rowlatt Acts, according to which, any Indian suspected of political or revolutionary activities would be tried in camera, and the accused would not be permitted the benefit of defence. Gandhiji declared that such laws violated the fundamental principles of justice, democracy and individual liberty, and smacked of racialism, since the acts were applicable to Indians only. He declared that these acts were "Black Acts" and asked the Government to withdraw them.

Following the call given by Gandhiji, for a nationwide hartal against the Black Acts, the whole country was politically mobilised. On 6 April 1919, a meeting was held at Kashipur where Govind Ballabh was the main speaker. The meeting demanded the withdrawal of the Rowlatt Acts. As a sequel to the movement against Rowlatt Acts, the Jallianwala massacre took place in

Amritser on the Vaishakhi day, 13 April 1919. All of you must have read about the ghastly tragedy of Jallianwala Bagh in Amritser in which General Dyer had ordered uninterrupted firing on the peaceful meeting held there. The firing continued till the ammunition was exhausted, leaving many hundreds of men, women and children dead and thousands wounded. No medical help was provided to the wounded and Martial Law was proclaimed in the Punjab. Against these atrocities, the whole nation protested. As a consequence of these events, Indian National Congress decided to launch the Non-cooperation movement against the British rule, under the leadership of Mahatma Gandhi. Govind Ballabh Pant was deeply moved by these events, and following Gandhiji's call, the hill regions also were drawn into the mainstream of nationalist political agitation.

Govind Ballabh moved from Almora to Kashipur for practice, but by 1916, he established himself at Nainital, where he had a flourishing practice. Within a few years, he planned to enrol himself as a member of the Allahabad Bar, which would enable him to practice at Allahabad High Court. But Gandhiji's influence dominated the Indian political scene after 1920, and most of the leaders of the Indian National Congress gave up their lucrative practice following his call for non-cooperation.

The most important legal case in which Govind Ballabh appeared as a defence counsel was the Kakori Conspiracy case of 1925. The revolutionary movement was also an important aspect of the Indian nationalist movement. Some of the young revolutionaries, who did not believe in the method of non-violence, preached and practised by Gandhiji and the Indian National Congress, decided to follow "the cult of bomb". Several incidents of violence were organised by them; they even tried to hurl bombs at important British officials including the Viceroy of India. They also derailed trains, and looted government treasury to finance their movement.

One such incident occurred on 9 August 1925, in which revolutionaries stopped the train coming from Saharanpur to Lucknow at a place near Kakori, and succeeded in removing the iron-chest carrying money, from the train. The Indian National Congress, under the leadership of Motilal Nehru, asked Govind

Ballabh Pant to fight the case as a defence counsel on behalf of the revolutionaries. Pant skilfully and forcefully fought out their case, but there was no chance of saving these revolutionaries from death or jail sentences since the British government was determined to deal with revolutionary crime with a heavy hand. One of the members of the Kakori Conspiracy was Chandra Shekhar Azad, who remained underground for a number of years till at last he was killed in police action in Alfred Park in Allahabad in 1931.

Devoted to Congress Programme

Pant was at the zenith of his practice and powers in Kumaon in 1922 when after his return from the Ahmedabad Congress he made decisions of his life. He decided silently—without making any public announcement to leave his lucrative legal practice. He devoted himself whole heartedly to the programme of hand spinning and hand weaving, communal unity, prohibition and eradication of untouchability for which the public support was sought at Ahmedabad. He started centres for spinning and weaving and gave all his time for Congress work. The Charkha had found a place in the Congress programme. In the exhibition at Ahmedabad he saw a unique demonstration of what India could produce. There the chief attraction was the party from Chikakole who demonstrated all the processes of cotton leading to the drawing out of yarn upto 100 counts. No machinery could possibly make the show like silver that the delicate hands of women of Andhra produced.

The pages of 'Young India' which he read were full of great stirring thoughts. The spirit of the time was mirrored in a statement made by Jawaharlal Nehru before a magistrate: "Affection and loyalty are of the heart. They cannot be purchased in the market place; much less can they be extorted at the point of the bayonet."

The stern terms of the Treaty of Sevres imposed by the allies on the Turks in 1920, which were in fact never enforced were the cause of the Khilafat and Non-cooperation movement in India. In February 1922 Lord Reading and his Executive Council thought it expedient to make a conciliatory gesture towards the Khilafat agitators by recommending a formal revision of the terms of the Treaty. They made some suggestions in the form of proposals. Montagu who was the Secretary of State for India, got the

Government of India's telegram on 1st March 1922. He did not order copies of the telegram to be circulated to his Cabinet Colleagues until 3rd Match. Montagu received a second telegram from the Government of India requesting permission to publish their recommendations forthwith. The Secretary of State privately telegraphed his consent saying that he would confirm it officially on Monday, 6th March. On that day the British Cabinet met. Lloyd George who was Prime Minister was indisposed and Austin Chamberlain presided over the Cabinet meeting. Before the business began Lord Curzon who was the Foreign Secretary protested to Chamberlain against any publication and so to Montagu, who said that he had already authorised on Saturday. Montagu did not realise the gravity of the situation. If he wished even on Monday he could have immediately asked in time the Government of India to stop publication of the telegram. In fact the Government of India was not publishing it until Wednesday, 8th March. Storm broke out in British press on Thursday morning, 9th March. That day Chamberlain rose to speak in the House of Commons when he said:

> "His Majesty's Government are unable to reconcile the publication of the telegram of the Government of India on the sole responsibility of the Secretary of State with the collective responsibility of the Cabinet, or with the duty which all Governments of the Empire owe to each other in matters of Imperial concern. Such independent declaration destroys the unity of policy. The Secretary of State has tendered his resignation to the Prime Minister and His Majesty has been pleased to approve its acceptance." On March 14 Lord Curzon in the House of Lords declared that it was intolerable that he should have to negotiate over Turkey while a 'Subordinate branch of British Government, 6,000 miles away dictated to the British Government what line it should pursue in Thrace.

British public life gives several such instances how a little lapse or indiscretion had cost the termination of such valuable political life. Montagu never recovered from the wounds of his pride. He died a year after.

A.I.C.C. met at Lucknow on June 7 1922 to take stock of the situation in the country. Pt. Motilal Nehru had just been released from jail and C. Rajagopalachari who was the Secretary of the Congress and succeeded Gandhiji to the editorship of his 'Young India' were present. The Civil Disobedience Enquiry Committee consisting of Hakim Ajmal Khan, Motilal Nehru, C. R. Das, Dr. Ansari, Vithalbhai was appointed to report on the political situation in the country. The report was ready by October 30 and was submitted to C. R. Das who was then released from jail. Half the members of the Committee opined that the movement be abandoned and a new party be formed to work in the Councils. Those who were in favour of Council entry were Pandit Motilal, Hakim Ajmal Khan and Vithalbhai Patel.

On November 20 the A.I.C.C. met in Calcutta and after five days discussion it was resolved that the country was not prepared for mass civil disobedience; but the question of council entry was postponed till the annual session which was held in December 1922 at Gaya under the presidentship of C.R. Das. In his presidential address he advocated council entry but said that he would give it up if the decision of the Khilafat Conference was against it. He wanted Congressmen to return in a majority in the Councils and there oppose all measures of the Government. The no changes were victorious. C. R. wanted the Congress to adopt full fledged non-cooperation, and his resolution on Council boycott was passed by 1740 votes as against 890.

On January 1, 1923 Das and Motilal raised a standard of revolt and formed the Swaraj Party with Das as President and Motilal Nehru as Secretary. They declared that the Swaraj Party wanted to work within the Congress "having full faith in the creed of the Congress believing that the Gaya programme was not conducive to the speedy attainment of Swaraj". They attracted an increasing number of able followers in every province.

Matters came to a head at the A.I.C.C. held in May 1923 in Bombay under the presidentship of C. R. Das. The majority was against him and the Swarajist Policy. Das resigned from the presidentship to devote fully for the organisation of the Swaraj Party for the ensuing general elections in the autumn only some months after.

In the summer of 1923 Pandit Motilal Nehru, Sri C. R. Das and Hakim Ajmal Khan came to Nainital and stayed there for a fortnight to chalk out their plans on the constitutional front. Pandit Pant then came in their close contact and they were much impressed by his ability and resourcefulness.

A special session of the Congress was held at Delhi in September. Maulana Azad presided. Lala Lajpat Rai who was recently released pleaded strongly for unity in the Congress. C. R. did not attend the session and left the affairs in the hands of Maulana Mohammed Ali who was then released. He was the central figure at the Congress Session and the whole session was dominated by his personality. All eyes turned on him. He made a statement that he was searching for the Key of Yeravada. He won the day by his heroic gesture for the Swarajists by announcing that he had received a telepathic message from Gandhiji in Yervada Jail approving of the modification of the boycott in favour of Council entry. It was a fictitious product of his lively imagination. It was a diplomatic stroke of high order. He moved a resolution permitting individual congressmen who had no religious or conscientious objection to stand for election, and suspending the propaganda against Council entry which was carried after a somewhat heated discussion. Vallabhbhai Patel, Rajendra Prasad remained neutral, and the resolution was passed by the majority. At the instance of Maulana Mohammed All Swarajist succeeded and they got the sanction for contesting 1923 general elections. They had collected funds and enrolled workers.

Congress Session at Lucknow

The Congress session was held in Lucknow under the presidentship of Ambika Charan Mazumdar, which was of great importance. It was a memorable session, where a historic decision was taken, which changed the future course of Indian political history. The Muslim leaders met at the same time in Lucknow—and a joint Hindu-Muslim reform scheme was sent to the Viceroy. Its most important provision was, which was known as Lucknow Pact, and approved by the Congress and the Muslim League—that Muslims should be represented in the Legislative Councils by separate electorates, and on this basis they demanded an immediate declaration of British intentions to confer self-government on India at an early date. Surendranath Banerji moved and Tilak and Besant supported the resolution. Tilak met rapturous reception at the railway station and on arrival in the Congress pandal. In the words of President Mazumdar, "The united Congress which was buried at Surat was reborn today at Lucknow."

Pant attended the Lucknow session as a delegate and a member of All India Congress Committee from Kumaon. It was here he first heard Gandhiji and Sarojini Naidu. On the second day Sir James Meston, the Lieut. Governor of U.P., accompanied by Lady Meston paid a visit to the Congress Session. The President offered him cordial welcome on behalf of the Congress and mentioned some instances when the highest administrators paid a visit to the Congress. Meston in his reply said that there was a curious link between the Congress and him in time and sympathy. The year in which Congress was born was the year in which he entered the I.C.S. to serve India. Mrs. Naidu's speech simply charmed the audience. She began, 'Ladies and gentlemen, and *unarmed* citizens of India'. Meston who was sitting received a jerk and he took protection by leaning on the pillows.

Early in December 1916 a political crisis reached its climax in England with the resignation of Asquith of his office of Prime Minister. In August 1917 Lloyd George's National Government made the historic announcement. Lord Curzon was the real author of the declaration which for the first time defined the goal of Indian aspirations 'the establishment of responsible government.' The word 'responsible' was written in the original draft by Curzon himself. The terms of the announcement were settled by the coalition Cabinet. The British Parliament accepted the Statement as a pledge and assurance offered to India by Britain. In April 1918 the Montagu-Chelmsford Report was signed. Its joint authors in the first chapter of the Report declared that the announcement made by Montagu on 20th August, 1917 to the House of Gammons was "the most momentous utterance ever made in India's chequered history."

The Joint Report of Montagu and Lord Chelmsford was published in June 1918. It created a great stir in India. In order to give effect to the recommendations made in the Report on the

Indian Constitutional Reforms, two Committees were constituted under the presidentship of Lord Southborough to recommend (1) what subjects should be transferred to the control of the Governor acting with his ministers and what subjects should be reserved to be administered by the Governor with his Executive Councillors, and (2) to recommend the franchise to be adopted for elections to the provincial and central legislatures. The First Committee which was known as the Functions Committee consisted of Richard Feetham, a judge in South Africa as chairman; Sir Tej Bahadur Sapru; Sir Chimanlal Setalvad; M. H. Couchman, a Madras civilian, Sir Rahim Bux, Chief Minister of Bhawalpur State; H.S. Stephenson, a Bengal civilian, and J. P. Thompson, Chief Secretary, Punjab Government as members.

The Second Committee which was called the Franchise Committee consisted of Lord Southborough as chairman, and Sir Frank Sly, Sahibzada Aftab Ahamad Khan, Malcom Haily, then Chief Commissioner Delhi, afterwards Lord Haily—and Governor of Punjab and U.P., Sir Surendranath Banerji, Sir Malcolm Hogg, and Rt. Hon'ble Shrinivas Shastri as members.

Lord Southborough was in general charge of both the Committees which met first in Shimla on November 8, 1918. The Committees visited the provincial capital cities and examined official and non-official witnesses. They came to Lucknow in November 1918.

Pant came to Lucknow to give evidence before both these Committees. The other prominent persons who gave evidence were Pandit Madan Mohan Malaviya, Pandit Motilal Nehru on behalf of the U.P. Congress; Syed (afterwards Sir) Wazir Hasan, Syed (afterwards Sir) Raza Ali, U.P. Muslim League, Prof. Stanley Jones, De La Fosse who was then Director of Public Instruction from the government side and various senior I.C.S. officers like Sir Atul Chand Chatterji who was then Revenue Secretary, S. P. O'Donnell appeared before the Committees.

The Kumaon was excluded from the operations of the Montford reforms. It was treated as a backward tract which the local government proposed to exclude from the operations of the scheme. Pant pleaded the case of Kumaon. He at length discussed the question relating to franchise in Kumaon; and was successful in getting Kumaon removed from the schedule of backward areas. He had made a thorough study of the issues which were to be discussed by the Committees. He left an abiding impression on the members of the Committees who afterwards recalled that he was one of the witnesses appeared before them who showed mastery of the subject. When Pant was elected the leader of the Congress Party in 1937 which was to constitute the Government—and he was to be the first Premier, I happened to be with Sir Tej Bahadur Sapru at Allahabad. He was going to issue a press statement whether the Governor under the 1935 Act could give assurances as demanded by Gandhiji. Sir Tej told me about Pandit Pant—of his evidence before the Franchise Committee of which he was also the member then 18 years back.

In December 1917 a Committee was appointed under the Chairmanship of Justice Rowlatt of the Kings Bench of H.M.'s High Court of Justice to investigate and report on the nature and extent of the criminal conspiracies connected with the revolutionary movement in India. The members of the Committee were Sir Basil Scott, Chief Justice of Bombay; C.V. Kumaraswami Shastri, Judge of the Madras High Court; Sir Verney Lovett, Member, U.P. Board of Revenue and P.C. Mitter, Vakil of the Calcutta High Court.

It was felt that when the war would be over the special emergency legislation would lapse and the persons interned would be released. Proposals for legislation for the period after the war were drafted. The measures which the Committee appointed for the purpose suggested were of two kinds, viz., Punitive—by which to better secure the conviction and punishment of offenders, and Preventive, i.e., measures to check the spread of conspiracy and the commission of crime.

The report of the Committee was published in 1918 and on the recommendations of the Committee a bill was moved, which was popularly known as the Rowlatt Bill in the Imperial Council, which was passed in 1919 during the Viceroyalty of Lord Chelmsford in which the liberties of the people were placed in a certain measure at the mercy of bureaucracy—the outstanding features being summary arrest and summary trial and hardly any appeal. No appeal, no daleel and no Vakil. It was felt that it contained drastic provision which totally curtailed the liberties of the people. It was considered a measure of great iniquity. Gandhiji raised an emphatic protest against it. He took full advantage of the situation. The reign of terror prevailed in the Punjab after the Jallianwalla Bagh tragedy and the martial law was proclaimed in Lahore, Amritsar and other cities of the Punjab under the orders of Sir Michael O'Dwyer. A wave of repression spread all over the country. It furnished a necessary fuel for the new upsurge which gripped India.

The Muslims felt great religious humiliation by the terms imposed by the Treaty of Severes, which led to the birth of Khilafat movement. There was large economic unrest which was inevitable coming as an aftermath of the Great War. Gandhiji who was watching the reactions of these conditions understood the mind of the Indian people. He made them the target of his new peaceful non-violent movement. He forged a new weapon—a new movement in the history of the world in which unarmed people who were oppressed and downtrodden raised their voice against a mighty Empire. It was unique experiment in the struggle for independence by oppressed people. Gandhiji marshalled the immense potentialities of soul-force in politics. He had made his experiments in South Africa and he wanted to apply them on a large scale in India. He insisted on the great motive power of Ahimsa.

Gandhiji proclaimed that 6th April 1919, the second Sunday after the Rowlatt Act had received Viceregal assent, as a day of general mourning and cessation of work. We were then mere boys; but the slogans still ring in our ears. It had reached the farthest corners of India. The country gave an extraordinary response. All cities, towns and villages on that day acted according to Gandhiji's instructions. For the first time it brought both Hindus and Muslims together—into one line of common political thought. As an anti-British movement it achieved great success. Gandhiji restored to India hex-lost soul. He asserted the superiority of the spirit over the flesh—of the mind over the matter. That was the victory of the East over the West.

It was in the last week of December 1919 two days before the Congress Session began at Amritsar under the presidentship of Motilal Nehru when the Royal Proclamation was issued giving Royal assent to the Government of India Act, 1919 "which will take its place among the great historic measures passed by the Parliament of this realm for the better government of India and for the greater contentment of her people. The path will not be easy; and in the march towards the goal there will be need of perseverance and of mutual forbearance between all sections and races."

Tilak read this in the train while going to Amritsar. He coined the term 'Responsive Cooperation' in his telegram to the King through Montagu while thanking His Majesty for the Proclamation and amnesty, and assuring him of 'Responsive Cooperation.'

Swami Shradhanand was the Chairman of Reception Committee. President Motilal referred to Gandhiji's Satyagrah, as a new force, introduced into our politics— a force with the most tremendous potentialities. Gandhiji in fact had become the leader of the Congress. On 1st August 1920 Tilak died in Bombay. He was taken ill as a result of chill caught in a motor car drive.

Gandhiji who arrived in Bombay in the morning had fixed that day for the inauguration of his Non-cooperation Movement. On 1st September Congress Special Session was held at Calcutta under the presidentship of Lala Lajpat Rai, who had just returned from USA after a long absence. There was a keen discussion on Non-cooperation resolution moved by Gandhiji which was carried by 1826 votes against 884. Das opposed as he objected to the boycott of the new legislatures.

On October 2 the A.I.C.C. met and resolved to raise two funds—All India Tilak Memorial Fund and the Swaraj Fund. In December the annual Congress Session was held at Nagpur. Das went with 250 delegates to undo what was done at Calcutta. But there was reunion and the resolution was moved by Das, seconded by Lajpat Rai.

Ahmedabad Session of Congress

Pandit Pant attended the momentous Congress Session at Ahmedabad in the last week of December, 1921. This was 36th session held under a specially erected pandal covered all over with pure white Khadi on the bank of the river Sabarmati. The main gate bearing the motto 'Swaraj is my birthright,' inscribed just above the central arch with a charka, stood as the noble gateway to India's freedom.

The revolution seemed to be smouldering everywhere, ready to burst into flames when the Congress met. It met under very exciting circumstances under the guidance of Gandhiji whose arrest appeared imminent and the Government was hesitant to arrest him. C. R. Das, the President-elect being in jail, Hakim Ajmal Khan was elected as acting President who made an ideal and patient president.

There was a big rush. The Reception Committee had arranged a provision of one lakh visitors; but the lowest calculation put down the figure to two lakhs. The issue of tickets had to be stopped. Out of the total 6,173 delegates as many as 4,726 attended the Congress. U.P. in spite of so many arrests sent 880 out of 960 delegates. The Congress Camp was half a mile in length and was built of Khadi, and was known as Khadinagar.

Mahatma Gandhi, bare-bodied and bare-footed, having only a loin-cloth round his waist, was the centre of attraction of all.

Vallabhbhai Patel who was then not known as Sardar was the Chairman of Reception Committee. He took no more than fifteen minutes to read his address in Hindi. The President's address also took no more than twenty minutes. It was in Hindustani. Every speech delivered was to the point. Everything there appeared to have business like appearance. It was regulated in perfect order. As Gandhiji put it 'Self restraint is the key to Swaraj.' The undelivered presidential address of the President-elect, C.R. Das, which was written just on the eve of his arrest was read out to the Congress by Bengal's great poetess Sarojini Naidu.

Gandhiji who was seen wearing a cap which was known after his name moved the main resolution which was seconded by Vallabhbhai Patel and adopted. Maulana Hasrat Mohani who was also the President of the All India Muslim League held there wanted the Congress to change its creed and method. Gandhiji replied, "Think fifty times before you take a step, which may rebound not to your credit, not to your advantage, but which may cause irreparable injury." Gandhiji pleaded for the golden mean. This sentence had a profound effect on Pantji who has such conducted himself in his life. He pleaded in the words Gandhiji then wrote in Young India under 'Introspection':

> "Swaraj does not consist in the change of the government and its real control by the people; but that would be merely the form. The substance that I am hankering after is a definite acceptance of the means and a real change of heart on the part of people".

In Local Politics

In 1921, Govind Ballabh was elected Chairman of the Nainital District Board in addition to being a member of Kashipur Municipal Board. During this period, he put forward a plan for establishing schools in rural areas, advocating free and compulsory primary education for all children. Also, he wanted that books and slates, etc. should be given to the children of the schools free of cost. Another programme which he wanted the government to adopt related to the promotion of cottage industries.

Later, when he became the Chairman of Kumaon Parishad, he asked the government to establish Panchayat in each village for resolving disputes and to initiate measures for rural development. He also wanted that the Parishad should undertake series of measures for "industrial, commercial and national education" in Kumaon. A vocational school was established at Kashipur by Govind Ballabh to impart training in skills and finally he demanded that use of drinks in the rural regions should be stopped.

Situation in Rural India

India was both a manufacturing as well as an agricultural country. The manufactured goods were produced in the villages as cottage industries. Indian agriculture was dependent mostly on the rains during the monsoon season. Irrigational canals were not many and there were few dams constructed by the British. Every home in the village, therefore, was free from farming activities for nearly six months in a year. Every village home, therefore, devoted itself to manufacture of cloth and production of different kinds of handicrafts, which were sold in the market. Thus every peasant home supplemented its income by producing some articles for sale.

The British, after gaining political power as rulers of India, allowed their merchants and trading concerns to invest money in manufactures in India and forced the artisans to sell their goods and raw materials to them often below the market rates. The Indian manufacturers and the cottage industries suffered losses and after sometime, the villages stopped manufacturing items like silk and cotton goods, for which they were once famous, and which had helped them for centuries to supplement their income from farming.

The cottage industries and handicrafts were thus destroyed by such a rapacious British policy. The villagers lost their position as manufacturers of goods and became merely producers of agricultural goods like rice, wheat, cotton and sugar cane, etc. India was reduced from a manufacturing to a purely agricultural country. This was one of the causes of poverty of India during the British rule.

The factories of England needed a lot of raw materials like cotton, jute and other goods. India became a supplier of these raw materials. The agents of British firms purchased raw cotton at a cheaper rate in India, transported it to Great Britain for manufacture of cloth and brought the manufactured goods back to India for sale. Thus they reaped advantage on both counts. On the one hand, they received continuous supply of raw materials, purchased at a much lower rate than the world market, and on the other, they got a ready market for their manufactures and made enormous profits.

Such an economic policy ruined the industries of India and the villages became poorer and poorer as time passed. The peasants did not have any other occupation than to cultivate the soil for their own living. Hence, they rushed for acquiring more land. Land being scarce, there was competition for land among the people engaged in agriculture. As a consequence, the rent on the cultivable soil was raised by the landlords. Such a development gave rise to exploitation of the peasantry.

In Uttar Pradesh, after the revolt of 1857, in which a large number of peasants participated, the British thought it advisable to create more landlords, who would remain loyal to them. These landlords were known as *taluqdars* in the Avadh region, and *zamindars* in Agra, Mathura, Allahabad, Gorakhpur, etc. Nearly 66 per cent of land was given away to these big landlords, who paid revenue to the government after collecting rents from the peasants. The landlords' revenue demand was fixed by the government, but the rent to be paid by the tenants was not fixed. It fluctuated according to the demand for land. In actual fact, the rent demanded by the landlords increased each time an agreement was reached between the landlords and tenants or peasants.

The peasants or tenants paid rent to these *taluqdars* or *zamindars.* There were several kinds of tenants. Some of them were called hereditary tenants, who cultivated their lands for life as long as they paid the required amount of rent to the landlords. They could not be evicted from land because they had hereditary claim on these lands. The second type of peasants were called "occupancy tenants", whose rent was regulated after 10 or 12 years in the *non-taluqdari* areas and after seven years or so in the *taluqdari* areas. Each time, i.e. after seven or 10-12 years, the rent was raised although these tenants were permitted to cultivate land on payment of the rents. They had no permanent rights over the land they cultivated. They could be thrown out of their land for non-payment of rent. There were also other kinds of tenants, who moved from one village to the other and could be evicted at the pleasure and sweet will of the landlords. On the whole, you can see that these tenants were not secure in their possession of land, and most of them could be turned out from their soil by the landlords, although they were the most important elements in the production process. Without their labour nothing could be produced.

Secondly, these peasants or tenants were subjected to payment of various kinds of dues or cesses, which were demanded by the landlords from time to time. For example, they paid either in kind or money a cess called *nazarana* to the landlords at festivals, marriages, etc. When the *taluqdars* bought an elephant, they paid a cess called *hathiana.* When they purchased a car, they paid a cess called *motorana.* These were illegal practices. In addition, the tenants worked in the landlords' fields as free labour *(begar)* for a number of days in a year. As a result of these exactions, there was great discontent among the peasantry in Uttar Pradesh. Besides, the peasants became poorer through their burdens and they merely survived somehow. In addition to the *zamindar's* exactions, the village moneylenders plundered them by demanding high interest on the loans they asked for. The villagers, thus, by and large, remained in perpetual debt. The "rural indebtedness", as it is termed, has been a chronic phenomenon of British land policy in India.

In 1920-21, in Rai Bareli, Pratapgarh and Faizabad districts of Avadh, widespread disturbances took place, during which the landlords and their agents were attacked. The moneylenders also did not escape their anger. Their houses were burnt, shops were looted and the government had to open fire on the peasants. It was against this background that the Indian National Congress demanded passing of legislation for the protection of the peasantry from oppression and exploitation by the landlords.

The most important issue before the government, was to grant security of tenure or rights over land to the tenants, or peasants, or *ryots*, as they were called. In the Agra region, the problem was to ensure the tenants' occupancy rights after ten or twelve years of cultivation and to fix the rent demand on a rational basis. By custom, 40 per cent of gross produce, or its equivalent amount in money, was taken as rent but that was too high a demand, and the rent needed *to* be lowered.

Also, law had to be passed to curb the powers of landlords regarding the eviction of tenants from land. In addition to these, illegal cesses or feudal dues demanded from the tenants, as was the practice in the *taluqdari* regions in Avadh, had to be stopped.

The Avadh Tenancy Act of 1921 tried to mitigate some of these evils by prohibiting the landlords from demanding dues other than rent, and granting rights to the cultivators to till the land for seven years. Govind Ballabh Pant, as Member of the U.P. Legislative Council, representing the Swaraj Party of the Indian National Congress, strongly supported the cause of the peasantry and demanded restriction of powers of the landlords over the peasantry in general. He also supported the Agra Tenancy Act of 1926, passed by the U.P. Legislative Council, which sought to guarantee security of tenure to the occupancy tenants. These measures were rather half-hearted attempts on the part of the government to provide justice to the peasants, since the government was not prepared to annoy the landlords.

In U.P. Legislative Council

The first elections for the new Legislatures under the Montagu Chelmsford Reforms were held in November 1920. The experiment began in the shadow of Non-cooperation movement and of a financial crisis. Motilal Nehru and C. R. Das were of the *view* that the elections should not be boycotted. Pt. Motilal had decided to contest for the U. P. Council and also asked his son Jawaharlal to fix up a constituency for himself. At the last moment the Congress decided to boycott the elections at the instance of Gandhiji. At this time party organisation was non-existent and the candidates for the most part came forward *suo motu*, and were elected on personal grounds. C. Y. Chintamani, who was the editor of the *Leader* and after his election became the first Education Minister, persuaded Pandit Pant to contest for the Council, which he did and was defeated.

The U. P. Council was then composed of 123 members of which 23 were ex-officio nominees of which 18 were officials. Out of 100 elected 10 were elected by special electorate, one by University, 6 by Landholders, 3 by Commerce and Industry. Out of 90 elected members 30 by communal electorate of which 25 Muslim Rural; 4 Muslim Urban and 1 European. By general electorate 60 were to be elected out of which 52 were non-Muslim Rural and 8 Non-Muslim Urban.

Sir Harcourt Butler was the Governor and his love for Lucknow was responsible for its status in India. As deputy-commissioner of Lucknow he had inspired many town planning and improvement schemes. The magnificent building of the Council House is the product of his imagination and effort. He felt that the then Council Chamber was totally unsuited for a young Parliament. There was the controversy about its location— whether in Lucknow or in Allahabad. Non-official members of the pre-reform Council decided by 17 votes to 2 that the Council Chamber should be located in Lucknow. The Council voted a sum of one and half lakh for building residences in Lucknow for the President of the Council and the Finance Member, which Pantji occupied as Premier. In March 1920 lands were acquired and plans were drawn up. Butler had a fine design from architect Lanchester. He felt that the experience of the world had shown that for the efficient disposal of public business, a certain measure of comfort, conditions that favour balance of mind and temper, opportunities of pleasant informal intercourse outside the actual Council Chamber, were essential. He was guided by one of those wise and pithy sayings that "A public authority meanly housed may be meanly esteemed." The work on the new Council Chamber was started on 25th August, 1922, and its foundation stone was to be laid by Prince of Wales but on account of the boycott of the visit it was laid by Butler on December 15, 1922 who said:

> "Make it worthy of a people's desire." The first Reformed Council came to an end in the autumn of 1923 when the Swaraj Party entered the arena for the 1923 elections and achieved considerable success. The moderates, who had entered the first Council, were heavily defeated. Sir William Marris succeeded Butler. He came from Assam where he was the Governor. He had helped Montagu and Chelmsford in drafting the Montford Report on Indian Constitutional reforms.

On the eve of the Election the Swarajists issued a party manifesto in which they laid stress upon the fact that they were entering the Councils in order to ensure that the new Constitutional machinery should not be exploited for anti-national purposes. They intended to present an ultimatum to Government demanding the right of the Indian people to control its own destiny. In the event of the demand being refused the Party pledged itself to a policy of uniform, continuous and consistent obstruction with a view to making Government through the Councils impossible. Instead of attempting to destroy the Councils from without they had set themselves to wreck the machinery of the Councils from within.

For two months the country was kept in merry excitement over the election campaign. The Swarajist gained almost everywhere sweeping victories. From Nainital district Pandit Pant was returned to the U.P. Legislative Council.

The first session of the Second Council began on 8th January, 1924—the day the new British Parliament began after general elections which resulted in the increase of the membership of the Labour party to 191 from, 144 and the Conservatives had lost nearly 100 seats. Ramsay MacDonald, who had been elected 13 years earlier the President of the Indian National Congress— the office which his wife and son's death prevented him from holding, became the first Labour Prime Minister of England.

Pantji who sat on a back bench was sworn in as a member by Michael Keane, the first official President of the Council. He was then little known. He came from a distant district. There were eminent persons in the Council from Allahabad and Lucknow. Pandit Motilal came to Lucknow from Allahabad to arrange the preliminaries and hold consultations with the members regarding the selection of the leader of the Swaraj Party and its programme. He watched the proceedings, heard speeches. He put his hand on an obscure person and felt that this young man was to play a decisive role in Indian political life. He made the choice, chose him to lead the party in U. P., and carved a brilliant career for this young man.

Thirty years after Pantji as the Home Minister, India, speaking on the birthday of Pandit Motilal, expressed his feelings of gratefulness thus:

> "Pandit Motilal Nehru was a Prince among men and his name will ever be enshrined in letters of gold in the history of India. He set an example which will always continue to inspire the unborn generations of our land. I revere his memory also for personal reasons, as I owe an everlasting debt of gratitude to him for the kindliness and affection with which he treated me in younger days and the unfailing guidance and encouragement I received from him."

Motilal Nehru was the leader of the Swaraj Party in the Central Assembly, Deshbandhu Das in Bengal, M. R. Jaykar in Bombay, Dr. Moonje in Central Provinces and Pantji was to lead in U. P. For the first time the party system was noticeable in a much more developed form. The Swaraj Party constituted the chief opposition. They maintained a united front against the government. They introduced an organised and disciplined party organisation in the

Council. The report on the working of the Reformed Constitution submitted by U. P. Government to the Simon Commission mentioned thus on the formation of political parties:

> "In 1923 the appearance of a compact body of about thirty Swarajists gave the Council its first real experience of party discipline and party organisation. Pt. Govind Ballabh Pant is the leader. His tactical skill is considerable, and was responsible for his party's decisive influence in the debates on the Agra Tenancy Bill."

The rent and revenue Bills introduced in 1926 were the most important measures that had come before the legislature for a generation. Experience had shown that the Agra Tenancy Act of 1901 had failed in several important respects. The retention of the provision under which a tenant acquired occupancy rights in the land held for twelve years, coupled with the increased competition for land, had led to an ever-growing volume of harassing litigation. The non-occupancy tenant had no stability of tenure and no guarantee of a fair rent.

Pt. Motilal Nehru and Deshbandhu Das convened a meeting in Lucknow in January 1924 and in Delhi in February. Pantji was present at both meetings. As a result of the deliberations at Lucknow and Delhi Pt. Motilal Nehru was to put forward in the Legislative Assembly a motion, which he put on the 8th February, 1924. This was in the shape of an amendment to a resolution of Rangachariar recommending an early revision of the Government of India Act with a view to securing for India full self-governing Dominion Status within the British Empire together with responsible government in the provinces. The result was that the amendment was carried by an overwhelming majority recommending the Government of India to take steps to have the Government of India Act revised with a view to establish full responsible government in India, and for the said purpose to summon at an early date a representative Round Table Conference. During the course of the debate Sir Malcolm Haily, the Home Member pointed out that he was not willing to accept the amendment but he was prepared to hold an enquiry into the working of the Constitution as to the inherent defects of the

Government of India Act and the difficulties experienced in its smooth working. The Labour Government was in office and high hopes were raised by some remarks of Lord Olivier who was Labour Government's Secretary of State for India. A Reforms Enquiry Committee was appointed under the chairmanship of Sir Alexander Muddiman of which Sir Tej Bahadur Sapru and Jinnah were also members.

The Committee issued its report in March, 1925. The majority maintained that the present Constitution had not been in existence long enough to enable any decision on its merits to be pronounced, but the minority opposed this view and declared that Indian political opinion would be satisfied with nothing less than the abolition of Dyarchy and the institution of provincial autonomy. On September 7, 1925, Sir Muddiman who had become the Home Member moved a resolution in the Assembly recommending the acceptance of the principle underlying the Majority Report of the Reforms Enquiry Committee. A long amendment was moved by Pandit Motilal Nehru as Leader of the Swaraj Party, the gist of it being that immediate steps be taken to move His Majesty's Government to make a declaration in Parliament embodying such fundamental changes in the constitutional machinery and administration of India as would make the government of the country fully responsible. The amendment also recommended the holding of a Round Table Conference to frame a detailed scheme. The amendment was carried against the Government by 72 votes to 45.

Perhaps the most significant debate in the U.P. Legislative Council during this period was that of April 1925 over the resolution of Dr. Ganesh Prasad, which opened the most important question of the day—the report of the Reforms Enquiry Committee. The mover was a great mathematician of India, that masterful personality, who represented the Allahabad University and by his learned and lucid speeches showed that he was a great parliamentarian.

Dr. Ziauddin, another noted mathematician and an old class mate of the mover, was the second speaker on the resolution followed by another professor of History of the Allahabad University Dr. Shafat Ahamad Khan. The debate continued for two days. At the very outset it was made clear on behalf of the provincial government that they did not propose to take part in the debate. Pandit Pant spoke in the last before the mover's reply. All the speakers accorded their unqualified support to the resolution and it was adopted.

Pt. Pant said:

> "The question is much more momentous one. It raises constitutional issues of a far reaching character as the happiness and contentment, progress and prosperity of our people, the relations of Britain and India, and the goodwill between the two races depend on a sound and correct solution of the constitutional problem today ft is in that light that the question has to be looked into: but the Muddiman Committee Report does not touch the fringe of this question. So it is an absolutely worthless and disappointing document. I personally think that it is not regulations, it is not acts, it is not rules which determine the position of a people in the race for freedom. It depends entirely on faith and determination of the people to win freedom for themselves, and there is no body on earth who can obstruct the course of those who are after a right cause. The right to freedom is an inherent, inalienable right and everybody is entitled to rely on that well-recognised principle of self-determination.
>
> "As to dyarchy itself, nobody on earth has a good word to say about it and from its very nature it cannot be justified. There is not complete dyarchy as it is not feasible. We have got the same agency to work the transferred and the reserved departments so far as the permanent services are concerned. So far as this Council is concerned it has practically the same amount of legislative power in respect of both only with larger powers of veto, certification and restoration reserved for the Governor in respect of the reserved departments. Under these circumstances, what is there to distinguish one from the other? It is only the idea

in the minds of those who have to administer the two sides that make a difference. The finances which are above all the sinews of war and of peace in matters relating to administration, are in charge of a member of Council controlled by the Governor. Again it is the stepson knocking at the doors of a doting father whose fondness is for the weakling's stepmother. We have an immoveable executive which is supposed to be controlled by the legislature. What is the natural consequence? Constant friction and bitterness, the sense of irresponsibility in one and arbitrary power in the other, which leads again and again to the vicious circle. We are here only to express our conviction that unless and until this Constitution is amended fundamentally and categorically we cannot have anything rational to work through which the needs of the country may be fulfilled."

He concluded:

"In the end, I will make one submission and it is this. Too late is writ large in the history of this country, and all this bitterness has resulted because Government shadowed and eclipsed by the Bureaucracy, has failed to take notice of the omens betimes and has stupidly opposed popular wishes till the very last. It is time for them to reconsider their position. After all, this calm should not mislead them. Now, we have reached a situation in the country when the limit to tolerance has been reached, if not outstripped and it must think seriously before flouting public opinion now. The Rowlatt Act was never put into force; it had to be withdrawn; yet it roused the great storm of controversy, and looking at the various acts of the executive, you will find that in course of time the Government has followed on the heels of the popular opinion. It was forced, in the end, to accept its soundness and correctness. In this case think before it is too late and save India and save England; and put an end to the bitterness and animosity which will otherwise lead to the doom of both countries. There

> are breakers ahead and if you will cling to your discredited oars, the barge will be foundered and disaster will follow. After all, you have to restore to us what is ours, then why not do so in good grace and good time."

Sir Samuel O'Donnel, who was the Finance Member was the main spokesman of the government. He had officiated as Governor for four months in 1926. The province was indebted to him for the Agra Tenancy Act. He shaped the scheme originally, watched over it, and nursed it at all stages. He never showed to be an eloquent speaker but he showed what a powerful brain and a careful preparation could achieve. He was responsible for the unfriendly atmosphere between the government and the opposition. He surprised his critics when he adopted an extremely conciliatory tone while his manner was almost the perfection of courtesy. Once he described the members of opposition as professional politicians. At once Pandit Pant speaking after him castigated him in the following words:

> "I do not know exactly what the Hon'ble the Finance Member meant by the term 'professional politicians'."
>
> "Well, I do not know which particular class in this hall is expected to belong to that honoured category. I personally think, so far as paid politicians are concerned on the professional side, it is the benches opposite. So far as the professional politicians of an unpaid variety are concerned, whether good, bad or indifferent, practically all of us come under that category, for we profess to deal with politics and we are here with that object. We have made it a profession, an avowed profession of our own, to espouse the cause of our people. That was what we professed when we sought their vote and it was with that profession that we secured an entry here. So in that sense, I think we are all professional politicians.
>
> But if anything different were meant something after the term "agitator.

The Hon'ble O' Donnel: I did not use the term in that sense. I said 'without any disrespect.'

> Pt. G. B. Pant: I do not fight shy of it, because I remember Lord Morley when he said that all good causes were in fact espoused by that class which is called agitators. Whether we are called agitators or professional politicians, I would not fight shy of it. I, in fact, do say that every member in this House should try to be a professional politician. Politics in India should cease to be an armchair leisurely diversion, if people mind their business; and if they mean to do what is expected of them. If there is no one in the House who would like to fight shy of that profession, when he is here to espouse the cause of politics in favour of his country, in favour of justice and in favour of humanity."

After four and half years in August 1925 Michael Keane retired from the presidentship of the Council. He succeeded Sir Atul Chand Chatterji as Chief Secretary in 1919 and after 15 months he left the Chief Secretaryship to Lambert to become the first President of the Reformed Legislative Council in January 1921. He filled the office with great ability and distinction. His first appearance in Council made a little sensation as he showed himself a fluent speaker and a clever debater with an abundance of keen Irish wit.

Speaking on the occasion of his retirement Pandit Pant referred to the almost infallible character of the chair and expressed his grateful appreciation and admiration of the manner in which he had conducted the deliberations of the Council during the last one and half years that he was connected with its actual working. He said that it was difficult for any man to treat all questions with equal coolheadedness and impartiality in the midst of the heat of the debate and there were occasions when even those who had subdued their temper were likely to go wrong over matters of importance. He said that he conducted the deliberations of the House with impartiality and independence and conducted the business of the House with skill, tact, dignity and firmness.

He Recalled:

> "In fact the very day I entered this Council, I was impressed with the keenness with which you carried on you work. It was simply marvellous to see you giving out the name of every single member as he stood up from his seat to take the oath."

The Council was fortunate in the choice of a successor to the first official President. Sita Ram, then Rai Bahadur was elected and re-elected by the new Council. He enjoyed the confidence of all sections of the Council, and his authority was accepted without question. There had been no instances of disorderly conduct, and the debates were conducted with decorum. The Council conformed to English parliamentary practice. He demonstrated the fitness of Indians for the parliamentary system of government. He conducted the proceedings with marked ability, and grace, decorum, and earned the reputation of one of the successful presidents in India. He afterwards writing about Pantji said:

> "I used to admire the manner in which he had succeeded in making the Swaraj Party a well-knit and solid party in opposition and in earning the respect or fear of various sections of the House. His presentation of facts and marshalling of figures, his persuasiveness and method of speaking, coupled with a peculiar incisiveness and directness in speech, when necessary, made him quite a towering personality in those halcyon days of opposition."

In March 1926 prior to the general discussion on the budget Pandit Pant made a brief statement on behalf of the Swaraj Party and withdrew from the House in accordance with the mandate of the All India Congress Committee. The events of the last five years clearly demonstrated the mentality of the government which aimed to coerce the nation into abject submission without making any advance on the vicious system of government.

He said:

> "I do not intend to enter into any detailed criticism of the administration or to allude to its sins of

commission and omission. My experience has convinced me that the government is growing more and more unresponsive to public opinion. It is prepared to throw its oft-repeated proposals and professions to the ness and almost helplessness of our position here. The Government is already in a strong position on account of the various safeguards, reservations, and loopholes in the Government of India Act. They have been further fortified by the unfortunate communal differences among the people. So we are driven to the conclusion that the first and foremost task today is to mobilise that opinion, to obtain that sanction which will enable the public to exact from the Government those rights which it claims and which it has received from God and from nature. It is only through the assertion of that force that we can work. The wooden and cast-iron system does not know how to bend except to force, and it is that force which we mean to gather by acting outside. With these few words, Sir, I crave your permission for the members of the Swaraj Party to withdraw themselves from this House."

The disqualification of women from membership of the Council was responsible that no woman was a member of the Council. The disqualification was only removed in 1927. The percentage of votes recorded was 33 in 1920; 41.36 in 1923; and 49.32 in 1920.

General elections were held in November 1926. They were more keenly contested than the two previous elections. Pt. Madan Mohan Malaviya and Lala Lajpat Rai had formed a Nationalist Party and Nationalist candidates opposed Swarajist candidates. Pt. Motilal Nehru, Pt. Malaviya and Lala Lajpat Rai toured through a large part of the province in support of their candidates. Nationalist party was purely Hindu party. Its adherents were members who were formerly Liberals. The Swarajist Party suffered a set back. It was returned in smaller number. We have a recollection of this election. Pt. Motilal Nehru came to Bareilly after a strenuous election tour. He stayed with Pt. Dwarka Prasad. He was not well. His throat was so bad that he could speak with difficulty. Sri Sampurnanand was elected from Banaras on Swaraj Party ticket. Nawabzada Liaqut Ali Khan and Hafiz Mohammed Ibrahim entered the Council at this election. C. Y. Chintamani returned to the scene of his old labours after an absence of nearly four years. He led the Nationalist Party in the Council. Pt. Pant and Shri Chintamani were old friends. Though their parties had no formal alliance, but they worked together as there was no real difference between their aims and policy.

Both parties therefore found it easy to combine in criticising and defeating the government. The opposition was the strongest and the debates were of high order. As a debater both Pantji and Chintamani had no equal. The qualities of their speaking were those of logic and lucidity. The Council will never have such a combination of speakers as it had at this time.

At that time the event which engrossed public attention more fully than anything else was the publication of Miss Mayo's book "Mother India" in the early summer of 1927. Practically every newspaper in India denounced it as a scurrilous libel on Hindus. Gandhiji described it as 'drain inspector's report—a book for Englishmen to forget and Indians to remember'. It was freely alleged that Miss Mayo was subsidised to produce it in order to degrade India in the eyes of the world,—to prejudice her case for self government before the Statutory Commission. Some spirited replies were written by Lala Lajpat Rai in his "Unhappy India"; K. L. Gauba, "Uncle Sam"; C. S. Ranga Iyer, "Father India" to the tirade against the Indian Nation. Shrimati Uma Nehru in Hindi wrote a reply. For months there was a violent agitation in the press and the platform. During the autumn session of the Central Assembly the Home Member was subjected to a volley of questions.

Anti Simon Commission Agitation: The announcement regarding the appointment of Simon Commission was made on November 8, 1927. A fortnight later presiding over the 21st Session of the U.P. Political Conference at Aligarh, Pandit Pant said:

> "During the last fortnight the announcement of the appointment of the Simon Commission has stirred the country from one end to the other. It has been received with a chorus of strong condemnation by the intelligentia of all classes and communities. So far as

> Congressmen are concerned it has caused them neither surprise nor disappointment. The Congress stands for self-determination and refuses to recognise the right of any alien agency to frame a Constitution for India. The Congress claims that it is the inherent right of every nation to frame its own Constitution."

After six weeks of the announcement of this Commission the 42nd annual session of the Indian National Congress was held in Madras under the presidentship of Dr. Ansari. It was a very momentous session held in the Tilak Mandap. Inspiring mottos greeted the eyes. As one came up the main passage one read, "Are we children to *be* examined," "India expects everyone to do his duty." Pandit Jawaharlal Nehru who had recently arrived in India from Russia, addressed the delegates as "comrades" took a prominent part in the proceedings of the session. His resolution declaring that the goal of the Indian people was complete independence was carried by the Congress.

The other important resolution was for the boycott of the Simon Commission. The resolution was a comprehensive one and laid a programme as to how the boycott could be made successful and effective, that the Commission should be boycotted at every stage and in every form, that mass demonstrations should be organised throughout India, and that elected members of all legislative bodies should refuse to help the Commission. It was moved, seconded and supported by some of the very best speakers in the land like Dr. Annie Besant, Pandit Madan Mohan Malaviya, Pandit Govind Ballabh Pant, Maulana Shaukat Ali and Babu Shyam Sunder Chakarvarti. Mahatma Gandhi attended the session but he did not take part in the proceedings. Pandit Motilal Nehru was in England in connection with some professional work.

Pandit Pant took an important part in the debate on the resolution both in the Subjects Committee and in open session. He made a great impression on the audience by his speech in which he effectively deals with the pros and cons of the then political situation. He was staid, sober, simple, logical and at the same time eloquent. He was introduced by the General Secretary as the Leader of the Swarajist Party in U.P. Legislative council and President U.P.C.C. He ascended the rostrum amidst applause.

The previous day in the Subjects Committee, he had won laurels by his brilliant performance and his speech had been unanimously voted as the best speech made on the occasion.

The delegates had not left Madras when the sad news of the death of Hakim Ajmal Khan was received. He died at Rampur due to heart failure. The A. I. C. C. met under the shadow of this great loss. He was "India's one of the greatest patriots and workers in the cause of unity" as described in C. Rajagopalachari's draft resolution passed at A. I. C. C.

The Commission landed in Bombay on February 3, 1928, for its preliminary tour. That day an all India hartal was observed. By the beginning of the year 1928 the opposition to the Commission had reached its full strength. All the political parties Congress, Muslim League, Liberals, and others had declared for non-cooperation with the Commission.

Pandit Pant as President U. P. C. C. made an extensive tour of the province, addressed public meetings. He exhorted his audience to observe hartal on the 3rd Feb.— the day of the arrival of the Commission. He delivered stirring speeches advocating the boycott of the Simon Commission. He said the mere idea of one nation judging the fitness of another was abhorrent. Swaraj was not given but won. It was their birth right. In his opinion the appointment of the Commission was clear defiance of Indian public opinion. Responsible British Statesmen made pious declarations during war time that England stood for self-determination. No nation could rest content without Swaraj, without which there was no self-respect or honour.

A day before the arrival of Simon Commission, the Viceroy Lord Irwin addressed the members of the Central Legislature on February 2, 1928. His speech was a striking appeal for cooperation. His Excellency dealt with the charge that the exclusion of Indians from the Commission was an insult to Indian self respect. He admitted that the wisdom or unwisdom of excluding Indians was a question on which every man was entitled to his opinion. "But what no man is entitled to say—for it is quite simply not true—is that His Majesty's Government sought to offer a deliberate affront to Indian honour and Indian pride."

Sir John Simon and his colleagues came straight from Bombay to Delhi, where they arrived on February 4,1928. Major Attlee, who later became the Prime Minister under the Labour Government and in whose regime India ultimately achieved independence, was one of the members of this Commission. From Delhi they went to Calcutta, then to Madras, and other places in the Madras Presidency. Practically everywhere, they were received by "Simon Go Back" demonstrations. Their preliminary visit ended on March 31.

The discussion on the Simon Commission was the pivot of the whole session in the Central Assembly and U. P. Legislative Council. In the Central Assembly Lala Lajpat Rai moved a resolution declaring that the Constitution and scheme of the Statutory Commission were wholly unacceptable to the House, and that the Legislative Assembly would have nothing to do with the Commission at any stage or in any form. The most important speakers were Javakar, Jinnah, Sir Basil Blackett—Finance Member, Pt. Motilal Nehru, and Pt. Madan Mohan Malaviya. The resolution was carried by 68 *to* 62. Hardly had this result been declared when a reporter of a nationalist daily newspaper in Delhi threw an attache case down from the press gallery on Sir Basil Blackett's head. Sir Basil was partially stunned for a moment but suffered no injury. His assailant explained that his misdeed was meant as a reply to the speech delivered at Doncaster a few days previously by Lord Birkenhead.

A Memorable Debate: It was on February 24 and 25 when a debate was held in the U. P. Legislative Council in Lucknow on the Simon Commission. Never since the introduction of reforms has a question of vital importance aroused such a keen and widespread interest as this one which was discussed on the floor of the U. P. Council. It was a question then of supreme national importance. The entire attention of the country was focused on it. Every shade of opinion was fully expressed.

It had engaged the attention of the whole of India for the last four months. I had gone to Lucknow with Pt. Dwarka Prasad who was an ex-chairman of Bareilly Municipal Board and in 1937 was elected M. L. A. We had the opportunity of witnessing this historic debate in which Pt. Pant appeared conspicuously. This debate aroused greater interest both in the House itself and in the country than any other debate within living memory. The visitors galleries were overcrowded. There was record attendance of members. There were scenes of wild enthusiasm. Every available inch of space in the five galleries reserved for visitors was occupied. They were crowded for beyond their capacity. The special gallery reserved for ladies was fully occupied. Maj. Paterson, Private Secretary to the Governor was present in the Governor's Gallery. The forces on each side were equally matched. For a week before the newspapers had editorials drawing attention to the forthcoming debate and the duty of legislators. Never perhaps in the annals of the U. P. Council had such universal interest been aroused in the public mind as on this occasion.

The debate was worthy of the occasion, the recollection of which will live in the memories of those who had listened to it. It was my first experience. The speech of Mukandi Lal, who moved the resolution, occupied nearly three quarter of an hour. He made a very strong case for the boycott of the Commission. Badri Dutt Pandey, with whom I had the privilege to come in close contact in jail in 1942, next supported the resolution in a thunderous speech which was very warmly received.

Nawabzada Liaqut Ali Khan, who became the first Prime Minister of Pakistan, delivered a very fine speech in support of the resolution. Sir George Lambert who was the Finance Member spoke on behalf of the Government and pleaded for postponement. He was appointed the Finance Member only some months before. Previous to that he was the Chief Secretary and held that office for the long period of 6½ years when he was succeeded in 1927 by Kunwar Jagdish Prasad. His reputation as Chief Secretary was that he was very able and still more industrious, that nobody could beat him in the knowledge of details.

But he had rarely spoken in Council as Chief Secretary. When he was elevated to the office of the Finance Member it was wondered how he would acquit himself in debates. He had taken some lessons at home. As Pandit Pant remarked at the very outset of his speech referring to Finance Member that he was a novice in the art and had just entered the arena He began by congratulating Lambert for his speech. The resolution was discussed threadbare.

The objections raised by the speakers of the treasury benches were fully answered by those whose ability, patriotism or public spirit could not be disputed.

Pandit Pant spoke in the last and after his speech the closure was moved. He was loudly cheered when he rose to speak. It was punctuated with frequent applause. It is difficult to summarise this speech. A period of 30 years has elapsed and still his sonorous words ring into my cars which I heard as a boy. I had not thought that one day I would have the opportunity to be in his close companionship. We cannot forget the feelings of elation which we then experienced and which inspired us afterwards. Pandit Pant said:

> "The monstrous plot brought forth by the Baldwin-Birkenhead Cabinet has been torn to pieces by almost every one from even among those Indian politicians who have received solemn testimonials about their sobriety and moderation from the accredited representatives of the bureaucracy. So far as the Indian National Congress is concerned, its differences are fundamental and go to the very root of this scheme. We stand for self-determination. The history of the growth of self-governing institutions within the British Empire has demonstrated that there is only one way for the solution of the constitutional difficulties, and that can be found only in the country for which the Constitution has to be devised and only by those people who are to be affected by that Constitution. This principle had been discovered by actual experience before the sacred doctrine of self-determination was formally proclaimed from the house tops by self-seeking egoists, at an hour of crisis, to save their own skins. That is a principle which history has vindicated as being the only sound principle on which a lasting Constitution can be based."

After narrating the experiences of various Dominions of the British Commonwealth the Leader of the Opposition observed, "History has established two or three principles and they are indisputable. It has been repeatedly proved that unless and until a Constitution framed and formulated by the representatives of the people of the country for which the Constitution is intended is introduced, makeshift contrivances cannot put an end for the struggle for liberty, nor can they secure satisfaction or stability. It is equally clear that whatever efforts have been made to superimpose something from without, it has only added to complications and bitterness and has made things worse."

Proceeding Pandit Pant quoted a speech of Sir John Simon which he delivered in 1921 speaking on the Irish Constitution Bill in which he had pointedly observed that "Constitutions which promote prosperity and loyalty and which have been found to be lasting Constitutions.... have been framed by those who were to live under them themselves." He gave a conclusive and direct reply to the authors of the scheme. He wondered how Sir John Simon should have agreed to be a party to the working of a scheme which went fundamentally against the principles which he enunciated in 1921.

Referring to a sentence from the speech of the Finance Member that "in politics the unexpected often happens',' Pandit Pant retorted by quoting the case of Ireland when the Government in power in 1920 did not agree to the conferment of Dominion Status on Ireland and within a year of the passage of the Home Rule Act in 1921 the British Parliament had to confer on Ireland a Constitution going far beyond the Dominion Status. "The unexpected happened," said the speaker looking towards the Finance Member, "and it happened within a year. I am not using the language of intimidation. I ask the Government in power here who are in close touch with the state of things in this country, to tell those who are their masters and who have appointed them our masters, that the unexpected happens so often and the unexpected may also happen in India. The British people and Parliament accepted to a letter the Home made schemes in the case of Canada, in the case of South Africa, and in the case of Ireland, why do they fight shy even of a Round Table Conference in our case? Is it because they think that old India is lying prostrate today? Will the lessons of history be of no avail to them? They were deluded by appearances in Ireland but within a year Ireland proved its might and British Government had to bend. "Too late" is inscribed in dark letters in so many chapters of British history. Will they realise their blunder in the case of India in time?

> "I ask my hon'ble friends to bear in mind the parting will and testament of that great and good man Hakim Ajmal Khan, who died with the words on his tongue "Boycott this Commission".

Concluding it Pandit Pant said:

> "If you are dissatisfied with the all white Commission, it is your duty, the duty you owe to your country, the duty that you owe to your conscience, the duty that you owe to your future generations, to assert yourself unambiguously before it becomes too late. And if you fail to do so, mind, you are taking a great and irksome and very terrific responsibility on yourself and it will be for you to answer the generations to come for having stood in the way of the progress of this great country at a critical hour. It is your duty in your own interest to support the movement of boycott so that there may be more places available for you there. So far as we are concerned, we are soldiers in this battle of Swaraj and we do not ask for anything until and unless we have reached that glorious goal which can be attained only through the path of righteousness, rectitude and self-abnegation. So in your own interest, I ask you, to think twice before giving your vote against this resolution."

There was a tense feeling of suspense when the President (Dr. Sita Ram) who had high fever by mistake announced the victory of the opponents of the resolution. The official benches were in high glee but their rejoicing was short-lived. The anticlimax came with the discovery of the mistake which was duly announced. "I apologise to the House," said the President, "The result is other way about. The Ayes 56, Noes 55." Those who thought that they were the victors suddenly found themselves converted into the vanquished. The two ministers Rai Rajeshwari Bali, and Kunwar Rajendra Singh remained neutral in the division and they had to pay thé price of this neutrality by their resignation from the office of the ministership.

On March 26, 1928, a grand political dinner was given by the citizens of Kanpur to the members of opposition to celebrate their victory on the Simon Commission Resolution in U. P. Council. It was a matter of great achievement. The composition of the then Council showed that the Government had a solid block of 25 votes and in addition had the support of a non-descript party of 30 or 35 members who had no political creed. In spite of the pressure brought on them, the progressive section of the house was able to carry the motion of non-confidence in the Simon Commission.

The dinner was attended by the members of the Council, leading citizens of United Provinces and citizens of Kanpur. Prominent among those present were Sir Tej Bahadur Sapru, Pandit Govind Ballabh Pant, Sri C. Y. Chintamani, Nawabzada Liaqut Ali Khan.

Pandit Pant was in Nainital. He started by car in the evening of 25th March to participate in the dinner at Kanpur. When he reached Kathgodam, the train had left. He proceeded further in the car to catch the train. When he reached Bareilly the same fate awaited him. The Lucknow train had left. There was no option except to proceed by car or abandon the idea of joining the dinner. To the surprise of all Pandit Pant reached Kanpur by car.

Vikramajit Singh welcomed the guests on behalf of the citizens of Kanpur. He admired Pandit Pant for robust optimism, undoubted courage, stout advocacy and able leadership for his sagacity, forethought, tactfulness and resourcefulness.

Narain Prasad Nigam speaking next paid a tribute to him. He said: "Pandit Pant has risen to the position which he occupies in the Council by sheer dint of merit. We have been knowing each other since college days, and I can say that the high hopes that were formed of him have been more than fulfilled. I think he has a great future before him. So quiet and unassuming, so sincere and able, he is a very fine type of public worker." How prophetic his words were!

Nawabzada Liaqut All Khan, speaking next said that from his experiences of 17 months membership of the Council he would say without fear of contradiction that the lead which Pandit Pant had given in the cause of the country deserved their gratitude. Warm tributes were also paid by Sir Tej Bahadur Sapru.

Pandit Pant speaking at the dinner was in a very humorous mood. Amidst laughter he said, "If you and other friends could arrange such substantial dinners from time to time, I assure you that that would give a source of great strength to us." He spoke on the stupidity", audacity and impudence of the authors of the Commission. "The idea of examination about our fitness for Swaraj is obnoxious to me."

The U. P. Government having lost the battle on the Simon Commission issue thought of another device. Lambert on behalf of the government moved that the Council elect a Committee of seven members to cooperate with the Simon Commission when the Council met in Nainital on September 18 in a mood of great expectation. Among those present in the visitor's gallery were Lady Haily, wife of the Governor, Sir John and Lady Shea. Pandit Pant sought permission to make a few remarks before the Finance Member moved his motion. He said that no alternative course was open to him and his party except to dissociate themselves completely from the motion having regard to their sense of personal decency, national dignity and the honour of the House.

He asked for what the legislatures existed, if their verdicts, recorded after careful, elaborate full dress debates were going to be reopened every day, if the executive took it into its head to bring forward the question again. On February 25 a clear, emphatic and definite verdict was recorded by the members of the House. That verdict was not the verdict of any precipitate hurry. After carefully weighing all the pros and cons of the proposition before them, they definitely determined that this House would never have anything to do with the Statutory Commission at any stage and in any form. Now they were asked to trample upon that resolution. However, emphatically the resolution might be couched the point was clear that the Government wanted the House to cooperate with the Commission. The trend of thought and opinion as exhibited in the results of the two by-elections held within the last two months amply convinced that the country was against the Commission.

Concluding Pt. Pant said:

> "I may also state here that it has been fully disclosed by the proceedings of this House as well as outside that there is a fundamental difference of outlook and of ideal between those who want to cooperate with the Commission and those who do not want to have anything to do with it. There are those in whose scheme of things the central figure is the starving skeleton in the field, and there are those in whose scheme of things there is the pampered fat man on the pedestal to whom everything and everybody must bend and submit. Between there two classes there is little chance of agreement. There are those who want the people to rise, there are those who want the economic uplift of the masses; there are those, on the other hand, who would only desire to have more of the loaves and fishes, who would care more for the service than for the service of the people and who would care more for high posts and for high salaries than for the service of those for whom these services are meant. If there are people who want to whine before the Commission, let them have unrestricted scope. Let those who desire to dance to the tune of their masters have the joy of it. But we, on the other hand, have only one goal before us, that is, the goal of liberty, of freedom for the country. We feel that in the present circumstances, when all constitutional methods, when everything has been thrown to the winds, has been trampled upon, there can be only one goal, that noble goal, that glorious goal of Independence for this great country. We cannot think of anything else. We have to live and to die for that; and for us these little juggleries in the forms of commissions and committees, these little devices in one name or another, have little meaning. We must steer clear of them all. We refuse to be deluded, to be misguided by these things. We see the vision of the glorious mother installed above all these bickerings,

> above all these little handicaps, high up in the clouds, and we want to seek that road which will lead to that; that road which is not to be found inside the nets of this House, that road which is not to be found inside the machinations of the bureaucratic nets; but which is to be found apart and away from that; that road, which, however long it may be, is sure to lead us to our goal. We depend on ourselves to carve our future. We know that nations by themselves are made. We care not for your commissions. We care not for your manipulated, manoeuvred factious intrigues. We are after something better. We know that it is only through self-sacrifice, through self-abnegation, that that object can be attained. For the present, we make to you a present of your Commission. Make use of it as you like. For us there is room elsewhere. Enough of it."

Another exciting debate followed in the autumn of 1928 at Nainital on the resolution of non-confidence, moved and passed against a newly appointed minister, Raja Jagannath Bux Singh. Tense atmosphere seething with intense excitement prevailed when for the first time that during the past seven years a vote of non-confidence was brought before the House against a minister. It was carried by 58 votes against 57.

The Land Revenue (Amendment-Settlement) Bill was enacted in 1929. The Joint Select Committee of the two Houses of Parliament appointed to consider the Government of India Bill 1920 were of the opinion that the rules were often obscure and imperfectly understood by those who pay the revenue and recommended that the main principles by which the land revenue is to be determined, the method of valuation, the pitch of assessment, the periods of revision and the graduation of enhancement should be regulated by law. Accordingly the U. P. Government appointed a Committee in 1922 to examine the whole question. It was not until 1926 that a Bill was introduced in the legislature making a number of important concessions to Zamindars, as they had a preponderant influence on the government. They were influential in the legislature and the Governor could always exercise his special powers if an unacceptable situation arose. The Land Revenue Bill introduced in 1926 was withdrawn as the Zamindars outvoted the Government and the amendments made by them were considered objectionable by the Government. After the withdrawal of the 1926 Bill, there was continued pressure for codification of settlement principles.

The annual demand for survey and settlements was rejected in 1927 by the Council on this ground and was passed in 1928, only on an assurance that the Government would introduce legislation at an early date. Eventually the Government introduced a Bill which finally emerged as the U. P. Land Revenue (Amendment) Act of 1929. It was piloted by Lambert and Pantji took a leading part in the whole debate. The principles of assessment laid down by the Act were vague and left wide discretion to the Settlement officer.

Pandit Pant, who was a member of the Select Committee, noted in his minute of dissent:

> "I am conscious of the fact that no code can claim perfection and that experience has revealed defects even in the products of consummate jurists and draftsmen, but I find that the Bill is imperfect by design and its defects are patent. It is an elementary principle of legislation that statutes should not lack in precision and definiteness. The doctrine is applied with special rigidity to fiscal enactments which should not leave any loophole for the vagaries of the executive. This Bill, however, yields very wide latitude to the settlement officer in vital matters. His percentage of net assets to be taken as revenue may ordinarily range between 35 and 45 and where he considers the circumstance to be special he may descend to 20 or ascend to 50 as he may deem fit. Similarly he is free to grant an allowance of 15 per cent or at double that rate, on the valuation of proprietary cultivation, again in accordance with his own notions unfettered by any rules or regulations. A proposal to leave it to the discretion of an Income-Tax Officer whether to assess the tax at the rate of six or twelve pies on the rupee,

> or of a Customs Officer to charge import or export duty on an article at any rate varying from 35 to 45 per cent, of its value, according to his appraisement of the circumstances of the person concerned, would be regarded as preposterous. Such laxity in a financial statute is indefensible. But the Government shuns a rational treatment of the subject of land revenue settlement and would not accept a concrete formula for the proper valuation of the circumstances of a proprietor. I am convinced that the scientific system of land revenue assessment can be founded only *on* the principle of progressive assessment on an elaborately graduated scale."

He found that the land revenue policy resulted in the misery and degradation of millions of cultivators, their increasing poverty and the inefficiency of agriculture. He endeavoured to give these teeming millions security of tenure and a fixed rent. Effective protection was not given until the Congress Government passed the U.P. Tenancy Act in 1939."

The result of his strong opposition was that the vagueness of the Bill was to a certain extent mitigated. But a graduated scale proposed in the Council was defeated, as all the big zamindars voted on the side of the government. He took full interest in the debate. His criticisms were very helpful and his knowledge of the Bill in which he had taken part in 1926 proved to be of great value.

Lambert in his speech in the end expressed his gratitude to Pandit Pant. "Maulvi Fasihuddin has referred to Pt. Govind Ballabh Pant's assistance in the select committee. He has given us plenty of trouble here, but I freely acknowledge the help which he gave during the seven long days of the select committee's deliberations."

Experiences of Lathi Charges: Pandit Pant was elected to preside over the 21st Session of the U. P. Political Conference held at Aligarh on November 26, 1927. As soon as it was brought to his notice that his name was recommended for the presidentship, he requested to fix the choice on Dr. Murari Lal. The country was then passing through a dark phase in our national history. There were internecine quarrels political workers were divided into several parties while forces of reaction were solidly arrayed against them. India was being treated to gross affronts and injury and the enemies of the country were busy poisoning the world opinion by insidious propaganda. At such a juncture Pantji was called upon to guide the destiny of the country. The conference was attended by Dr. Ansari, President-elect of the Madras Session of the Indian National Congress, B. Shive Prasad Gupta, T. A. K. Sherwani, Maulana Hasrat Mohani and others.

In the previous year the 20th Session of the Conference was held in his home town Kashipur in Nainital district under the presidentship of Pt. Motilal Nehru and Pantji read out the welcome address as President of the Reception Committee. At that time communal question was the most conspicuous feature of social and political life. It overshadowed every other question, not excluding the Statutory Commission and Constitutional reforms. It was the main obstacle to Swaraj and often lead to violent outbursts and disturbances of the public peace.

In his presidential address he dwelt on various questions of the day like Sangathan and Tanzeem, violence, newspapers, scurrilous writings and separate electorates:

> "The qualities needed for a judicious consideration of these matters," said Pt. Pant, "are clarity, toleration, a rational outlook and a true sense of perspective."

He felt that Swaraj was the only remedy of Communal discord. He said:

> "I want to impress upon you emphatically that the sovereign remedy for our distemper is Swaraj. History has proved from time to time strife, factions and dissensions thrive in the hot bed of foreign domination and disappear in the bright sunshine of freedom."

Pandit Pant held that the Commission was a gross and deliberate affront on us. He said that it was a blessing in disguise. "To us it has proved a veritable blessing. The depth of feeling roused by the white Commission has revealed a hopeful unanimity among Indians regardless of differences of caste, creed and politics. This shows that the heart of the country is sound and that it can brook no insult to the motherland. History has repeatedly proved that there is a limit to the capacity for forbearance even of fallen and oppressed people, and when tyrants become too bold and aggressive their victims shake off their lethargy and raise their heads against the oppressor. He added:

> "The Government have by their calculated insult to national dignity facilitated the task of Congressmen and revivified to a certain extent the national movement."

Referring to the need for concerted action Pt. Pant said:

> "This is the psychological moment in the history of our unfortunate country. Let us offer a united front. There can be only two parties in this country—those who stand by the bureaucracy and foreign rule and those who stand by the motherland and Swaraj. He suggested that they should have a national fund and paid workers as he was convinced that no work could be performed in a systematic and regular manner unless and until they had a National Fund and paid workers. He added "The sacrifice cannot lose its merit because of their acceptance of a living wage. It was our duty to carry on constructive programme of the Congress which is the key to our success."

Concluding Pt. Pant said:

> "Even the darkest night ushers the soft dawn which leads on to bright sunshine. The lowest ebb is followed by a rise. No nation having once entered the arena of freedom has lost the battle. Let us then hopefully, prayfully and in a spirit of humanity resolve that we will carry the struggle uncessantly, in fair weather or oul, undaunted by failures and chastened by success, relying on our own powers, in the righteousness of our cause and on the strength and momentum which Right gathers as it marches onwards, till we reach our goal."

The Simon Commission landed on October 11, 1928 for the second time and remained in India till 13th April 1929. They visited Lahore on October 30, when Lala Lajpat Rai heading a huge 'Go back Simon Commission' procession, was assaulted and beaten by lathis on the chest. In the same evening the Lion of the Punjab addressed a huge gathering in Lahore. One sentence which he uttered echoed throughout India:

> "Every blow that they hurled at us, drove one more nail into the coffin of the Empire."

On 17th November Lala Lajpat Rai died. His last article published in the 'People' of November 1, 1928 mentioned:

> "This is the time when we ought to know who's who and this is the time when we are inclined to think that those who are not with us are against us."

His end was hastened by the injuries he had received. Apart from his contribution towards the attainment of freedom, he pushed ahead the cause of social, cultural and educational advancement of the people. He was a great journalist and a writer of eminence.

Pandit Pant in the U. P. Council paid the following tribute on the death of Lala Lajpat Rai:

> "He was one of the most distinguished sons of Mother India and he was most loyal to his country throughout his life. He did all that any human being could do for the uplift of his people. He devoted every particle of his energy, every minute of his time and every pie of his income to the service of his community. To the very last he had only one ambition, that was to see his country emancipated from foreign rule. He was not a man of words only but above all he was a hero of action and he demonstrated his real, genuine, ardent enthusiasm for his motherland by the sufferings to which he was subjected continuously, at least for a period of twenty years. His deportation followed by his exile and his enforced sojourn in a foreign land spoke of his real love for his country. He was a very

energetic social reformer, a great educationist and ardent supporter of all good causes, a very generous philanthropist, a selfless patriot, a valiant champion of people's cause and one above all who knew not only how to live but also how to die for the freedom of his country. His courage knew no bounds and fearlessness was writ large on his feature. It is most agonising that a man like him should have been chased throughout his life by those who happen to be in power in this country today. If Lala Lajpat Rai's death can be connected with the brutal, barbarous assault which he received at the age of over 60 it can still be traced to the fell disease which he contracted while he was confined in Mandalay Jail. There can be no doubt that his end was accelerated by the persecution he was subjected to by our foreign masters. *I* would not say more about this painful aspect of this sad incident on this solemn occasion. There are no signs of any wisdom in the other quarter and I only pray that many of us may have the courage and the strength to sacrifice their all and in the end themselves for the freedom and emancipation of their mother country. For so long as the present system continuous, there can be no hope for the best among us and the hope for the best lies only in following the footsteps of Lala Lajpat Rai and in courting death alone and nothing else can move."

The Simon Commission visited Lucknow on 30th November after their visit of Agra. Elaborate preparations were made for the boycott of the Commission. A Boycott Committee was constituted with Mohanlal Saksena as its convener. Pandit Nehru and Pandit Pant were also in Lucknow on this occasion when the city witnessed savage lathi charges. Among the victims were the men like Jawaharlal Nehru and Govind Ballabh Pant. These were the events of the greatest possible importance which attracted India-wide attention. Pandit Nehru and Pandit Pant would have been killed on the morning of November 30, but for the chivalry of some students of the Lucknow University who formed a cordon around them.

Pandit Nehru in his Autobiography thus described:

> "After what seemed a tremendous length of time, but was probably only a few minutes, our line began to yield slowly, step by step, without breaking up. This left me somewhat isolated, and more exposed at the sides. More blows came, and then I was suddenly lifted off my feet from behind and carried off, to my great annoyance. Some of my young colleagues, thinking that a dead-set was being made at me, had decided to protect me in this summary fashion. Now that the excitement of the moment had passed, I felt pains all over my body and great fatigue. Almost every part of me seemed to ache, and I was covered with contused wounds and marks of blows. But fortunately I was not injured in any vital spot. Many of our companions were less fortunate, and were badly injured. Govind Ballabh Pant, who stood by me, offered a much bigger target, being six foot odd in height, and the injuries he received then have resulted in a painful and persistent malady which prevented him for a long time from straightening his back or leading an active life."

Speaking in the Council on Chintamani's adjournment motion Pandit Pant said:

> "If I have ever stood before this House with a genuine feeling of embarrassment it is today. My name has been prominently mentioned with the splendid activities that are associated with this city of Lucknow in connection with the visit of the Simon Commission. I can say this much, that I am not swayed by any feeling of anger or resentment. If a personal explanation or confession of or faith can be permitted, I am prepared to say with all humility that I am proud of the part that I took on November 29 and 30, and it is my prayer, my sincere, earnest, humble prayer to the Almighty that He may give me strength to face the brute force of which we are the victims not only

when it is displayed by means of batons, but also when we have to face more serious ordeals for it is only thus that one can put an end to a raj which is based entirely and exclusively on brutal and physical force and on might and nothing else."

Gandhiji from Wardha congratulated Pandit Nehru. "It was all done bravely," he wrote, "You have braver things to do. May God spare you for many a long year to come and make you His chosen instrument for freeing India from the yoke."

G. W. Gwynne was the Deputy Commissioner of Lucknow at this time, who was the Chief Secretary when ten years afterwards Pandit Pant became the Premier of this province. In 1938 he died on his voyage home. He was Chief Secretary at an exceptionally difficult period. His long experience, sound judgement and administrative ability were of the utmost value to Pt. Pant as Premier who was then new to office.

Heading the Provincial Government

Govind Ballabh Pant became Premier of U.P. in 1937-38 and Chief Minister from 1946-1954. During his rule, a series of laws were passed granting full rights to the peasants. During his Chief Ministership, several measures for rural development were initiated. The zamindari system was abolished and land reforms were introduced. Govind Ballabh Pant's vision of rural India was for creating suitable social and legal climate in which peasantry would be prosperous and Indian urban centres would be surrounded by flourishing countryside. With this aim in view, he was determined to make the peasants fully secure in their possessions of land. With the dawn of freedom, an all-out drive was made to encourage village industries including handicrafts. A regeneration of the economy was on the agenda, and series of welfare programmes were initiated for rural uplift. The rural development programme under Govind Ballabh Pant became for the first time an important plank of government policy. In addition, new schemes for irrigation were launched. Research centres for production of better variety of rice, wheat, pulses and maize were started. Villages were linked up with market centres through a network of new roads. Programme of rural electrification was taken up. Rural banks for providing loans to the peasants were started. More schools and colleges were opened for creating an infrastructure for social and economic development. Several steps were taken to usher in social and economic transformation of the villages of U.P. This was a signal contribution of Govind Ballabh Pant as Chief Minister of U.P.

Member of Legislative Assembly

When Pant became a member of the U.P. Legislature, he supported the District Board Primary Education Bill introduced by the government. The programme was the same which had been advocated earlier by him. He also brought forward a bill in 1925 for the development of rural areas in U.P.

The untouchables, called Harijans by Gandhiji, were not treated properly by the high-caste Hindus, although the Harijans were Hindus themselves. They were not allowed to draw water from the wells used by the high-caste Hindus. Similarly, they were not allowed to worship in the temples. Govind Ballabh organised a Conference at Almora on 10 November 1932, called "Kurmanchal Samaj Sammelan". At this Conference, a community kitchen was organised in which the Harijans were asked to cook meals. All those who attended the Sammelan under the leadership of Govind Ballabh, ate food cooked and served by the Harijans. Similarly, he led the Harijans to enter temples. For the first time they were permitted entry into the Murli Manohar Temple at Almora.

Thus, it will be seen from the above account of Govind Ballabh's activities that he proved to be a true follower of Gandhiji and the Indian National Congress, which had adopted these programmes as part of national reconstruction of India.

Under the Non-cooperation programme, as devised by Gandhiji, the courts and schools were boycotted; national schools were started; khadi was spun and khadi clothes were worn by nationalist Indians. British goods and clothes were burnt in the bonfires and "swadeshi" became an act of faith for all Congressmen. Govind Ballabh followed these programmes as a true follower of Gandhiji; in letter and spirit he became a true Gandhian. Once, he said:

> "The history of India is the common heritage of all Indians born of common ancestors. Hindus and Muslims are equally entitled to share the pride of the glorious past of this great country. It is true that their religions differ but they have drawn their sustenance from the same soil for many a millennium.
>
> "Ours is a secular State. This solemn declaration... forms an integral part of our Constitution. There can he no difference in our State between man and man on account of religion, creed, caste or other similar considerations. It is the privilege of everyone to serve the nation... so that every citizen, whatever his faith, may live in peace and may have full opportunity to develop his personality... and to enjoy his full share of the privileges, amenities and comforts that our State can provide."

On National Scene

By 1930, Govind Ballabh Pant was recognised as an eminent leader of national movement in U.P. He worked with great leaders of U.P. like Purushottam Das Tandon, T.T.K. Sherwani, Sri Prakasha, Rafi Ahmed Kidwai, and others. He had come into close contact with Mahatma Gandhi, Motilal Nehru, Sarojini Naidu, Jawaharlal Nehru, Maulana Azad, Sardar Patel, who were outstanding leaders at the national level. They all appreciated Pant's qualities of leadership. His complete dedication to national cause, which was to achieve independence for India, was recognised. Everyone was impressed by his patriotism, his faith in the composite culture of India and complete loyalty to the Indian National Congress, its ideals and programmes. Pant proved to be an Indian first and last. He was untouched by any trace of communalism in his personal or public behaviour. Like the Congress, he was determined *to* remove untouchability, which he considered as a curse for the Hindus.

Sole Leader in Hill Region

He also emerged as the undisputed leader of Kumaon through his constructive political programmes. By his advocacy of abolition of the *coolie-begar* system, or fight for the rights of the people for the use of grazing lands in forest areas, or collection of fire wood from forests, or promotion of primary and elementary system of education for the people, he had endeared himself to the people of Kumaon. Also, he had brought the people of Kumaon hills into the mainstream of nationalist movement. He had steadfastly supported the cause of untouchables and had succeeded in opening the doors of temples to them. In schools, public places, they were welcomed mainly through the efforts of Govind Ballabh Pant and his devoted followers of the Congress programme.

During 1920-22 he had organised the people in favour of the Non-cooperation movement. Similarly, in 1930-31, when Civil Disobedience movement started, following Salt Satyagraha, widespread support was ensured through his leadership. His fame as a great organiser and political leader had already spread beyond the confines of Kumaon and U.P. by this time.

Under Gandhiji's Influence

The influence of Gandhiji on Govind Ballabh Pant became manifest from the beginning of his contact with him. The entire nation had supported the non-violent, Non-cooperation movement offered by Gandhiji. Govind Ballabh participated in the Non-cooperation movement as a soldier of freedom. Also, his ideas and approach to rural development, through the growth of cottage industries, establishment of national system of education, and programme for social uplift of the untouchables, appealed to him and he followed Gandhiji. Like Gandhiji, he also led an extremely simple, pious and honest life. He moulded his conduct on the lines which Gandhiji had taught millions of men and women of his times.

During the Non-cooperation movement of 1921-22, Govind Ballabh Pant organised political movement in the Kumaon region. During the Salt Satyagraha in 1930-31, several meetings were held under his leadership and salt was manufactured. The action taken was symbolic, since salt could not be manufactured on the hills.

The main aim was to defy the salt laws. Series of arrests were made by the British in the Kumaon region and Govind Ballabh was sentenced and imprisoned for leading satyagraha movement in these regions.

Non-cooperation Movement

In 1921, the Non-cooperation movement against the British rule was started by Gandhiji millions of peasants, workers, artisans, from all parts of the country participated. People from other classes like professionals, educationists, lawyers also followed him. The movement truly became a mass movement under the leadership of Gandhiji. He wanted the movement to remain non-violent and peaceful, in spite of the atrocities perpetrated by the government on the people. Lakhs of people were put into jail. Property and houses of several thousand persons were attached by the government.

The movement, however, had at places become violent and at Chauri Chaura, in Gorakhpur district, the crowd surrounded a police station and set it on fire, killing a few policemen, who were inside the building. Gandhiji withdrew the movement after this incident. Many leaders criticised Gandhiji for this, but he continued to maintain that the movement led by him must remain non-violent and peaceful.

In 1929, he launched yet another mass movement against the British rule. The movement was seemingly against the imposition of salt tax. But the main purpose was to show to the people of India that the British rule was unjust, callous and, therefore, must be overthrown. He declared that salt, like air and water was a product of nature, and was born out of the Indian soil, and the taxes imposed on this basic necessity of life, which every Indian, rich or poor, used, was "unethical" and that the tax was "iniquitous" and must be withdrawn. Otherwise, he declared he would break the salt laws by manufacturing salt himself. The famous Dandi March, as you know, led by him, was undertaken. He walked from Sabarmati Ashram covering 200 miles and reached Dandi on the coast of Bombay and broke the salt law. Millions of Indians did the same in other parts of the country and that transformed the whole country into one rebel camp against the British.

Gandhiji had identified himself with the poor. He lived in a thatched mud hut in the ashram named Sevagram in Wardha and wore only a loin cloth, just as the poor people of India did. And he set an example of sacrifice, suffering, truthfulness and dignified conduct. His followers came from all classes and communities. Hindus, Muslims, Christians, Sikhs all appreciated his leadership. He was deeply religious but believed in the greatness of all religions and believed in the cultural oneness of India. He was a true Indian and the greatest among them.

During the nationalist movement, Gandhiji was able to gather around him some of the great men and women *of* India. Every province, every city, every district, town and village in India produced its heroes during this epic period.

It was Gandhiji who was the first person to impress on his countrymen that India could not make progress if villages remained backward and poor. More than 80 per cent of the population of India lived in villages, he declared, and unless the quality of life in the villages was improved, the nation would not be able to march forward. He worked, therefore, incessantly for village uplift; drew out a plan for the growth of village handicrafts and cottage industries; adopted *charkha* for weaving, and through these measures, he hoped that the weak, the downtrodden and the untouchables, would begin to eke out a respectable living for themselves. What was most important, he said, this would instil in them a sense of pride in their own skills and train them to become self-reliant; and in the process a new awareness for eventual social resurgence of India would emerge.

Efforts for Reforms

Under the leadership of Jawaharlal Nehru, the Indian National Congress sought to create essential conditions so that the rural areas flourished and prospered. This could be achieved, Nehru declared, if rights of ownership to all tenants were granted, so that these small peasants could remain secure in their lands and their households, and were free from feudal burdens. The rights of ownership meant that the peasants would be able to sell, transfer, or mortgage their lands as they wished. Also, peasants would be free to cultivate his soil and produce whatever crops he wished to produce in his land. In many villages, as has been seen, especially in Bihar, peasants were forced to undertake indigo cultivation against their wishes, which had resulted in oppression. It was against this practice that Gandhiji had started his first campaign at Champaran in Bihar. Similarly, in U.P., the government sometimes imposed conditions that certain areas should be earmarked to produce cotton and sugar cane, etc. according to the market demand. This happened specially in the nineteenth century.

The problem of granting ownership rights to peasantry, in spite of the movement of Indian National Congress, was not resolved as long as the British remained in power in India. It was only after independence that right of ownership over their lands were granted to all peasants under Govind Ballabh Pant's Chief Ministership. During the 1930's, the Indian National Congress led by Jawaharlal Nehru also had demanded that the zamindari system should be abolished. It was rightly asserted that only after the abolition of the zamindari system, full security of tenure could be granted to the peasantry. When India became independent, most of the States in India passed laws abolishing the zamindari system.

On the issue Pant said:

> "The Government have to build a network of canals and wells so that not an inch of cultivable space is left uncultivated for want of irrigation; we have to build vast flood protection weirs, reservoirs and dams to save the people from recurrent distress and agony; we have to build roads... to connect every village to the other... We have to provide houses for all... not only in the towns and cities but also in rural areas... We have to industrialise the country, set up basic industries that can build aircrafts, modern machines and things on which the life of a civilized nation so much depends."

During the period of national movement, the abolition of zamindari system became an important issue but it was not rigorously advocated as a matter of policy by the Congress; mainly because it was feared that the zamindars as a class might support the government. The Congress policy was to unite all classes and communities against the British Raj. Mahatma Gandhi declared that all sections of Indians must fight the "most powerful zamindar" of the country, i.e. the British government in India. It was felt that zamindars should not be alienated on the issue of the zamindari at this phase of national struggle for freedom. Otherwise, a class war would ensue, which would provide an opportunity to the government to divide Indians further. Gandhiji observed that all Indians must unitedly fight first and foremost for independence of India. Govind Ballabh Pant also fell into this line of thinking and advocated that through legislation the rights of peasants should be protected and guaranteed.

During 1930-34 the prices of agricultural produce fell. An acute economic depression prevailed in the whole country and the world. As a result of fall in the prices of rice, wheat, pulses, cotton and sugar cane, etc., the peasants of U.P. suffered great losses. It became very difficult for them to pay the rent to the landlords. Even the *zamindars* and *taluqdars* were unable to pay the land revenue demanded by the government, because they could not collect rents from the peasants. Under the leadership of Jawaharlal Nehru, Purushottam Das Tandon and other leaders of the Indian National Congress, including Govind Ballabh Pant, a "no-rent campaign" was started, and after a lot of agitation and negotiations with the government, remissions from payment of rent were granted to the peasantry. It was indeed one of the great achievements of Indian National Congress that during the period between 1931 and 1933, rent amounting to nearly ten crores of rupees was remitted by the government. The benefits of remission also were reaped by the landlords and about three crores of rupees of revenue was not demanded from them by the government. This was possible mainly because of excellent survey carried out by a team headed by Govind Ballabh Pant, on the basis of which the remissions were granted. The report he submitted was entitled "Agrarian Distress in U.P.".

Activities in Congress

He was elected member of the All India Congress Committee and he rose to be a member of the Congress Working Committee, which was the supreme policy-making body of the Congress. The

Congress, Working Committee, consisting of top Congress leaders of the country took decisions on political matters. The plan of action in respect of launching of mass movements against the British rule and all organisational details were chalked out by this Committee. Negotiations with the government of India or provincial governments were carried out through the Congress Working Committee or by the representatives nominated by it. In 1945, Govind Ballabh participated in the Shimla Conference, where the Viceroy and his Executive Council, representing the British government, were to discuss issues pertaining to the eventual transfer of power to India.

Mass Movements

In the national movement under the leadership of Gandhiji, people from all walks of life participated. From 1920-21 onwards, beginning with Non-cooperation movement, till India achieved independence in 1947, series of mass movements were launched by Gandhiji. In 1930-31 the Civil Disobedience movement was started with Salt Satyagraha. After a decade, in 1942, Quit India movement was started and the British were asked to leave India. In the national movement, all parties, with different political ideologies, participated. The revolutionaries and others contributed to the movement. Lakhs of people were sent to jail. Houses and properties of thousands of Indians were attached by the government.

In Prison

Govind Ballabh Pant was sentenced to six months' imprisonment for taking part in Salt Satyagraha in 1930. In 1931 and 1932, he was jailed again. In November 1940, he was sentenced to one year imprisonment for offering individual satyagraha and kept in Almora jail. He was released in November 1941. On 9 August 1942, as you all know, the Quit India movement began. All leaders of the Indian National Congress including Pant were arrested on that day and put into jails in different parts of the country. At Ahmednagar Fort some of the eminent leaders like Jawaharlal Nehru, Maulana Azad, Rafi Ahmed Kidwai, Vallabhbhai Patel, Acharya Narendra Deva and Govind Ballabh Pant were kept. After the arrest of the leaders, people became leaderless and they themselves took up the reins of the movement. Widespread disturbances in all parts of the country took place. The government had to use the army to control them. Administrative machinery broke down. In places, bombing was resorted to. It was estimated that more than 10,000 people were killed; villages after villages were burnt down. Police and army ruthlessly suppressed the movement.

Govind Ballabh Pant was released on medical grounds on 31 March 1945, after nearly three years. Other leaders were also released in May-June 1945.

Most of these great leaders of national movement had spent a number of years in prisons. Jawaharlal Nehru spent nearly ten years between 1920 and 1945 in different jails. Stories of their hardship and courage; despair and cheerfulness and yet how well they occupied their time in the jails have been written by Jawaharlal Nehru in his famous book, *The Discovery of India*. He wrote it while in imprisonment in Ahmadnagar Fort, between 1942 and 1945. Earlier he had written an equally popular book, *An Autobiography*, which was published in 1936. These are great writings and tell us the story of those stirring times when Indians as a nation fought for independence in a peaceful, non-violent manner under Gandhiji's leadership.

Every student should try to read the story of this non-violent national struggle. It is a remarkable story characterised by heroism, strong nationalistic spirit of the common man and their leaders. Their deep concern for the weak and poor, and complete lack of bitterness against the people of England show the greatness of these leaders of our national movement. They were determined to bring about social, economic and cultural resurgence of India when India became independent. They stood for the nation, not for their selfish ends.

For three long years the Congress leaders were in prison detained at Ahmednagar Fort. For the first seven months the world outside did not know the place where the Congress leaders were detained. The Secretary of State for India refused in British Parliament to disclose their whereabouts. At first their addresses were c/o the Home Secretary, Government of India, New Delhi.

Those who were detained in Ahmednagar Fort were Pt. Nehru, Maulana Azad, Sardar Patel, Pt. Pant, Acharya Kripalani, Acharya Narendra Dev, Dr. Pattabhi Sitaramayya, Dr. Profulla Ghosh, Dr. Syed Mahmood, Asaf Ali, Shanker Rao Deo and Hari Krishen Mehtab. In the camp there were 36 persons, 12 were sent to help them from Yeravada Central Prison.

For the first three weeks they were totally cut off from the world when no newspapers were allowed to them. No interviews were permitted till first 20 months. Only letters from near blood relations were permitted on domestic business. It was on 27th August 1942, after 20 days of their arrest, that only Bombay papers were allowed when they learnt the distressing news of the passing away of Mahadev Desai. The news of the death was incidently referred to in a leaderette in the *Times of India* under the caption, 'The Nazi Propaganda and Mr. Desai.' Then they could know that he died suddenly on the 15th August while talking to Inspector-General of Prisons. Their thought went to Gandhiji who was his lifelong companion. What a great shock it must have been to him!

"The news of Mahadeva's death cast a gloom over us in Ahmednagar Fort," wrote Dr. Pattabhi in his book, "They were moved to teats. Vallabhbhai was deeply shaken. He fasted for the night as he could not touch food. They recalled that he qualified for the Bar, and Vallabhbhai remembered him attending courts and watching while he himself was practising in 1914."

We have got a glimpse of their daily life from day to day journal kept by Dr. Pattabhi Sitaramayya who was one of them and given in his book 'Feathers and Stones.'

He wrote that Sardar Patel had an attack of his spastic colon and for more than a fortnight he could not resume his routine. He was a regular walker and he had daily four mile walk. Acharya Narendra Dev suffered from a fit of asthma. He tided over it by walking with Sardar Patel. They all lived a very busy and pleasant life. They made their lives very attractive and joyful. The Dining hall was the centre of their talks and they discussed all sorts of topics. They participated in games and held tournaments. Pt. Pant was very active. He was optimist and never gloomy, always cheerful and never worried. He refused to think of his health. He conquered over his ailments through his sheer will to be well. He had enough faith that all would be well. He spent at least 10 hours in serious study and two hours in play. He played badminton and his play was a marvel for a man who was 6 ft. 2 inch tall and 208 lbs. in weight but who was actively able to rotate round his own vertical axis.

There was a good collection of books. Pt. Nehru received very fine books from abroad. Maulana Azad ordered some old history books. Pt. Pant took studious notes of what he read and he covered more than 2,000 pages of his copybooks in these notes. All the English newspapers of India except the *Hindustan Times* of New Delhi were supplied to them. Weighing was the weekly routine on Tuesday. The temperature usually shot up very high in summer. Maulana Azad received the disturbing news of the dangerous illness of his wife and a week later they learnt with profound grief her passing away in Calcutta. The death of Satyamurti who was a colleague of Pt. Pant and Asaf Ali in the Central Assembly, came as a great shock in the camp. He was a great debater and a finished parliamentarian. He died in the prime of his life. His illness began at the time of his detention in September 1942.

Their daily time table was that they woke up between 5 and 6. Then they had the morning tea. At 7-15 there was the bell for breakfast. At 11 they had their lunch. Till then some engaged themselves in spinning, some attended to gardening, all read and wrote. Each had his time for bath ranged from 6-30 to 10-30. They had tea at 4 p.m. and dinner at 8 p.m.

Dr. Pattabhi, who afterwards became the President of the Indian National Congress and the Governor of Madhya Pradesh thus described his association with Pt. Pant in the Ahmednagar camp:

> "Shri Govind Ballabh Pant's towering personality is quite familiar to the Indian public. His is a statuesque figure in intellect as in stature. His studious habits belie any reports of ill health. His intellect is as keen as his memory is retentive. As things are in the world flashy intelligence and shallow minds generally go together in life while the quality of thoroughness is

generally associated with dullness of understanding and slowness of cerebration. Pt. Pant is a complete exception to this rule. He is quick of perception, sharp in debate and thorough in understanding. His presentation of resolutions at the Congress Sessions have always been remarkable alike for their lucidity and eloquence while his balanced mind and self confident temperament give him an advantage rarely possessed by Congress speakers. It is the habit of the legal profession which serves the politician in good stead to be able to think while on legs, and therefore more easily while seated, to develop a theme in all its vividness and carry conviction to the judges and the audience. Pantji's interests are varied as his talents are versatile. He can hold a conversation on the latest developments in medicine and science while he can en-liven a talk on Socretes or Voltaire. The gift of wide reading is possessed by many but many shuffle it off like the horse and few that chew the cud like the cow. *Dharama* and *Marana* are the two great assets of a successful scholar according to Indian psychology and these Pantji possesses in abundance. He is fastidious in his tastes, has a meticulous sense of cleanliness as well as neatness, is assertive in temperament and sustained in debate. No wonder that he had been selected to lead the ministry in U.P."

The other Working Committee members who were not detained at Ahmednagar were Shrimati Sarojini Naidu, who was detained with Gandhiji in Agha Khan Palace, Pune and Dr. Rajendra Prasad, who was detained in Bankipur Jail in Bihar. At the time of the passing of the August resolution Dr. Rajendra Prasad was lying ill in bed at Sadaqat Ashram in his home province, where he was arrested.

Bareilly Central Prison was United Province's Central Detention Camp No. 1 in which security prisoners from all over the province were lodged. Rafi Ahmed Kidwai, former Minister of Jails in U.P., and S.K.D. Paliwal, then President U.P.C.C., who were arrested long before the August resolution were sent there.

Satya Ranjan Bakshi, editor of the *Forward,* was transferred from Bengal. By the time the August Movement started almost all the security prisoners had been released from there. Purushottam Das Tandon, Speaker, U.P. Assembly, Sampurnanand, former Education Minister and afterwards Chief Minister, U.P., R.S. Pandit and many other prominent Congress leaders were transferred to Bareilly Central Prison from different jails of U.P.

Congress leader Shyam Sundar's account:

> "I was arrested in the first round while I was in bed suffering from fever. A senior police officer awakened me from sleep and he did not tell me that I was to be arrested. He took me out on a false pretext and drove me straight to the District Jail. People at my home waited for my return the whole night and they were not even informed that I was arrested and sent to the District Jail. My father was ill at that time and I could not meet him at the time of my departure. Two years after I was released on parole for a fortnight to perform his last rites. In that night I was kept with the security prisoners who had arrived in the previous evening from Almora, Nainital and Garhwal. Prominent among them were Badri Dutt Pandey, M.L.A. (Central); Har Govind Pant, M.L.A.; Devi Dutt Pant, (afterwards M.P.); Pyarelal Gupta, (afterwards M.L.C.); Mohanlal Sah, M.L.C.; Jagmohan Singh Negi, M.L.A. (afterwards Minister of State). Mohanlal Sah provided for me the bedding for the night. Everyone was awakened and we had a good talk. The next day I met friends from Bareilly who were arrested earlier and were lodged in another barrack. Ram Murti, (afterwards Minister of State in U.P.), Munshi Udho Narain; Brijmohan Lal Shastri, Darbari Lal Sharma, Satish Chandra, (afterwards Deputy Minister in Indian Government), Dharam Dutt, Pratap Chand Azad, Rang Bahadur Bhartiya, Raghunandan Prasad Taiyal, Dina Nath Mishra, Sahu Gopinath and Shive Saran Agrawal.

"The very hour we stepped into the jail gate in August 1942, we found that the Security Prisoners' Rules made by the Provincial Government only some months back were deleted in most material form, and all communications from outside were stopped. Rules concerning letters, interviews, deposits, permission to sleep outside, writing material and examinations were deleted. One found then in a strange and piquant situation. For nine months we lived in a citadel of utter impenetrable darkness. Credit went to the *Hindustan Times* which then endeavoured to let out a ray of light for the outer world in a series of leading articles "For Humanity's sake" which drew pointed attention to the conditions in which we as security prisoners lived. There was total blackout on what was happening in prisons, because no communications of any sort were permitted. No newspaper could publish any account. When the *Hindustan Times* published them in June 1943, it was characterised as 'atrocity mongering.'

"We were transferred here quite unexpectedly. For about three months we lived in Bareilly District Jail. No one outside knows that we have been transferred here. We do not get any newspaper. We cannot send or receive letters, what to say of interviews. We cannot even inform that we have been transferred here. We have been totally cut off from the outside world that we cannot know what is happening outside. Whatever little news we get is through those persons who join us on transfer. On our arrival here we met friends from Saharanpur, Bijnor, Hardoi, Kheri and other districts who had arrived only a day before. We met Ajit Prasad Jain, formerly Parliamentary Secretary (afterwards Food Minister of the Government of India), Phul Singh, M.L.A. (afterwards Deputy Minister), Chedalal Gupta, M.L.A., Radha Krishen (afterwards M.L.A. and Chairman U.P. Public Service Commission), Chandrahas Mishra (afterwards M.L.A., of Hardoi, Bansi Dher Mishra M.L.A., Kr. Khus-waqut

Rai M.L.A. of Kheri, Nemi Saran Jain, (afterwards M.P.), Chandra Shekher Goel, Shiv Kumar Sharma, Khub Singh, M.L.A. from Bijnor, Sharda Prasad, M.L.C. of Etawah Dr. Jai Gopal (afterwards M.L.A.), Govind Sahai afterwards Parliamentary Secretary who was transferred from Dehra Dun and many other friends. I learnt two strange things about my family members about whom I heard nothing since I was arrested. A friend from Bijnor told me that my younger brother, Deoki Nandan, was arrested in Bijnor district on the very day I was arrested and was prosecuted under rule 35 D.I.R. (Sabotage) for alleged setting fire a railway station and he was undergoing two years rigorous imprisonment in C class in Bijnor district jail and another case for setting fine a post-office was pending against him. I was told by another friend that my wife had got herself admitted in Lady Hardinge Hospital in New Delhi to avoid her arrest as there was a warrant for her arrest in Bareilly. These were startling news which upsetted me. The strangest thing was that I was living in the same city at such a short distance and was in total darkness. What about that little child who was only two months old when I was arrested. Those who joined us afterwards were Mahavir Tyagi, Govind Sahai, Manzer Ali Sokhta, Kesho Gupta, Prof. Ram Saran, Damoder Swroop Seth and others. In one of her notes from her sick bed in Lady Hardinge Medical College Hospital New Delhi, which I got in prison after a year Shrimati Shyam scribbled:

"You have done your duty. My fate is against me and it will bring me several calamities. I am to suffer. If I die in Shyam's absence tell him that Savitri's greatest desire has gone with her. I passed last night with great restlessness. If I remain in this condition for 2 or 3 days more I will suffer from mental shock. I will remember this period throughout my life. I admit it was my great fault that I gave birth to this child. Day passes and night comes. I desire to sleep but cannot. Whenever it is kind to me I always see happy visions. My Munni and Shyam remain stamped before my eyes in the dream. But sleep is so cruel to me that it flies away with the happy visions. Oh! how long I will suffer from this heart pain."

"Last evening we learnt of the starting of Gandhiji's fast for 21 days and the correspondence that passed between him and the Viceroy. The fast had commenced at noon on 10th February. It greatly stirred our minds and created a tense excitement. We were all stunned. We had a very disturbed sleep last night. We are not supplied with any newspapers and we are very anxious to read the correspondence. Six months have passed when we were arrested. We all observed a 36 hour fast. We expect Gandhiji would be released. Gandhiji is 74 and he may not stand this ordeal at this age.

"We have no further information. Sumat Prasad Jain, (afterwards M.P.), Dwarka Prasad Mittal, (afterwards M.L.A.) and Madan Mohan Lal (afterwards M.L.C.) arrived in our barrack on transfer from Muzaffernagar District Jail. They brought with them a newspaper in which the whole Gandhi—Viceroy correspondence was published. This enabled us to read the correspondence."

Gandhiji wrote to the Viceroy:

"I begin it on the 9th instant, with the clearest possible conscience. Despite your description of it as 'a form of political blackmail,' it is on my part meant to be an appeal to the Highest Tribunal for justice which I have failed to secure from you. If I do not survive the ordeal, I shall go to the Judgement Scat with the fullest faith in innocence. Posterity will judge between you as representative of an all—powerful Government and me as a humble man who has tried to serve his country and humanity through it."

"Dr. Gilder who was detained in Yeravada Prison was brought to Agha Khan Palace on the second day of fast. On the 4th day nausea began to appear bringing disturbed sleep. Dr. BC Roy arrived in Pune on 15th February and was permitted to attend. On 18th anxiety deepened as Gandhiji did not show any inclination to talk. On 19th a Leaders' Conference attended by three hundred public men from different parts of India, representing various communities, creeds and interests met at New Delhi and unanimously passed a resolution urging immediate and unconditional release of Gandhiji whose condition was fast approaching a crisis. Three members of the Viceroy's Executive Council, Mody, Aney and Sarkar, resigned. From all quarters came thousands of appeals demanding Gandhiji's immediate release. It was a universal feeling that Gandhiji's life should be somehow saved. Churchill's reply to an urgent appeal from Leaders' Conference shocked every Indian.

"The health bulletin of February 20 described his condition very grave which took a turn for the worse. He spent most of his time in bed in silence listening to the *Gita*. On 21st Feb. crisis developed and the doctors said that if the fast was not ended without delay it might be too late to save his life. After a restless day he entered a crisis at 4 p.m., when his condition was reported serious. In the evening we learnt of Sir Tej's message to countrymen in which he asked to 'be prepared for the worst.' He said: "Speaking for myself, I think, we should be prepared for the worst, namely the passing away of Gandhiji, unless a miracle happens." This saddened us all. No one of us could sleep the whole night. The next day we could get no news.

"Gandhiji's condition was reported to be serious on 22nd February. It was his weekly silence day. It was stated that the Government signalled precautionary measures and it was widely current that sufficient quantity of *sandal wood* was collected for the cremation. At this time an English friend of Gandhiji, Horace Alexander and William Phillips, Personal Representative to President Roosevelt, who were in India made an effort to bring about a settlement. Their mediation was rejected by the Government. Phillips who arrived in India in January 1943 was one of America's most competent diplomats—a former Under Secretary of State and then Ambassador to Italy. He at once realised that if Gandhiji died due to the obturate attitude of the White Hall there would surge a violent revolution which would place the Allies in a very critical situation. On 16th February he cabled to White House asking whether President and Secretary of State would approve his informally approaching the Viceroy to express their deep concern they felt over the political crisis in India. The President concurred. But the Viceroy forbade him to call on him on the ground that it would be exceedingly dangerous to the British India situation and the British Ambassador in USA was instructed to express that H.M.G. was very desirous that Phillips should avoid any public reference to the Gandhi affair at that time. The President expressed the wish to discuss the matter of Gandhiji's fast and felt that Gandhiji should not be allowed to die in prison. On 22nd February Prime Minister's cable was received by the American President that the British Government would not in any circumstances alter the course it was pursuing about Gandhiji. Churchill hoped that Britain's difficulties would not be added to at so critical a moment. The President replied that USA Government would say nothing but that in the event that Gandhiji died he would have some statement to make.

"With the beginning of the third week the prospect of Gandhiji successfully terminating the Fast appeared brighter. He was quite cheerful on 28th Feb. when only two days were left to break the fast. Nausea was absent and he was able to take in more water without difficulty. On March 3 at 9.34 a.m. Gandhiji after completing 21 day fast sipped orange juice given by Kasturba Gandhi. He took 20 minutes to sip the juice.

"During the fast a 86 page booklet under the title 'Congress Responsibility for the Disturbances' was issued. We read it in the month of March when a friend who came on transfer brought it with him. It reached Gandhiji on 13th April after 50 days repeated requests. After 48 days he sent a long reply to it on July 15 which ran into 77 paras. Gandhiji said that he came to the conclusion that there was nothing in his writings and his doing that could have warranted the inferences and innuendoes of which the indictment was full. As the *New Statesman and Nation* commented:

"The Government of India has done a questionable thing in publishing a White Paper of 76 pages, which is from first to last a personal indictment of Mr. Gandhi. It is a propaganda document primarily designed, we presume, to damage him in American eyes. This attack is made on a man who is, after all, one of the world's greatest personalities, but who is not now in a position to reply or defend himself. Again, if the graver charges are well founded, ought not the Indian Government to have tried Mr. Gandhi before a court of law, instead of holding him, silent and isolated, in internment by an administrative act?"

"During Gandhiji's fast the members of the Congress Working Committee from Ahmednagar addressed a long letter to the Viceroy on February 13 in which they gave their reactions. It was their first communication to the world outside. The Government of India refused permission to Phillips to see Gandhiji in prison and in April he had to leave India. At the time of Gandhiji's fast he wrote a long letter to American President the text of which was published in America in July 1944 after fifteen months by an American columnist Drew Pearson. Farewell 1943:

"The whole year was spent in Central Prison, Bareilly. The greatest ordeal which we experienced was is in the days of Gandhiji's fast. He survived to the surprise of all. We have been waiting for the last 18 months for the interviews but they have so far not been granted. In the month of May after ten months of our detention we were supplied newspapers and one letter per month we were permitted to write and also to receive. I look back to the year and I wonder how we have spent such a long dreary period. My little child who was only two months old at the time of my arrest must now be blooming. In the year at two times I felt greatly distressed when I learnt of the illness of my father and of that little child who was a solace to her mother in her solicitude. How she lived, waiting, worried and exasperated.

"In April a new situation arose when the validity of rule 26 of D.I.R. under which we were detained was questioned before the Federal Court which held that the said rule was invalid in law as it went beyond the rule making powers of the government. The Governor-General promulgated an Ordinance which substituted for the section dealing with detention in the Defence of India Act. A new section having retrospective effect was enacted which validated orders already made. The validity of this Ordinance was also questioned but the Allahabad and Madras High Courts upheld it.

"A terrible disaster overtook Bengal in the last months of 1943 where a grave famine took place. The *Statesman* contributed a very thoughtful editorial on Food Crisis in Bengal under 'Reflections on Disaster.' It commented, "Under the present system of Government responsibility for breakdown inescably rests in the last resort upon authority in Britain and its immediate representative here. Every British citizen is necessarily shamed and sullied when his Indian fellow subjects die of starvation in Bengal."

"We spend time here in longing, hoping, dreaming, reading and waiting. So life goes on without any change. During this long period I have maintained equilibrium, health and happiness. Reading has given strength, joy, courage, defiance and perspicuity. To preserve one's life one should be active. I.G. Prison's visit here resulted in the award of 2 months solitary imprisonment for 48 of us. Lord Wavell who was previously Commander-in-chief in India was appointed as Viceroy and succeeded Lord Linhthgow in September."

"Shrimati Sarojini Naidu, the only member of the Congress Working Committee, who is outside jail and has, in spite of ill-health, had an opportunity to observe developments in India gave an authoritative reaffirmation of the Congress position at a Press conference in New Delhi. She marshalled India's case for freedom with great confident tone as the spokesman of the Congress Working Committee. She threw great strength by her inspiring message in many a frustrated heart by long suffering which greatly enthused us behind the prison bars. 'On fundamentals we cannot surrender' she said, 'I would rather that every one of us died in jail than that merely for the sake of coming out we should compromise the integrity of our position. We have spoken in the name of the nation. We cannot go back on it till we are convinced we are wrong.'

"Referring to the people who demanded release of Congress leaders she said, "Nothing is more humiliating than intercession on our behalf asking for release as a matter of mercy. I would beg kind friends, who when the Congress is out are so much against us, to desist from pleading for our release. The country's demand should be: 'Try Congress leaders; face them with the charges against them.'"

"A new Ordinance (III of 1944) was promulgated from January 15 and we were detained under it at first instance for a period of six months. To those who would be further detained, the grounds of detention would be supplied by the Government and the detenuc would have a right to send a representation.

"On March 29th 1944 after almost two years we were served with notices under section 7 of the Restriction and Detention Ordinance, 1944 (No. III of 1944). It was as follows:

"Government of the United Provinces. Confidential Department. No. 1301-CX Dated Lucknow, March 25, 1944.

"Notice under section 7 of the Restriction and Detention Ordinance, 1944. (No. III of 1944).'

"In pursuance of section 7 of the Restriction and Detention Ordinance, 1944 (No. III of 1944), you Shyam Sunder son of Ram Chandra are informed that the grounds for your detention were that you were an office holder and a prominent and active member of the organisation which passed the resolution of August 8, 1942 sanctioning a mass movement which was calculated to impede the successful prosecution of the War.

"You are informed that you have a right to make a representation in writing against the order under which you are detained. If you wish to make such a representation, you should address to the undersigned and forward it through the Superintendent of the jail as soon as possible.

D.S. Barren, I.C.S.,

Jail: Central Prison, Bareilly. Home Secretary to Government, United Provinces.
District: Bareilly.

We were further served with the following order:

Government of United Provinces.
Confidential Department.
No. 3860—CX.

Dated Nainital, July 14, 1944.

"In exercise of the powers conferred by the proviso to section 9 of the Restriction and Detention Ordinance, 1944, (Ord. III of 1944) the Governor after a further consideration of all circumstances of the case is pleased to direct that the order under clause (b) of Subsection (I) of section 3 of the aforementioned ordinance directing the detention of Shyam Sunder of district Bareilly shall continue in force.

"D.S. Barren, I.C.S. Home Secretary to Government, United Provinces.

"Learnt that Shrimati Kasturba Gandhi whose condition was reported to be very grave on 20th February, died yesterday at Aga Khan Palace. With her death Gandhiji's 62 year old companionship came to an end. She breathed her last lying on the lap of her husband and as a Hindu woman she had the best death. Hartal was observed all over India today and we also fasted. Our thoughts were with Gandhiji in his great personal loss. This was the second great loss which he suffered in this detention. In the very first week he lost his most valuable comrade and friend Mahadev Desai."

"At long last in this last week of March after 20 months, the Government permitted the security prisoners one interview once a month. We had our first interview today. We got up early and became ready. We learnt that members of our family had arrived at the gate at the appointed time of 8. 30 a.m. Our interview was delayed owing to Rafi Sahib's interview and we had to wait upto 11-30. We had an hour at our disposal.

After so much waiting the veil was lifted and we faced each other. I intended to talk many things but forgot in the stress of the moment. I composed myself under smiles and laughter. I noted that Savitri greatly restrained herself, though at one time was on the verge of breaking down. The little child very intelligently saluted me and greeted me by calling *Pitaji.* What significance she knew of that word. I was a total stranger *to* her. She must have been trained for this meeting. I offered her an orange which I took with me, and she very fondly accepted it. She was thirsty and hungry and it was natural as she was waiting since morning. She came to me and went away and began to play. At the time of my arrest she was only two months old. The time ran swiftly. There was so much abruptness that I could talk nothing. The outpourings of the lacerated heart were more eloquent in silence than speech. The thought of parting was hanging *on* me. The time was up. I stood up and so they. We looked to each other—a tear was trickling into Savitri's eyes. She smiled and pointed to little child to salute again. Then we parted. I stood watching. The door was opened and then closed and every one disappeared before my eyes. With halting pace and with a heavy heart I returned to my barrack with past memories refreshed. Our return was very anxiously being awaited as ours was the first interview. They all collected and we related our account of the first jail interview. The whole day passed in a disturbed mood."

"It was some days ago when we were permitted to sleep outside the barracks in the night for the first time. Today is Sunday and I was expecting my interview and I kept myself in readiness. At 11 we were informed and we reached the office at 11-45. The interview began at 12 noon. My father, mother and my youngest brother, Nihal Chand, came for the interview. My other brother was outside the gate as only three persons are allowed at the interview. Nihal came from Delhi especially for this interview. It was after a period of two years that I met him. I noted that they were much changed. My father's health was utterly ruined. Parents consumed themselves in their agony for their sons' separation. They looked towards me with eager eyes and were happy to meet me. Father told me many things how he was harassed and distressed. Mother mentioned that the marriages of my two younger brothers had been much delayed due to my detention. It was announced that "there were only five minutes *left*. In these five minutes we talked under great pressure of time. The time finished and I stood up. While I was taking leave Rail Sahib who was coming after his interview met me at the gate. I introduced my father to him. He cut a joke at my expense. He said to my father, 'So your sons may have been great source of worry to you.' So we parted. [stood and saw them going off through the first gate. He looked back—to see me whether I was still there. He stopped for a while looked at me. I could feel the beatings of his heart. He raised his hands towards me. I bowed with folded hands. They all looked at me and went out of the gate. I saw them disappearing from mv view. The gate closed; and the curtain fell. It was half past one *in* the afternoon and the heat was sufficiently troublesome. I returned to my barrack picturing the scene and remembering that in this heat they would be returning. To what inconvenience the people are put who come to interview in these jails. What a great respite this interview had given me. I was reminded of every dear and near who was suffering and pining for us. Received 10 Gillette Blades, Forhans' Toothpaste, Aksir Dandan deposited by Nihal Chand."

"On first May we learnt from a Bombay Government communique that Gandhiji was *ill*. Another report said that Frontier Gandhi was also ill seriously. It caused great anxiety. The next day we waited for the newspapers.

"Some improvement in the condition of both leaders was reported. Dr. BC Roy was permitted to examine Gandhiji. In the evening of 4th we learnt that Gandhiji's general condition was again giving rise to some anxiety. We learnt on 7th of Gandhiji's unconditional release on medical grounds. He was in his 75th year.

"Today was the interview day, third of this month. I expected but I was not sure; though mentally I was prepared. I was thinking that this time my sister and her husband would come. At 9 I was called to the gate for the interview. Just as I was leaving my enclosure I got a post-card sent by Savitri on 15th and received here on 17th. I was surprised to read that she was coming to interview. It appears that she changed her mind as in her earlier letter she had written that she would come in the month of June. We were called early. At ten we were ushered into the room where she and her brother with little *Pritibha* were waiting for me. This time there was no such rush. The same scene was enacted. We met after a period of two months again in the same circumstances. The weather has become hot. I talked to Sukhbir first and made many enquiries. Then I turned towards Savitri. She asked the child to come near me. She was looking towards me with amazing eyes. She saluted me with folded hands. She appeared considerable weak as she suffered from fever.

"The time of the interview was passing very swiftly. She said that she had brought one bottle of Kesranjan oil for me which she deposited at the gate. It was announced that the interview time was over and we took leave and parted. The little child—came to me—saluted. Sukhbir took her up and the door was closed. I returned to my barrack and took my food. I could not concentrate the whole day. The whole scene was moving before my eyes. I recapitulated the events of these 21 months which we have spent in this Prison. I am surprised how we have lived. The world has moved so fast and so swiftly. Small children have come of age. The little baby dandling in mother's arm has begun walking and talking. Seasons have taken round their course more than once. What great changes have been wrought in the world outside of which we are still in darkness. Many new faces have come in the world and many old familiar faces have disappeared. But we have been in the same place, same prison, same cell, same walls, without any change in the life of waiting, exasperation, pining and remembering the events of the past. So are they, outside, near and dear, waiting day in and day out, waiting for our return, hoping and disappointed and disillusioned. How days have turned into weeks and months and years? What a trial in fortitude it had been? Still there seems to be no end. Such is life! I have read with great profit the wise words of Dr. Johnson, 'It has been the endeavour of all those whom the world has reverenced for superior wisdom to persuade man *to be acquainted with himself—to* learn his own powers, and his own weaknesses, to observe by what evils he is most dangerously beset and by what temptations most easily overcome.' Can there be a better place and also can there be a better opportunity for a man to be acquainted with himself than this prison land? We have been here for such a long period at a stretch, packed to the full, overcrowded in a barrack in a motley crowd."

Mahavir Tyagi was with us in Central Prison Bareilly. He always infused new life in that dreary atmosphere. In 1952, when he was the Minister of State for Finance in Government of India, he wrote in a letter to me in which he made a very significant observation:

New Delhi,
May 19, 1952.

My dear Shyam,

As usual, your letter was again as sweet as you are. It will be too formal to thank you for the kind regard you have always been having for me. I was sorry to know that you had to give up your post. The world seems to be fast changing, and along with it the conception of human values, that, I am afraid, very soon society would get smashed into splinters. Every individual would look to his own interest and loyalty, howsoever true it be, shall be misunderstood to be a diplomatic pose for the achievement of ones selfish ends.

I remember, when I was in Persia we were offered not to carry dogs with us when we were getting ready for a long route march. I shot my little pet; and I can never forget in my life that after receiving the small bullet of my pistol, the dog looked towards me for help and hurried a few paces towards me for rescue. Poor little animal! It hardly knew that his 'protector' was the real culprit. In your case it seems as if, one has shot one's own loyal dog. When I had resigned from Lucknow, I came crying under the pressure of the same intensity of feeling as my dog did when I shot it. Such is the world. You have my sympathy and love.

With regards to your wife and children.

Yours sincerely,
Mahavir Tyagi.

"The second year of this deadening detention is coming to close. It is perhaps not realised how severe is the sustained strain thus imposed on us who are here. All, big or small, are suffering the same degree of degradation and economic depletion. Some times sad news are received from home and we find ourselves in an utter state of helplessness. We have passed our days very cheerfully. Congressmen have shown heroic acts of endurance. They have exhibited great character. Many could have been released long ago by giving some undertaking of good behaviour. On the face of it there might have seemed no objection to do so. Many had to face very difficult situations—serious illnesses of their dear ones or bereavements in the families. But they refused to be so released, as such an undertaking was associated in our minds with some recantation of our political faith and no one could have given that undertaking without a feeling of shame at having gone back upon his loyalty to the cause for which he suffered so much.

"Very unexpected came the news of the invasion of Europe by the Allied forces. At last they launched their Second front against Western Europe. Sixth morning, according to a German overseas news agency message, Allied parachutists were reported to have landed at the mouth of the Seine, near Le Havre on the coast of France. This news enlivened our camp and created intense excitement. The position of the Allies was very strong and it would surely turn the tide and assuredly would bring the culmination of war. It is the last straw that breaks the camel's back. The second front was opened after two years and at very apposite moment. Only a day before the news came of the liberation of Rome by Allied Armies. It was a curious coincidence we read in the newspapers of June 5 a news item of June 3, of a girl who flashed the invasion story from New York, a flash that General Eisenhower had officially announced Allied landings in France. It was later announced that it was circulated by error by an American news service. Radio Stations throughout America interrupted their programmes to give the news but retracted a few minutes later when the news service cancelled the flash, which had originated from London. It was stated that the message was due to transmission error. It was later stated that a girl employed in London was practising on the teleprinter and typed the erroneous flash. Without the knowledge of the editorial staff it was inadvertently run through the transmitter serving New York. Only two days after the news of actual invasion came."

"Today was the interview day. I was ready as I was expecting my interview. At 9-45 we seven were called. Savitri, Vidya and Nihal had come. Our interview began at 10.25 a.m. I was told that Deoki had come and was waiting outside. Nihal came for the second time. Savitri told Pritibha that I was her father. She as usual saluted me and looked towards me. I gave her some flowers which I brought with me from my barrack. She took them eagerly. It was this which I could give her. Vidya was silent and was hearing our talk. I saw her after 22 months. She had grown weak. I could only read what was passing in her mind Her silence was more eloquent. She spoke few words and replied what I asked her. I knew how she loved me and served me and was ready to suffer for me. Savitri told me that she did her best to comfort her and spent most of her time to give her company. I said that I could do nothing for her—but she said that everything was done for her—tears came into my eyes but I checked them and turned the talk to another topic. Many things I forgot. The time was fleeting very swiftly. I was conscious that very shortly all would be over. I looked towards Savitri and she blushed. Hurriedly and nervously I talked. I took Pritibha in my hands. There were 12 minutes—8 minutes—6 minutes—all of a sudden it was announced that the time was over. I finished my talk, stood up and then with a heavy heart took their leave. They disappeared before my eyes. All was over. Excited and exasperated I returned. Nihal brought Neem toothpaste and Aksir Dandan for me and a bottle of sherbat—which could not be deposited."

"In the morning I read the news of the sad demise of Acharya P.C. Rai. Today I began to read 'Mother Russia' by Maurice Hindus. Some years ago I read his another book 'Humanity Uprooted'. In the very first chapter he depicted the picture of the families in Russia after evacuation. A very pathetic scene was presented. Mother who was feeding the daughter of his son who was killed in the war, began to weep—and also the wife. There was no other person in the family to look after them. In what helpless condition they were. It brought tears into my eyes. I could not proceed with the book and began to think and pictured many scenes. It troubled me. In the afternoon I received a letter from Savitri and one post-card. She referred to the reactions which she had from her last interview on 11th. She asked me to write a letter to father—and I was thinking to write to him. As usual I finished my meal—by 5 p.m. but I left it without taking it full as I found a fly in the *dal.* I was just walking when all from a sudden one fellow prisoner Ranjit Singh—a student of Almora came upto me and announced that I was released. It surprised me as there was no such indication. At first I laughed it away but then came a convict-warder who said that I was wanted immediately. He showed me a chit from the Deputy Superintendent. "Please send Mr. Shyam Sunder for release immediately." I began to pack and met my companions. Then came a warder running that Deputy Superintendent was waiting and I was wanted immediately. I could not thus delay and I was sorry that I had to go in haste. The door of the barrack was opened, closed and I left.

"When I reached the office I met the Circle Jailor who pleaded ignorance about my release. He enquired from the office and he was told that there was no such release order. So I met the Deputy Superintendent and he asked the Jailor to release me immediately. He said to me 'I am very sorry, Mr. Shyam Sunder'.

Surprisingly I said 'what'. He replied, 'Nothing—because you are going'. I enquired what was the matter. 'You go at once. We meet after 14 days'. I could not describe my feelings at that moment. It became clear that I was being released on parole. At once I thought of my father—who was so often taken ill. I was reminded of my mother and also of Savitri. Someone of them must be dead. That explained the hurry—and I was wanted to perform the last rites. I composed myself. I came at the outer office. There was only one big gate between me and the outside world. From the opening I peeped outside. I saw Satish Chandra, and other persons waiting very much downcast, I saw that two tongas were standing. I called Satish to the gate and enquired what was the matter. He told me that my father died that morning—and I was wanted for the last rites. They would be waiting for me at Ganga Ghat. I heard it and at once hastened to the office. My papers for release were ready. I withdrew my cash deposit. Some time was wasted by the arrogant attitude of the office Jailor as he said that he had not received the release order. I hurried to the Deputy Superintendent and was released. The Commissioner had telephoned to the Superintendent to release me immediately.

"Very silently I got into the tonga which was waiting and accompanied by Satish Chandra left for Sardarnagar Ghat—a distance of *ten* miles from there. Chandra Narain Saksena left us at the Town Hall. My luggage was sent to my house direct by another tonga. So we drove straight to Sardarnagar Ghat. Satish who had spent the whole day in getting me released on parole, narrated to me the whole account of the death. My sister went to him in the morning and she asked him to move to get me released on parole to enable me to perform the last rites. We reached the Ganga Ghat. Every one was waiting for me. They were quite ready. I had the last *darshen* of my father. His face was as serene as ever. When I met him three weeks before when he came to interview me in jail, I had never thought that I was meeting him for the last time in life. Everything finished—we reached home. My family members were waiting for me. I met my mother, Savitri, sister and daughter. It was after two years that I had entered that house. It was very difficult to describe what passed into my mind. I could not sleep that night. Early in the morning my youngest brother Nihal who was in Delhi came and so also Anand Prakash and other relations and friends."

On 4th July I returned to Central Prison, Bareilly after the expiry of my 14 days parole. At the time of my departure my two year child was taken seriously ill. I left her in a helpless condition. On my return to the prison my mind was occupied with this illness. I was again in the world of darkness and I knew nothing what was happening outside. Everyone had sympathy with me. A week thus passed in great agony. I was informed that there was no improvement in her condition. I was again released on parole for 14 days to attend on the ailing daughter. What happened afterwards was that she died after some days of my arrival. Then I fell severely ill. Ram Murti from Central Prison wrote a letter to me. In my reply I wrote:

Bareilly,
September 11, 1944.

My dear Ram Murti,

I thank you for your kind letter of sympathy in my misfortunes. On June 19 when I parted from you I never knew that I was parting under the shadow of my dear father's death—and that I would never meet him in life. As you told me in prison you yourself noted when you met him during your parole period—how anxious he was about me and his sudden death released him from the worry and anguish which was his lot all these years.

After the expiry of my two weeks time, I rejoined you in July, though my daughter was laid up with typhoid fever and her condition was rather serious. When I saw her on my return from Prison on 12th July after my release again on parole due to her serious illness, I was thunderstruck to see her. She was a changed creature. Her eyes were closed. She was unconscious. I found her in a very pitiable condition. Next morning only 8 hours after my arrival her condition became very serious. A doctor was attending on her day and night, and his timely help saved her from that crisis. He told me that she was sinking fast and this fact we concealed from Savitri. Dr. BC Pant was immediately called. She had such three crisises before and surpassed them all. Then by and by she recovered. She came into consciousness and her old memory revived. We all thought that she had been saved. I asked my friends and relations who were attending on her during my absence that they could go—after all they were long detained. On July 17 they parted, satisfied that everything was all right. With her coming into consciousness she refused to take fruit juices and resisted. We had to resort to forcible feeding; and this cost her a great deal. In the morning of 21st July the doctor said that she would take only one week to recover. In the evening of that day Anand Prakash came to see her from Meerut. She had a talk with him fully recognising him. In that evening—as luck would have it, the bottle of brandy slipped from Savitri's hands and was broken. It cost Rs. 44. In that ill fated night I was attending on her. My turn was up to 1 a.m. I gave her medicine at 12. She resisted and with difficulty I could administer her medicine. I noted some deterioration in her condition. I awoke Savitri. She was much asleep. I asked her to apply some medicine on her lungs which she did half asleep. She waited to give a doze of brandy but brandy was not there. It was 2 a.m. but she was still asleep. I also began to doze. I never thought that her end was so near. At 3 a.m. I felt fast asleep—awoke Savitri and asked her to go to attend on her—and without making sure whether she had gone to attend on her, fell down on my bed and was soon fast asleep. She also did not go and remained sleeping. So between the hours of 3 and 4-30 the patient remained unattended when my younger brother happened to go in her room and found her alone sleeping quietly. He felt her pulse—which appeared to him very slow and her feet cold. He awoke us rather puzzled. Savitri felt her and became very nervous. My mother came at once. They realised that there remained nothing. I hastened to Dr. Rai—awoke him and brought him in no time, but he came only to announce formally that all was over with her.... After that you can well imagine our lot. At once Dr. B. C. Pant came and he consoled Savitri. With my own hands at Chaubarighat I laid her down in earth to rest. This was the only thing I did for her. What she knew of me. Surya Prakash and Ram Narain Mehrotra were with us.

A week later I became the victim of typhoid—and at one stage my condition became very serious. The attention of all was now absorbed on me, and they forgot their woe. In this respect this illness was heaven sent. It troubled me greatly. For three weeks I did not move from my bed.

Today I take your leave. It was really a great privilege to live for such a long time in the company of you all who were so considerate and affectionate. Really it was a great schooling for me. I have learnt many things and the sacred associations of these years in this Prison in such exacting circumstances will ever remain enshrined which will long be treasured. It was only an accident that we all met in these circumstances. I am grateful to you all for your love, sympathy and fellow-feeling which I will ever cherish.

I take this opportunity to express my feelings of gratefulness to you and through you to all my friends and companions whose picture is before me when I am writing these lines.

Please remember me to all.

Yours sincerely,
Shyam Sunder.

We received a large number of letters of sympathy. Rafi Ahmed Kidwai who was then in Central Prison, Bareilly wrote:

Central Prison,
Bareilly.

My dear Shyam Sunder,

I was grieved to learn of the death of your father. It was only some months back when I met him when he came to interview you. I was impressed by his forbearance especially when two of his sons were undergoing imprisonments for more than two years. It must be a matter of great satisfaction to you and to the members of your family that you could be present to perform his last rites.

I am sure you would have the courage to face this ordeal and to comfort your mother.

Where is your brother? Has he been released or still undergoing imprisonment.?

Yours,
Rafi.

"Rafi Sahib wrote another letter from Lucknow:

My dear Shyam Sunder,

"I am much concerned to read about your illness in papers. I trust you will be all right soon. I have admired how boldly you have faced the death of your father followed so quickly by the death of your only daughter. You should take care of yourself—I hope and trust that you will overcome all these calamities. I can imagine the feelings of your wife who has suffered such a grievous loss. I saw the child at the time of your interview. I hope you will recover soon from your illness.

Yours,
Rafi.

Dr. Kailash Nath Katju wrote:

19, Edmonstone Road
Allahabad. 7th November '44.

My dear Shyam Sunderji,

I am so grieved to learn of the domestic sorrow with which you have had to face in the last *few* months. The burden sustained by some friends has been heavy indeed and their sacrifice in the national cause has been so great. I hope you have now by this time completely recovered from your illness.

With kind regards.

Yours sincerely,
K. N. Katju.

Dr. Sampurnanand wrote

Jalipadevi, Banaras.

My dear Shyam Sunder,

I am grieved to learn that you have had such a painful time these last few months. Really we know so little about one another and are so little able to help one another even with a few words of cheer and sympathy. Politics threw us together and then we are pulled asounder by our individual circumstances. I can only offer you my belated sympathy. It is some comfort to know that you have now an opportunity to look after your own health and comfort your wife.

Sincerely yours,
Sampurnanand.

"Fourteen interviews took place between Gandhiji and Jinnah at Bombay, the first on September 9, 1944 and the last on September 27. During this period twenty-one letters were exchanged between the two. August 19 was the date originally fixed for the meeting, which had to be postponed owing to Jinnah's illness. Nothing came out of this talk and they could not reach an agreement.

"With the release of Congress leaders after several years detention the political activity assumed increasing importance. The Representative Assembly of released Congressmen which was formed in U.P. continued the efforts to revive activity. In January 1945 a three day meeting was held in Kanpur at which it was decided to open centres in rural areas to organise village handicrafts. Kasturba Gandhi National Memorial Fund was organised all over India for the welfare and education of rural women and children and it provided further opportunity for work. On the occasion of Gandhiji's 75th birthday on October 2, 1944 it was proposed to present a purse of Rs. 75 lakhs to Gandhiji for Kasturba Fund. In fact a sum of Rs. one crore and 28 lakhs was collected. Independence Day was celebrated on January 26. Events moved fast. On March 22 Lord Wavell left for England for personal consultations with H. M.'s Government on the Indian problem.

"By the end of March it was recognised that the war in Europe was virtually over. The Allied armies were driving into Germany so fast that all realised that the news of surrender might break upon the world at any moment. On May 1 came the announcement of the death of Hitler and on May 7 of the unconditional surrender of all German fighting forces. On May 23 Churchill tendered his resignation to the King on behalf of the Wartime Coalition Government and asked for the dissolution of Parliament which was dissolved on 15th June after a lapse of 10 years.

"During March and April 1945 the members of the Congress Working Committee, interned in Ahmednagar Fort prison camp, were dispersed and sent to their respective provinces. Pt. Nehru, Pt. Pant and Acharya Narendra Dev were brought to Bareilly Central Prison, Izatnagar on 31st March. They left Ahmednagar on 28th and on their way stayed in Naini Central Prison where they met a number of their old colleagues including Rafi Ahmed Kidwai. It was for the first time since their arrest in August '42 they had an opportunity of having first hand accounts of some of the occurrences of 1942. On their reaching Bareilly on 31st March Pt. Pant was released on account of ill health. Pt. Nehru and Acharya Narendra Dev lived in a barrack in Izatnagar Jail for over two months. Early in June they were transferred to Almora Jail due to excessive heat.

"Prior to his leaving for Nainital, Pt. Pant on his release from prison proceeded to Delhi for medical treatment. We were not in Bareilly at the time of Pt. Pant's release due to the illness and death of my sister. We met him while he was returning from Delhi on route to Nainital.

From Nainital Pt. Pant wrote:

Nainital,
May 1, '45.

My dear Shyam Sunder,

Thanks for your letter of 19th. Govind Sahai may have conveyed to you my message. I regret really that

I could not see your wife during my short stay in Bareilly, mainly because you were then out of the station. We are having splendid weather here now and I should suggest that you both should come up for a change for a few days.

I do not yet know when I shall be able to leave this place for the plains. I have no intention of doing so at least for the present. If I can manage it, I may go to Almora sometime about the end of this month, but not earlier.

I am anxious to know all about the life of Jawaharlalji in the Bareilly Central Prison. Have you any information as to the facilities accorded to him there? How is Narendra Dev? Let me hope that he has had no attack of asthma since his arrival there. It must be getting warm and even hot round about you now. Formerly, on more than one occasion Jawaharlalji was removed to Dehra Dun on the approach of the summer. Bareilly's climate may not agree with Acharya either.

Remember me to all. I trust this finds you both well. Yours sincerely, G.B. Pant.

"In another letter Pt. Pant expressed his feelings of sympathy in our misfortunes. He wrote:

Nainital.

My dear Shyam Sunder,

I regret that in the course of the few hours I have had at Bareilly the other day I could not manage to find a few minutes for a personal talk with you. There was nothing of any special importance to be communicated. I wanted only to offer you my heartfelt sympathy for the series of misfortunes and bereavements you had to face in recent months. I was deeply moved when I got your letter just before my leaving for Lucknow. I had the subject in mind when I saw you but it would have been incongruous to broach it in public; and I had hardly any breathing space or private moments during my short stay. I may have occasion to meet you soon. I shall be going to Lucknow on the 20th but not via Bareilly proper.

Yours sincerely,
G.B. Pant.

"After ten weeks of consultations in London, the Viceroy returned and on June 14 made *an* announcement on behalf of the British Cabinet that certain proposals designed to case the present political situation and to advance India towards the goal of full self-government would be placed before Indian leaders. He went on to say:

"I, therefore, propose with the full support of His Majesty's Government to invite Indian leaders both of the central and provincial policies to take counsel with me with a view to the formation of a new Executive Council, more representative of the organised political opinion. The proposed new Council would represent the main communities and would include equal proportions of Caste Hindus and Muslims."

"Lord Wavell invited twenty-one leaders of public life in the country to a Conference to be held at Shimla on the 25th June to advise him in setting up a new Executive Council with members more representative of organised political opinion in the country. Eight members of the Congress Working Committee who were still in prison were released. Pt. Nehru and Acharya Narendra Dev were released from Almora Jail where they had reached only a week before. There was a huge crowd at the Bhojipura station to receive them.

"At Gandhiji's instance the Viceroy invited the Congress President Maulana Azad. Prior to the Conference in Shimla Gandhiji informed the Viceroy that it would not be advisable for him to attend the Conference as he belonged to no organisation, but he promised to stay in Shimla for giving advice. "I have constituted myself both advisor to the Congress and advisor to the Viceroy," said Gandhiji in a press interview, "and through him to the British people".

"A meeting of the Congress Working Committee was held in Bombay on June 21 and 22. Maulana Azad presided. It was attended by all including Pandit Pant. Gandhiji was present at most of the sittings of the Committee. It met after a period of three years during which its members were in detention. The Working Committee met principally to discuss the Viceroy's proposal and to decide whether the Congress should participate in the Conference proposed to be convened at Shimla on June 25.

"The Committee considered the Viceroy's Broadcast of June 14 and the Statement of the Secretary of State in the House of Commons made the same day. It had also before it the Correspondence between Mahatma Gandhi and the Viceroy wherein Gandhiji had sought clarification of certain points arising out of the Viceroy's Broadcast. The Committee decided that Congress as an organisation should participate in the Shimla Conference.

"The Leaders' Conference opened at the Viceregal Lodge in Shimla on June 25 at 11-30 a.m. All the invitees were present except Mahatma Gandhi. In the short speech with which Lord Wavell opened the Conference, he reaffirmed his hope that its outcome would pave the way to a final solution of the complex constitutional problem. He was followed by the Congress President. The Conference began with an optimistic note:

"The statesmanship, wisdom and goodwill of all us are here on trial, not merely in the eyes of India but before the world," said Lord Wavell in his opening address. At the outset it became clear that Jinnah was determined to wreck Lord Wavell's efforts for a settlement. The Congress made it clear that it entered the negotiations with the hope of setting up an Interim Government which would be the first step to independence. On the other hand Jinnah took the uncompromising stand that 'this preliminary issue of Pakistan should be settled first, and the sooner it is done, the better for all concerned.'

"On 26th the Leaders took up for discussions one of the items on the agenda, e.g., scope, functions and responsibilities of the Viceroy's Executive Council on the basis of the H.M.G.'s proposals.

"On the 27th it was officially announced that after an hour session the Leaders Conference at Viceregal Lodge, Shimla adjourned till June 29 to enable the delegates to continue their private discussions.

"What the Wavell plan did was a fresh attempt to stereotype religious divisions on the eve of independence, to quote Gandhiji's words, exposing the dishonesty of the whole thing.

"On 28th the deliberations of the Conference reached a stage of impasse between the Congress and the Muslim League. Pt. Pant on behalf of the Congress was deputed to carry on talks with Jinnah with a view to reaching a preliminary understanding. The position taken by Jinnah was that the League on behalf of the Muslims should nominate Muslim members in the Executive Council. The Congress found that such a position would be inconsistent with its basic national character. The Congress was prepared to accommodate the Muslim League but Jinnah's intransigence gave no room for agreement.

"On June 29 Azad and Jinnah reported their failure to agree as to the strength and composition of the

Council. It was officially announced that the Conference was adjourned till July 14 'to enable the delegates to carry on further consultations.'

"Pt. Pant who had talks with Jinnah in a press interview in Shimla on July 1, clarified certain issues regarding the composition of the new Executive Council and dealt with fears expressed in Muslim League quarters that under the Wavell Plan the Muslims would be in a minority and thus would not get a fair deal.

"Pandit Pant said, "As you know, the present scheme provides for parity. The number of non-Scheduled Hindus will be no more than that of the Muslims in the Council, although the actual proportion of Hindus to Muslims is three to one. The majority community will thus be distinctly in a minority in the Executive Council. It is just possible that about two-thirds of the representatives in the Executive Council may consist of minorities and only one-third may belong to the majority community. In the circumstances, it is unthinkable how the latter can override the wishes of the former. In fact the majority community will be manifestly at the mercy of the minorities, and if there were conflicts between the interests of the two, it is the majority community that will stand in need of some safeguards under the proposed arrangement."

"Replying to a question Pandit Pant said that he did not see why there should be a Muslim block as against the rest. "I personally believe," he said "that our interests are more or less identical and we should be able to work in complete harmony. I have no reason to doubt the sincerity of the professions of the Muslim League about independence being their goal. If that be so, I sec no reason why fundamentally their outlook on problems as they come up from day to day should differ from other members of the Council.

"There is again no justification in holding that all other members of the Council will act in concert against the Muslims. In fact all, Muslims or Hindus, need not hold the same view between themselves. But no Council can work satisfactorily unless members are determined to work in unison according to the best of their light for the material and moral welfare of all sections of the community.

"Ultimately, it is the individual citizen who counts, and if we are really distressed over the present state of affairs and sincerely anxious to raise the general standard of life in this country, I personally believe that there will be no real cleavage on any communal or religious grounds inside the Council.

"In any case, the minorities will be in a majority and the majority community, whose strength is about three times that of the other minorities, will itself be in a minority in the Council and may not be more than a third of its total strength. If such a surrender by the majority community to the will and judgement of the minorities does not satisfy the latter, I do not know what more can be possible. One cannot find precedent for such reduction of a majority to such a minority position anywhere in the world."

"Talking of the personnel of the Executive Council, Pandit Pant said that it was essential that the members nominated should be those inspired by a common desire to raise the country to a position befitting its place in the sun with due regard to her vast numbers and ancient civilization. He concluded that passion for independence and for the improvement of the lot of the average citizen should be commonly shared by all the members.

"Unfortunately the Conference was unable to agree about the strength and composition of the Executive Council. The Viceroy undertook with the approval of the Conference on the last clay to endeavour to produce a solution. He asked parties to give him lists of names, and received lists from all parties represented in the Conference except from the European group which decided not to send a list, and the Muslim League declined to submit its list without an assurance that all the Muslim members of the Council would be members of the League. The Congress list included the names of the representatives of all the major parties including Jinnah and two other members of the League and that the names of only five actual Congressmen were submitted two of whom, however, were Maulana Azad and Asaf Ali. The Congress consistent with its national character claimed to include Muslims in its list.

"At the last moment again the wires were pulled by the Churchill Cabinet in London and the reactionary European-cum-Service groups in India. So when the Conference met again on July 14 Lord Wavell announced its breakdown. "All the parties," he said, "had submitted lists except the League, and as a last resort he had made his provisional selection including representatives of the League".

"The Viceroy could not accept Jinnah's impossible claim that all the Muslims in the Viceroy's Executive Council should be League nominees. The Premier of the Punjab who was the leader of the Unionist Party, as a member of the Conference claimed one of the Muslim seats to his Party.

"Meetings of the Congress Working Committee were held in Pune from September 12 to 18 and of the A.I.C.C. in Bombay from September 21 to 24. They were held after more than three years of wantom suppression by British Government at the same place where the historic meeting of August 1942 of the Quit India Movement was held. It conveyed its greetings and congratulations to the Nation for the courage and endurance with which it withstood the fierce and violent onslought of the British power and its deep sympathy to all those who suffered during these three years.

"Complaints were received in A.I.C.C. office regarding the hostile activities of the Communist Party members during the August Struggle and their open defiance of the Congress policy as embodied in the August Resolution. They were placed before the Working Committee which appointed a committee consisting of Pt. Nehru, Pt. Pant and Sardar Patel to go into the charges of indiscipline brought against the Congress members of the Communist Party. In view of the events happened in the country since August 1942 the revision of the Congress Constitution was called for. The Working Committee appointed a subcommittee consisting of Pt. Pant, Dr. Rajendra Prasad, and Dr. Pattabhi to suggest necessary changes in the Constitution to facilitate fresh elections.

"*National Herald* ceased publication in August 1942 Movement. It reappeared in the last months of 1945. Pt. Pant in his message on this occasion said:

"Hail Herald. It gives me great pleasure to extend a most cordial welcome to the *National Herald* on its resuming publication after more than three unforgettable years of ruthless governmental repression and suppression. The *Herald* had in the course of its relatively short but remarkably eventful career secured a conspicuous place for itself in the journalistic world. It had earned the esteem and affection of the people of the Province and had raised the general level of the public press by its indomitable courage and intrepid advocacy of all deserving causes. It had set a high standard for itself from the beginning and had always been in the vanguard in the nation's fight for political independence and social justice. The *Herald* was much more than a newspaper. It had built noble traditions and had grown into an institution, equally loved and respected by large sections of the community. It has made a solid contribution towards the achievement of national freedom and will no doubt lead us on in our onward march to our destined and cherished goal speedily and unfalteringly. May it live for ever as a perennial source and symbol of national and individual life, liberty and vitality."

3

In Government

Chief Minister of U.P.

When India achieved freedom, the Indian National Congress inevitably became the leading national party, which was voted to power by the people. Govind Ballabh Pant was the foremost leader of the Congress Party in U.P. and became the Chief Minister of U.P. on April 1, 1946 and continued to hold this position till the end of 1954 for eight long years. He laid the foundation of a modern, forward-looking state, wedded to the task of socio-economic transformation.

Farewell from U.P.

One could never forget the spontaneous outburst of feeling and enthusiasm with which he was accorded farewell when he left U.P. on the last day of 1954 to join the Central Cabinet. The vast upsurge of feeling burst forth when it was known in November 1954 that he was to join the Central Cabinet. This had aroused universal attention. The minds of the whole country, particularly of northern India, were widely agitated. This touched the headlines and editorial comments in every paper. In recent history there was no such topic which arrested so much attention as the reported news of Pandit Pant's departure from U.P.

Writing editorially the *National Herald* commented thus:

> "It is a tribute to his solid achievements as Chief Minister for a long period of seventeen years that Pandit Pant leaves the State stable and secure. The administrative machinery seems to be functioning smoothly and there is no political unrest. Pandit Pant's record as Chief Minister is broadly known to the entire country. U. P. is not only the largest State hut politically the most important for whichever way it swings, the rest of the country seems to swing. In major measures like land reform and panchayat raj U. P. gave (he lead. On the stability of this part of the country depended the course of freedom after August 15, 1917, and it is widely acknowledged that with his capacious mind, mastery of administrative detail, and political shrewdness, in which he is, perhaps equalled only by Mr. Rajagopalachari, Pandit Pant rode storm after storm with extraordinary tact and firmness. On the public platform, he is not only eloquent but pungent and popular. In the legislature, he is a tower of strength, and there are few in this country or elsewhere who can equal him in sheer dexterity of debate. Not unoften there have been troubles within the party, but Pandit Pant has been always the smoother and exerted an influence for unity.
>
> "Pandit Pant will be an immeasurable source of strength to the Central Cabinet. With his vast political and administrative experience, his amazing skill in debate and his unfailing ability to deal with men, he will add strength to a Cabinet which does not always look strong and well equipped in debate. Pandit Pant's addition to the Central Cabinet will mean added compatibility to a Cabinet which has not shown the maximum amount of compatibility. No body else has understood the Prime Minister's policies so well as Pandit Pant or given them his support so steadily, if often unobtrusively On foreign affairs Pandit Pant

has been foremost in the debates in the A. I. C. C. In serving U. P. he has served the country well; and in serving the country hereafter he will be serving U. P. too."

The Hindustan Times, New Delhi observed:

"Pandit Pant is the wisest and the most experienced administrator in the Congress Camp. He is not only well-versed in provincial administration but has unrivalled experience of central politics. Next to Nehru the U. P. Chief Minister has been the main exponent of the country's foreign policy in the counsels of the Congress. Resolutions on foreign policy have always been piloted by him at the quarterly meetings of the all India Congress Committee and the annual sessions of the Congress."

Since, India achieved independence in August 1947 the responsibilities of Pandit Nehru as Prime Minister greatly increased. He wanted to share them with some of his trusted friends in whose judgement he could repose full confidence. Pandit Nehru approached Pandit Pant several times to join him in the Central Cabinet; and every time Pandit Nehru yielded. In 1948 after the death of Gandhiji when Pandit Nehru felt distressed Pandit Pant's name was mentioned as a likely successor of Shammukham Chetty as India Government's Finance Minister. In 1950 Pandit Nehru wanted him again as Finance Minister to succeed John Matthai. This time he was adamant, but he could not resist the pressure of the universal desire to retain him in the province. Rightly observed *Hindustan Times*, "If Pandit Pant had not preferred him to serve his own State, as Chief Minister, he would have been in the Central Cabinet long ago."

The similar views were expressed by the *Statesman*: "It is no doubt true that Pandit Pant would make an able Finance Minister at the Centre. But he is a much able Premier and his exit from U. P. politics would not only be unthinkable to some, but one that may well upset the precarious balance between the groups in the Congress Party which he alone has been able to hold together."

> A Bombay Commercial Journal wrote: "Pandit Pant, of course, is well known as a capable administrator. He is a man of strong will and common sense. He has a practical outlook and his grip of economics and public finance became evident in the pre-war days when the Congress sat *on* the opposition benches in the Central Assembly. He proved himself quite capable of opposing Sir James Grigg, the then Finance Member. But it is doubtful whether his own province will be able to spare him."

Prior to his going to China in the first week of October, 1954, Pandit Nehru in some of his public statements suggested that he should unburden himself of the high offices he held. In his letter which he addressed to the Presidents of Provincial Congress Committees and provincial Chief Ministers he explained why he thought it would be better for him not to function as Prime Minister at least for some time as the strain on him had been considerable and it was not surprising that he felt somewhat tired. He wanted to function with vigour and speed.

After his return from China Pandit Nehru met Pandit Pant in the first week of November, 1954, when he went to New Delhi to attend the meeting of Congress Working Committee. He gave a bit of his mind, his helplessness, his predicament in which he found himself. He wanted Pandit Pant to join him in the Central Cabinet. He needed a person of the stature, calibre, and eminence of Pandit Pant to help him in his arduous work as Prime Minister, in whom he could repose his full confidence and in whose judgement he had full reliance. Without a moment's hesitation Pandit Pant agreed. He had refused several times; and he thought that it would not be fair to refuse. They had been colleagues and co-workers for more than 30 years. They had lived together in prisons. In Ahamednagar Fort they were together for about three years. A common friend of both wrote thus:

> "Of the part which Pantji has played in our highest councils in the Working Committee of the Indian National Congress it is not for me to speak. But it is noteworthy that of all the companions among whom Pandit Jawaharlal passed three years of his life in the

> Ahmednagar Fort he has singled out Pantji as one whom he then learnt to love. That is not a small thing. Long incarceration of a jail barrack shows the real mettle of the man, the real stuff of which he is made, and if you can stand that test, then you can stand any test conceivable."

If Pandit Pant had the choice he would have not left Uttar Pradesh; but he considered his duty like a disciplined soldier to work where he was mostly wanted without any personal consideration or inconvenience. Moreover, Pandit Nehru had been his weakness. In his own words which he wrote several years ago:

> "It is my good fortune to be Jawaharlalji's colleague for many years. We were together in jail more than once. The more I have known him, the deeper my affection and admiration for him has grown. The nearer one comes to his stupendous personality the more deeply is one impressed by his greatness. His vast learning, indomitable courage, high devotion to duty, unparalleled sacrifice, abounding energy and sober statesmanship are well known and universally respected. But the quality that endears him to me more than his learning is his large-heartedness. Such sensitiveness as his, comprising tolerance and kindness, is a quality rarely seen. Those who have seen him in temper on the public stage can hardly conceive of the innate humility and deep human sympathy he possesses."

On the 2nd December evening a crowded meeting of the U.P. Legislature Congress Party was held which was specially convened to discuss the departure of Pandit Pant. There was a record attendance—which indicated the gravity of the situation. There were tears in many an eye and they were sad on the departure of their leader who guided them for the last 30 years. In closed doors the meeting continued for more than 2 hours. About 20 speakers participated and some were so much overwhelmed that they broke down. Pandit Pant firmly intervened and told the party members to accept the decision of the Prime Minister for as soldiers of the Congress it was their duty to abide by the wishes of their leader. At the conclusion of the meeting the following statement was issued:

> "The U. P. Congress Legislature Party, which met here tonight to consider the situation arising out of the Chief Minister, Pandit Pant's going to the Centre, was unanimously of the view that Pandit Pant should be spared for the State. At the insistence of Pandit Pant, however, no formal resolution was moved by the party though there Were over 40 resolutions requesting the Prime Minister to let the State continue to enjoy the leadership of the veteran Statesman. Over 20 speakers took part in the discussion.
>
> "The party was practically of the view that Pandit Pant's presence was absolutely necessary. The party also realised that Pandit Nehru's desire to take Pandit Pant to the Central Government was justified in the sense that men of Pandit Pant's ability and capacity were rare in the country and Pandit Nehru needed a man of his calibre. At the insistence of Pandit Pant, who explained all the reasons under which he had given his assent to go to the centre, the party abstained from passing a formal resolution to request Pandit Nehru to spare Pandit Pant."

Both the Houses of U.P. Legislature assembled on the 27th December, 1954 in a special session to bid Pandit Pant farewell. There was a record attendance of members and the public galleries were crowded. Opposition and Treasury benches were united in their loving farewell. A large number of speakers in both the Houses from all sides participated in paying glowing tributes to Pandit Pant. Hafiz Mohammed Ibrahim, who was the oldest colleague in the Cabinet spoke first. Dr. Sampurnanand, who was elected to succeed Pantji joined in the tributes. He described Pandit Pant as the maker of the present U. P.—one to whom the State owed her present position of pre-eminence in the country." He said that Pandit Pant was one of those rare parliamentarians in this country who was feared and respected by the Treasury benches in the days when the executive was irremovable and he led the opposition against it.

The late Dr. Brijendra Swaroop, one of the eldest members of the Bar who joined it in 1901 speaking in the Council associated with all the observations made in appreciation and admiration of the great and disinterested services of Pandit Pant to this State. He said:

> "Pandit Pant's profound learning and knowledge and deep insight into the springs of human action, his persuasive eloquence and ability to sway the man's judgement, his sanity of judgement and patriotism and above all his wonderful capacity for sustained hard work are assets of inestimable value not only to our State but to the country. The departure of such a distinguished administrator from the State would create a void which I can say will be difficult to fill. We all know that Pandit Pant never allowed himself to be infected with narrow mindedness, of the communalism or sectarianism. He always placed national interest above his personal interest or the provincial interest. It is, therefore, not surprising that Pandit Pant responded to the call of the nation in accepting the assignment to the Centre in the larger interest of the country. Pandit Pant's sagacity and wisdom, his character and skill and above all his untiring and unceasing efforts for the uplift of the country and for its great brilliant future rose him in the public estimation and the public life of the country to a height attained by a few and surpassed by none probably with the exception of Pandit Jawaharlal Nehru. In individual capacity there might be some leaders who may be superior to Pandit Pant, but in the combination of rare qualities of head and heart and in the many sided activities of life and above all *in* the actual output of work *none* excelled him. Pandit Pant's regime has been characterised by numerous achievements in the development of the State which

will always be remembered with a feeling of pride and gratitude. It was due to these achievements that our State occupies a pre-eminent position in the country."

Dr. Ishwari Prasad, the eminent historian of India, as an independent member of the House said:

> "He occupies now a position second only to that of the Prime Minister of India by his unrivalled knowledge of public questions, by his mastery of detail, and by his unfailing skill in the handling of practical human affairs. He has been a great parliamentarian. More than a parliamentarian, more than a statesman, more than a councillor, and more than a Minister, he shines as a man. As a man he is greater than anybody else. Sweet and reasonable, amiable in temper, he is always accessible. You may go to him at any time. He is always full of the milk of human kindness. He is always good, he is always gentle; he is always generous.
>
> "Lately, Sir, I have been reading his speeches delivered in the Council and if you read them today, you will find that he is a man of natural eloquence, who can rise to great heights like the greatest statesmen of other countries and this shows his conspicuous ability in doing the business of the Parliament. As the Leader of the House, members will remember, he never loses his temper. It is his serenity, his amiability of temper that has distinguished him all his life.
>
> "He is going to a new sphere of activity. It is not new to him because for a man of his genius, for a man of great parliamentary capacity, for a man of the extraordinary talents endowed with patriotism, his new duties will present no difficulty. There is no position in the country which he cannot fill with distinction. When I think of him I compare him with other statesmen of the world whom he equals in

eloquence, in the splendour of genius, in patriotism and in parliamentary skill."

He concluded by quoting from a poet whose lines very appropriately apply to a distinguished gentleman like him:

"A statesman of soul sincere. In duty firm, in honour clear."

Union Home Minister

In 1955, he was invited to join the Central Cabinet by Jawaharlal Nehru, the first Prime Minister of India. Nehru needed Pant to help him as Home Minister. Pant's vast experience in administration and political wisdom now had to be used for national reconstruction.

Language is no doubt a powerful factor... It is not only means of communication but it reflects the culture and the character of the people. So, we have to attach sufficient importance to it. But language can also be a dividing factor. If we are cut away from each other and if we think of our language alone... then, instead of serving the cause of unification and advancement, languages become a source of disruption.

The Demise

Pantji was however able to serve the country as Union Home Minister only till 20 February, 1961 when while discussing certain problems with the Law Minister Asoke Sen, he suffered a stroke, caused by cerebral thrombosis. He remained in coma till 7 March, 1961 when the end came and the country lost one of its greatest stalwarts. The entire nation mourned his death and Parliament did so rather deeply as it had lost one of its most accomplished members. Both Houses of Parliament - Lok Sabha and Rajya Sabha - and members from all sections in each House paid rich tributes on his passing away.

In Lok Sabha, Shri Satya Narayan Sinha, the Minister of Parliamentary Affairs, read out the following message from the Prime Minister, Shri Jawaharlal Nehru on the passing away of Pantji:

> "What we have been expecting fearfully, during the last two weeks, has come to pass and the last glimmer of hope that Pantji might recover has been snuffed out and we are left desolate and forlorn. Dear friend and comrade, great captain of our people during *the* days of our straggle for freedom, great in leadership after freedom came, the wisest of counsellors, gentle and yet firm of purpose, with malice to none, child of our beloved Himalayan mountains, carrying with him something of their calm and imperturbability, rock of stability and lighthouse to guide people's minds and paths, how shall we replace him or find his like again. He shone in Parliament but, even more, he shone in life itself and loved with passion our motherland and the well- being of all her children. We pay our homage to him and give our pledge to devote ourselves to the cause to which he gave his brilliant mind and all his strength and energy, in spite of physical ailments and disabilities. To the last moment of his days, so long as consciousness lasted, he gave Ms unremitting labour to the service of India. Even so, may it be given to us to labour with joyful heart in this dear service till the last breath of life."

Some of the other obituary references in the two Houses could be summed up as follows:

Lok Sabha: Morarji Desai, Minister of Finance: His services of the country will never be forgotten and they will be equalled by few. He had been in public life for about forty-five years, as far as 1961 I find he was a Member of the A.I.C.C, as it was even then called... He was a tower of strength to the party and the Government here by his wise counsel, his debating skill and the great amount of thought that he gave to every problem that he dealt with. I was always wondering how he could remember every point without making any notes. People who might make written speeches might forget something but he never forgot a single point and dealt with every thing in proper sequence. He will be missed always in this House in the Government and in the Congress where he was a tower of strength. The country has lost one of the greatest patriots produced by it, who gave his whole life to the struggle for freedom and after freedom had been obtained, to the work of consolidation and bringing prosperity to the country. I never saw him ruffled even once. I was connected with him from 1937 from which time I had the privilege of getting his affection and I can never forget the wise counsel that he always gave me and others. I shall always miss him; we shall all miss him, I have no doubt We can only remember what he has done for all of us and for the country. He lived a rich life and has left us traditions in the matter of wisdom which if we follow I have no doubt that we will all enrich ourselves.

S.A. Dange: Sir, in paying tribute to the memory of Pantji we pay tribute to one of the stalwarts of the old independence movement led by the Congress and the people in this country against British rule, And throughout his life he carried the sign of the struggle not only in the memory of the people, but on his own personal body. He embodied in fact, the spirit of independence. After independence, and in particular lately, he had to discharge heavy duties. Everybody knows, Sir, that it is very difficult to be popular when you wield the Home Ministry particularly. But then he had that particular quality that even when he did an unpleasant job, he did not leave bitterness behind. He had the peculiar quality, as I saw him in many surroundings, to bind people together, to synthesise and not to dissipate, even where differences existed. Even when we differed, when ever we differed and parted, we did so not as permanent opponents, and without bitterness, That was the greatest quality which endeared him to all circles. He did not mind even keeping contacts with smaller subjects... The nation will remember his services not only during the period of struggle for Independence but also during the later period when it was his ambition to develop the country and strengthen its Independence, and a tribute to his memory will ever be given.

Ashoka Mehta: It is not easy in words the sence of loss and grief that we feel. I am remained of the words that Gandhiji used at the time of the demise of Pandit Motilal Nehru. He said, "The rock of ages has cleft for me". In that way, as our own Prime Minister pointed out the other day, Pandit Pant was the great anchor, in tills storm-tossed sea, when our journey is so full of difficulties and dangers, here was someone to whom all of *us* instinctively turned. We turned to him for security, for guidance. Even those of us who belong to another party would always go to him: his commanding and yet affectionate personality was there before us. I know, as many of my colleagues know, that we used to go to him with our doubts and difficulties, and sometimes with our woes, and we were always assured not only of warm welcome, of wise counsel; somehow or other, we came hack after meeting him, with a feeling as if we had left our worries to him. He was willing to carry the Cross for ail of *us and* it is very rare that one can have a person of that *kind,* massive in body, massive in *mind* and massive in spirit On a number of occasions I had the privilege to see him, I saw in his eyes and in his heart the great agony that he felt about many things that are going wrong in the country, many things for which perhaps many of us are responsible. But I also saw that there was always in him an unshakable faith in the future of our country and in the wisdom of our people. It is that faith and it is that anguish that I hope we shall try to remember. He was one of the great torchbearers of the freedom-fighters and one of those who have been privileged to consolidate that freedom. He has been removed, but I hope the torch which has been made brighter by his great personality, by his remarkable services, will be kept aloft by those who will always remember him and cherish him in their thoughts.

Prof. N.G. Ranga: On the death of Shri G.B. Pant, many people like me and I see so many here feel a terrible loss. We have been together for the last 35 years as colleagues, as comrades, as friends, as almost members of the same family. It was a privilege to be embraced by him. He was a great man, a good *man* and a wise counsellor. It could be seen from the debates that he did recognise political differences but he never recognised personal differences. He had a tremendous capacity for love, to love everybody. More than anything else, he set an example as a great follower of our great leaders, Mahatma Gandhi, Sardar Patel and Bhulabhai Desai.

Shiva Raj: I wish to associate myself both on my own behalf and on behalf of the Parliamentary group of the Republican Party with the sentiments expressed by the Leader of the House and by other speakers. *Shri* G.B. Pant was a man of great ability, endowed with clarity of thought and lucidity of expression. Even at the Wavell Conference, he chirped *in* on many important occasions to make useful suggestions to other equally intellectual giants like Rajaji and others at the conference the so-called backward classes, the Scheduled Castes and Scheduled Tribes who were lucky to be in his charge during the period of his administration had had the benefit of his human approach in the solution of their problems. I am glad that in that respect he had set a very great and noble example for his successors to follow in the solution of these problems.

Frank Anthony: I have had the opportunity and the privilege of working closely on many occasions with Pantji for about 20 years. We had our differences, but in that not negligible period, inevitably perhaps; I came to regard him not only with the highest esteem, but with deep affection. One finds it impossible to describe and pay a tribute even inadequately to his many and multifaceted gifts, but I would like *to* refer to two outstanding examples of his work, with which I was closely associated. The House will remember the vitally important States Reorganisation Bill. The more I saw him work the mote amazed was I. Some of us were conversant with some of the provisions, but not one of us except Pantji was conversant with every provision. I think he was flanked by four Secretaries in our deliberations lasting about a fortnight. I do not think he referred to them once. He was seized not only of every provision, whether it was legal, administrative, financial or constitutional, but he was seized of the nuance and meaning of every word. Again, he presided over the parliamentary committee on official language. Never in my fairly long public life have I been in a committee which was bedevilled by such fierce conflicts. I say this that perhaps none but Pantji with his skill, his patience and his unruffled nature could have brought its deliberations to any conclusion. It is not for us to attempt to assign a place to Pantji. I have no doubt history will do that I also feel that it will assign to Shri Govind Ballabh Pant a place in Indian history perhaps greater than what we have assigned to him today.

Acharya Kripalani: I associate myself with all that has been said here about our beloved leader. I have been associated with him personally ever since, the national movement started under Gandhiji. There are innumerable occasions which come to my mind. It is, therefore, not only a national loss, but a personal loss to me and at such time, words are not adequate to do justice to the great qualities of head and heart that he had. In him we have lost a great patriot, a great guide and a great parliamentarian, a man who was never ruffled and who always had a sweet word for everybody. Therefore, our loss is very great and I pay my humble tribute of reverence to his memory.

Surendra Mahanty: Pandit Pant was a great patriot and a distinguished administrator. The urbanity, charm, courtesy and dignity that he brought to bear upon the heated debates in this House were indeed a tribute to his high forensic ability. This is an occasion when small forgotten incidents in the cupboard of our memory are apt to assume most poignant dimensions. I remember one such incident That was years ago when I was harassed by a State Government other than my own. I was at my wits end what to do. I approached him and knowing fully well that he was undergoing the risk of interfering with the normal flow of law, he spared no pains to see that political differences were settled not in a legal plane, but cm a political plane. Indeed he was a man great by every standard. We pay our tributes to the man who was great by every standard. It will not be an exaggeration to say that light has gone out of our public life and to that extent light has gone out of this Parliament.

Tridib Kumar Chaudhary: Those of us who were in the past partisans of the underground revolutionary movement had the opportunity of knowing the largeness of his heart which was combined with warmth of affection and largeness of his vision. He never agreed with us; he often chided us for our activities, but we were never denied any help in respect of our cause. Of course, as a follower of the Father of the Nation and a follower of the philosophy of non-violence, he never agreed to our ways. Even then, we were assured that here was someone to whom we could go in our difficulties. Sir, his place is assured in history and if he were here today he would not have liked us to say that the void created by his death would never be filled up. But, even then, those of us and those of his co-workers and colleagues who had contacts with him would never be able to forget the loss they have suffered by his removal by the inevitable hand of death.

Braj Raj Singh: He was a great organiser, an astute parliamentarian and an able administrator. After Gandhi and Nehru, he was the most popular man in Uttar Pradesh - one might say, in the whole country. The vacuum created by Shri Pant's death could hardly be filled up. Great pillars of our national movement were giving way one by one and it was a matter of concern that men of similar calibre were not coming up to replace them.

Atal Behari Vajpayee: He was as firm as the Himalayas and as deep as the ocean. He devoted every moment of his life to the service of the country. For the coming generations his life would always be a beacon of light and a source of inspiration.

Ananthasayanam Ayyangar: I fully associate myself with all the sentiments that have been expressed on the life and services of Shri Govind Ballabh Pantji. In him we have lost one of the main architects of India's freedom. My association with Pantji started as early as 1935 when, for the first time, the Congress resolved to contest seats in the Central Legislature and both of us ware returned Members of the then Legislative Assembly. He became the Deputy Leader of the party and the Government of the day always paid the greatest regard for his words. He proved very easily to be one of the greatest parliamentarians. Without offence, rancors or bitterness and with an easy-flowing style he would meet all the arguments of his opponents. He was invincible in his argument and even his opponents developed great regard and respect for him. After renting hero to our Parliament he became an asset to us and on all crucial matters Parliament looked up to him for an answer. In spite of his poor health he never hesitated to *undergo any* amount of sacrifice and service for the country's freedom. As the Home Minister sometimes he had vary unpleasant duties to do but he was strong and, at the same time, good.

Rajya Sabha: Hafiz Mohammed Ibrahim, Minister of Irrigation: It is ray earnest desire that every Indian should die like Pandit Pant. So far as Pandit Pant is concerned, his end was fortunate because until the last moment, he was engaged in the service of the nation. He strained himself more than he could bear. Since he had a yearning love for his country, he joined the Congress and rose to the front rank of leadership by his ability and sacrifice. He was respected by all leaders who also sought his advice. His death at the present juncture has created a void which it is difficult to fill.

Bhupesh Gupta: He was not only the Leader of the House, he was an outstanding personality in the leadership of the national struggle, and when we are today rising to express our deep grief, naturally we recall to our mind those days in which he braved lathi-charges in the streets, went to prison and suffered, and he continued the struggle till freedom was won. That made him a great personality in the country and naturally, it is a tribute to him that today we remember those great traditions and we remember the personality such as he was. Sir, apart from that, in his passing away we have lost a personality in this House and his place would be difficult to fill. We have always admired from this side of the House his high intelligence, his patience and tolerance and his magnificent parliamentary skill. These are assets in a parliamentary democracy which we all cherish. From tomorrow, probably these qualities which radiated very great confidence in *the* House and affected us also on this side will be missed. But even so, I fed that his words in this House as well as the manner in which he functioned in this House *in* relation to us as to the rest of the Members will echo down the years that follow.

Rohit M. Dave: Pantji impressed every Indian and others *with his* passionate dedication to the service of the nation and his indomitable will to overcome any obstacle that came in the way of peace and prosperity of our country. He worked, the whole of his life, first to liberate our nation and suffered heavy losses in that struggle; after independence, he continued to serve the nation till the last ounce of energy in him. His work in Parliament and in the Legislatures will serve as an object lesson for all those who want to serve our nation through this august institution. This House feels a special sense of bereavement because he was the Leader of the House and while working at a speech which was to be delivered in this House, he lost consciousness and ultimately lost his life also. He literally worked himself to his final end and contributed the last ounce of his energy for the service of the nation. May his soul rest in peace.

Dahyabhai V. Patel: Apart from his achievements, his work in the public life and in the political life of this country, to which reference has been made by the previous speakers, I feel, Sir, one of the greatest qualities of Pantji was that he was intensely human. He was a very kindly person. I had occasion to worry him on a few small matters and in the midst of all his cares he was always willing to listen and, if possible to help. We have lost one of the greatest sons of this country. He leaves a void which it will be difficult to fill.

Dr. H. N. Kunzru: Mr. Chairman, having had the privilege of knowing Pandit Govind Ballabh Pant for more than forty-five years, it is difficult for me to give expression to my feelings cm this occasion. Sir, the very first day that I came to know him, I realised that he was far above all of us. Having followed his career, I can say without fear of contradiction that in his judgement of a situation, his grasp of facts, Ms administrative ability he had few equals in the country. I should add Till the last moment his devotion of duty at the risk of his health stood out... Reference was made to his great parliamentary skill. I have noticed it here; all of you have noticed it. Very soothing," very conciliatory, very civilized in his appeal, he made few errors, ruffled few tempers and disarmed every kind of opposition. You had in him a combination of common sense, clarity, balance of judgement and patriotism. It will be difficult for us to get another of the same calibre-Reference was made to his physical sufferings which he sustained during the struggle for freedom, but as was said these physical ailments did not produce in him any embitterment of spirit. He was human, humane and always anxious to find any fault with himself more than with others. Of course, as a parliamentarian when the opponents played into his hand he was devastating with a great sense of humour and yet he left no bitterness behind. His life is an example of service for the country. Till the end that was his one ambition and he has left behind an inspiring example for us all to follow. There is no doubt that we will feel his loss for many many years to come.

4

Great Administrator

Able Administrator

Pantji was one of India's ablest administrators. Like Sardar Patel he was also a man of action and firm determination. He possessed a wonderful understanding of the human mind. He knew men's weaknesses and their strong points and knew how to tackle men and matters even in the most difficult circumstances. He never allowed the bureaucracy to master him. His experience of handling the legislature, the party and the bureaucracy made him an eminently successful administrator, first as Premier ami later as Chief Minister of U.P. and Home Minister at the Centre. When he came as Premier of U.P. in 1937, he had had a long career behind him and was already one of the leading Congressmen in the country.

Once at the helm of affairs in U.P. he soon acquired a reputation as an astute administrator in addition to his old reputation as a leader and a speaker - a reputation for shrewdness and tact. U.P. was a large province, the most populous, with complete autonomy and "it seemed Pant was its Peshwa; he not only ruled but reigned over it" Among the officials he was called a Nana Phadnawis, the well known Maharashtrian statesman famous for his astuteness and ruthlessness. He could at times be quite stem. When a high central official's brother came to ask him to take interest in a case that was going on, he curtly told him: "The course of justice can not be interfered with". At the same time, he was of Madly disposition and dealt with his senior officials with good humour.

Good Administrator

Pandit Pant was a dynamic, driving and inspiring force in Indian politics and administration. He was ranked one of the foremost leaders of the country, a great figure with superhuman industry and tenacity. Wherever he was, he dominated the scene by his towering personality and remarkable charm. He was a giant among men, Prince among patriots, still young in his ideas, progressive in his views, and revolutionary in his outlook.

A trusted lieutenant of Pandit Motilal Nehru and a friend of Pandit Jawaharlal Nehru, Pandit Pant had risen to his present eminence which he had so eminently maintained during these four decades of his crowded public life through sheer hard work, intelligence, integrity and high character. He was a great example of selfless devotion to public service.

He had achieved distinction in many spheres, as a lawyer, politician, parliamentarian, administrator and statesman. His lucid speeches, polished manners and affectionate behaviour commanded the spontaneous homage, love and respect of the people. He was not only respected and loved but also feared. His great qualities of the head and the heart marked him out as one of the greatest men in the modern history of India. He was most brilliant political brain today. He would be reckoned as one of the best statesmen of the age, a great Parliamentary leader—was *at* the helm at a very critical period of history—when a new nation was born out of thousands of years of thraldom; and he proved worthy of that great heritage. He would be acknowledged by the posterity as one of the greatest administrators and parliamentarians. He left behind a name for steadfastness, for integrity and for piety, which few statesmen of his rank have emulated, and which certainly none has excelled. No man except Pandit Nehru had played a greater part during the last half a century than Pandit Pant. He is most far-sighted statesman with great vision, prudence and imagination, which is 'God's greatest gift to man.'

People learnt from him courage in the face of danger, patience in the face of frustration, great compassion and warmth of heart. His charm lay in his friendly-eyes, sympathetic smile and all pervading humanity. He is generous, equable and loving. People found that he was always courteous and sympathetic even when people are tedious and truculent. The keynote of his character is magnanimity. He combined brevity with comprehensiveness; strength with sweetness; genius with character; tact with talent; justice with generosity; wit with wisdom; confidence with courage; scholarship with practical wisdom; knowledge with resourcefulness and the qualities of a great politician with the patience of a first class clerk; and purity of heart with integrity of conduct. He prefers cooperation to conflict, and peace to power. He combined the shrewdness of the organiser, the strength of the leader, and vision of the prophet. He was an apostle of austerity and ascetic in his way of life. He is strict vegetarian. His life was regular, simple and strenuous.

He killed by kindness. No one could surpass him in ability, in sagacity and in human touch. He had a power of judging men far in advance. His consummate knowledge of human nature had enabled him to win the hearts of the people. He possessed three great qualities for leadership—personality, sympathy and above all idealism. He was always serene and calm even in the midst of severest trials. His cool, cloudless and unprovocative temper was his greatest asset. He was never excited. People had never seen him in temper. He has perfect control over his emotions. He had always emphasised and practised these basic factors which Gandhiji stressed—high character, integrity of mind and purpose, a spirit of tolerance, cooperation and hard work. He was a man who hates to hurt anybody's feelings. These were his basic characteristics which he has laid stress in his life.

It may rightly be said of him as Lord Rosebery said of Napoleon that "in all the offices of the State he knew everything, guided everything, inspired everything; and that his inexhaustible memory made him familiar with all the men and all the details as well as with all the machinery of the Government."

He was a model Prime Minister. He gave a clear lead on all questions and gives decisions quickly and unequivocally and then defended them with confidence and success. If he postponed a decision he understood the implications of it and it was with a definite purpose to have the desired effect.

Pandit Pant had established a high reputation as the ablest administrator in India. There could be no two opinions of his uncommon intellectual qualities. As Premier of U.P. he held this office with great distinction for such a long period, which no one would ever hold hereafter. He had acquitted himself as no one could have done. He had rare ability, unsurpassed power of work, and never failing devotion to duty. He had acquired a reputation for a detached view of men and matters "Wholly non-sectarian in his outlook", wrote the Pioneer editorially, "he has the rare gift—rare in a politician— to take a detached and dispassionate view of the administrative problems." This was the secret of his strength as administrator. Administration was the art in getting things done. To secure concerted action from group of men sometimes of divergent views, was a difficult task. It involved both deciding and doing. Superhuman tact was required to navigate in treacherous waters without shipwreck. When he was forced to make a difficult decision, he thought it over quietly, weighed up all the facts, considered pros and cons of the case and came to a decision. He never worried after that, because in the right act there was no question of worry.

He was intimately familiar with the working of each department. He kept a vigilant eye on details of administration. He was the most informed person and his retentive memory greatly helped him. He read every official paper, report, blue book, and took every opportunity of acquainting himself. He was expert in file work.

His disposal was very quick and very thorough. He would examine from every angle and not a single paper would escape his eyes. The technique of filing was not easy and was acquired by experience and hard work. It required the ability to seize the gist of a long statement by a single reading. It was the art of rapid digestion. He immerses himself in files, probes deeply and always would point out a fault, which was not pointed out or suggested below by those whose duty it was. Like Churchill he was a strong believer in transacting official business by the written word. He had capacity to take a decision and then sustain it. He was easy of access. Everyone-big or small, could meet him and speak to him. "The greatest temptation," once said a Prime Minister of England of a man who reaches supreme office is "to cease to listen". He would listen to the last and make adjustments.

He was very particular about his correspondence. He must see all the important letters. He read at least eight leading daily papers from the beginning to the end and his eye would not miss the trilling detail. He worked with terrific pressure, and the amount of work which he did even at that age was enormous. He never forgot seemingly little things, which really meant so much in life. He must visit an ailing colleague or a co-worker. He must write a letter of solace in one's sorrow, and of cheer in one's joy.

The following letter which he wrote during the course of his crowded election tour may be a fitting illustration of his style and habit of thought.

Almora,
February 12, 1952.

> My dear Shyam Sunder,
>
> I managed to find a few minutes to dictate two or three letters to some of the leading workers at Bareilly yesterday at Ranikhet. I am constantly moving from place to place and the programme is sufficiently tight. It leaves little time for any other work. I am, however, somewhat impatient to offer thanks to those to whom thanks are due. Even if I were to omit you for the present I cannot forget your wife, but you would not like to be left out in the cold if I were to single out your better half alone. So I should express my appreciation for the excellent work done by your wife and yourself in the midst of adverse forces and numerous other difficulties with which you were faced at Bareilly. You had many sleepless nights and restless days. I wonder if you had occasion to work equally

> hard even before. It is difficult to say which of you two had the better of the other. Please convey my grateful thanks to all who contributed towards your success and let your wife help you in this equally heave though pleasant task.
>
> With good wishes for both,
>
> Yours sincerely,
> G. B. Pant.

He had amazing capacity to see the basic points of a problem. Experts are surprised at his knowledge in their own fields. He would point out the fatal defects in technical experts' designs—and sometimes they would feel small. Many of them confessed that "he was a very extraordinary person". His ability, knowledge and memory have never failed to impress any one who had occasion to come in his contact. He knew as what Sir William Harcourt once said—"the value of the political heads is to tell the permanent officials what the public will not stand." He had always made a distinction in essential and non-essential. He was ready to concede on non-essentials.

The late Kunwar Sir Jagdish Prasad, an eminent Indian Civilian, who was the Chief Secretary in U. P. when Pandit Pant was the Leader of Opposition in U. P. Council and who afterwards became a member of the Viceroy's Executive Council, writing in a signed article in the Pioneer (dated 15 August, 1951) wrote about Pandit Pant's administrative capacity thus:

> "Among the ministers both at the centre and the provinces the foremost place must be given to the Premier of Uttar Pradesh, Pandit Govind Ballabh Pant. Many competent observers uninfluenced by political passions and prejudices of the moment would place him above Pandit Jawaharlal Nehru as politician and administrator."

One example of his constructive statesmanship and genius was the realisation of a dream which he cherished in his youth of converting the large tracts of land lying along the foot of the hills in his home district Nainital, of which at one time he was the chairman of the District Board. They were noted for the excellence of their soil and high fertility, but remained undeveloped and were considered undevelopable due to extreme difficult circumstances. They were covered with dense forests, infested by wild animals and dacoits, and visited every year by dreadful malaria of a malignant type. The mortality rate was very high and it was a place unfit for human habitation. He felt that it could be an important granary of the province, which could be transformed into a beautiful spot, and would be a proud place for the province. When he was at the helm of affairs in U.P. he devoted his attention to this tract. He was happy to see the realisation of his dream. The whole area was colonised and new shape was given to it. There is a 16,500 acre State farm, which is perhaps the biggest of its kind in Asia, where an unique experiment is being made in collective farming. It will now have the first Agricultural University—unique in itself in the whole of India. In winter of 1955 Marshal Bulganin and N. Khurshchev, Soviet leaders visited this area during their Indian tour. Every one was greatly impressed.

When Pandit Pant was a member of U.P. Council in early twenties he drew the repeated attention of the then government to these undeveloped tracts. Speaking in 1924 he asked whether the Government proposed to take measures to improve the conditions by framing drainage schemes and by establishing a model village to turn that area into a most healthy locality as the Government of USA did in the Panama Zone. The reply of the Government, as expressed in the words of its Finance Member, was that the area consisted of forests which contained a large number of wild animals; and it was not practicable and it was quite impossible to have anything like a healthy population. "Of course the Tarai can never be quite net and surround every village with a wire fence or wall."

When he came in power he engaged his attention to this question to give a practical shape to the dreams of his youth. He appointed a committee of experts and departmental heads with himself as Chairman to investigate the problems connected with the development and colonisation of these areas. He knew that it was an extremely difficult task on account of unhealthiness of the tract, depredation of wild animals, enervating climate, lack of communications and unscientific alignment of canals, which led to water-logging. Doubts were expressed by experts. Any attempt at deforestation in the Tarai region was likely to cause sheet erosion of a magnitude, which might have serious repercussions on the future well being of not only the submontane tracts but also of the plains far down below. Sir William Stamp, Hall, and Watal who were distinguished Chief Engineers, and had made special study of the Tarai problems, were not optimistic. Pandit Pant stood firm, overruled them, and asked them to go ahead.

This great work was inaugurated by Pandit Pant in 1948, and two years later on November 26, 1950 he switched Rudrapur Power House. Speaking on the occasion he said: "Let further light come to jungle. It is a proud day." We were present on both the occasions, and witnessed the bitter tarai battle since 1948. Lo and behold—to the amazement of all Tarai is the wonder of the land, a beauty spot with good roads, beautiful canals, charming buildings, wholesome climate, with plenty of milk, good air and clean surroundings. It is a place of attraction for foreign visitors and a site of the first agricultural university with a dairy, fruit orchard, and an airport.

The verdict of history would assuredly be that great as his leadership was, judged by merely nature and extent of its legislation and administrative achievement, it was definitely greater by reason of the exalted standards of duty, honour and high ideals by which it was inspired. He gave to the Congress party unity, direction and strength. It was not merely U. P.'s good fortune but India's too that in those formative years of our independence the reigns of office in the largest constituent unit of the Indian Union should be securely held by an experienced administrator and seasoned statesman like Pandit Pant. There is no one who can dominate as he does in all spheres of public life and no one can come to his standard in any one of them.

> "For most of the stability," the 'Statesman' wrote in 1917 "the Ministry has to thank the Premier Pandit Govind Ballabh Pant, whose mellowed personality, deep political sense and disarming reasonableness place him among the ranks of the country's leading statesmen and administrators."

We faced complete chaos in the country in the post— partition days when our newly born independence was in great peril and it appeared only to be 'seven days wonder'.

'Statesman' in its editorial dated 10th Nov. 1947 wrote:

> "Fair minded men have recently been much impressed by Pandit Pant's handling of communal problem in the U. P. with the whole of Northern India in turmoil it was impossible to expect perfect peace in the pivotal province of India."

The real position was pictured in Pandit Nehru's letter to Pt. Pant written at that time:

> "I doubt if people realise—particularly in these provinces which fortunately have not felt the impact of Punjab tragedy—the gravity and full significance of recent events. If the disturbances had not been halted in Western U. P. they would eventually have spread eastwards right upto Bihar and West Bengal and the whole of the Northern India would have been in chaos. Nor could the forces of disorder have, in that case, been kept confined to Northern India. We would then have faced quite apart from the butchery of innocent lives and the destruction of property, wholesale disruption of communications, disorganisation of food supply and the spread of epidemic diseases. We would, in fact, have faced complete chaos in the country and the destruction of all constitutional government."

After the first General Elections commenting on the formation of the new Cabinet in U. P. the Hindustan Times of New Delhi in its leading editorial wrote on 22nd May, 1952:

> "Uttar Pradesh which has had the great advantage of continuity of leadership and policy for a number of years has the good fortune of having its first Cabinet under the new Constitution under the tried leadership of Pandit Govind Ballabh Pant. The personal ascendency of the Chief Minister in the States politics is almost comparable to that of Mr. Nehru in national

politics. This position has been gained by him not through fortuitous circumstances, but through an unbroken record of public service and brilliant parliamentary gifts. Indeed, it has been U. P.'s good luck that while all but one of the first Pant Cabinet of 1937 have been drafted to high political and diplomatic offices, the Chief Minister has remained at the helm of its affairs. Of course, Pt. Pant has carved out for himself a high place in all India politics. He is a member of the Congress High Command whose counsel is valued and always sought for. But it is a tribute to his solicitous concern for the amelioration of the lot of the people that he has stuck to his sphere of responsibility. In many ways Uttar Pradesh is the crucible of India and the success and failure of democracy in India will be largely determined by what happens in this most populated State in the heart of the country. It was this State that did pioneer work in tenancy legislation. It is again U. P. that is making an earnest effort to abolish Zamindari."

We do not judge his greatness by the high and exalted offices which he held. We do not judge by the supreme power which he had swayed. We judge his greatness by the service which he rendered to the country and its people, by the love which his heart over flowed for the poor and down trodden, by the standards which he established for the good government.

He never took credit for the act which he did, but gave that to others. One of his letters illustrates this. In 1955 he was responsible for making one person a member of the U. P. Legislative Council. But he wrote:

Minister for Home Affairs,
India, New Delhi,
3rd September, 1955.

My dear Shyam Sunder,

I have your letters of August 31 and 1st September. I am glad that Savitri will now have the opportunity of serving in a wider field and I am confident that she

> will acquit herself well. She has always taken a keen interest in public affairs and with your collaboration she will be able to handle even difficult problems with ability and competence. She was chosen for this place because of her merits. I hope you both appreciate the consideration shown by Dr. Sampurnanand and other members of the Board and I am not entitled to any credit for this.
>
> Please accept and convey to her my heartiest congratulations.
>
> Yours sincerely
> G. B. Pant.

He had struggled hard with physical maladies and had exhibited admirable endurance. He must be having the severest pain; but he would give no expression. He would hardly even admit that be was suffering. He seemed to have the Victorian idea that illness and pain were something to be ashamed of. One day he was going to preside over the meeting of the U. P. Cabinet in the Secretariat. He had an attack of lumbago of which he was the chronic patient. He went straight to the Cabinet meeting, presided over it for several hours without giving the slightest indication of pain to his colleagues, went to address a public meeting. It was on his return that it was known that he was suffering from such severe pain when he called for the doctor.

He lived by his sheer will. During early thirties he was taken ill after his imprisonment. A doctor told him that he would die within a year. He said that he would not die, and it was this will power that overcame his all ailments. In the first Congress ministry days his vitality was shattered and he had to retire to the hills as the amount of work was too heavy for human shoulders.

His philosophy of life was based on the lines of Tennyson which he read as a student, and which he quoted once addressing the students of his university forty years later.

> "Self knowledge, self reverence, self control; These alone lead to sovereign power."

The motto of his life was truth. His whole approach was moral. He thought best, felt noblest, and acted right. He believed in every cause which aimed at the relief of human suffering, the removal of injustice or the increase of happiness.

He was, as Poet Pope said:

> "In action faithful, and in honour clear;
> Who broke no promise,
> Served no private end;
> Who gained no title,
> And who lost no friend."

As Premier of U.P.

It was the good fortune of U.P. (earlier called United Provinces and later as Uttar Pradesh) that a stalwart of the stature of Pandit Govind Ballabh Pant guided its destiny at the most critical period in its history with consummate skill and wisdom. It is not often appreciated that in terms of size and population, U.P. is bigger than Italy, France or Britain - in fact bigger than every country in Europe -except the Soviet Union. And, in terms of its problems in its early years, the task of governing and developing it was most gigantic. U.P. had long been the nerve centre of Indian politics and cradle alike of strong nationalism and acute communalism. Several top national leaders came from this State. A land of awesome contrasts, U.P. has been India in miniature - an amalgam of 3 or 4 regions very different from each other in many respects but united by a common past, language and culture.

When the Congress accepted office in the provinces in 1937, Pantji was elected Leader of the Congress party in the U.P. Assembly and he assumed office as Premier of U.P. when the colonial administration run by the civil servants was still powerful. At the time of formation of his Ministry practically all the important posts were held by Europeans. Pantji increased the number of Indians in the administrative services, including in the Civil and Police services. In the Secretariat too important departments were entrusted to Indians. It did not take him long to establish his authority over the whole range of administration by sheer dint of his intellectual calibre and to win the admiration of *the* "steel frame" civil service. Pantji believed that a senior civil servant was like a horse that immediately recognised the calibre of the rider and behaved accordingly. So he was able to carry the whole civil service with him with much ease partly because of his own intellectual talents which the civil service was soon to appreciate and partly because he was cool and impartial in handling various administrative problems. During the entire period of his premiership, there was no aspect of administration too small or remote to escape his searching attention. His decisions usually came with much study, almost agonisingly, but once made, they stood like a rock. The courage with which he overcame the obstacles and difficulties he faced, marked him out even then as an able administrator and a great statesman.

Premier Pant came into conflict with the British Governor *on* several occasions but he showed exemplary courage of conviction and did not fight shy of taking up cudgels with the mighty agent of the British Crown in India. One of his first acts on assumption of office was to order release of political detainees. But the Governor put his foot down and a showdown followed, Pantji sent in his ministry's resignation and ultimately the Governor had to eat an humble pie-There were several other occasions when the premier had to take a stand against the Governor and maintain the dignity of the office he held.

In November 1928 the Hindi "Chand" magazine had published an advertisement containing synopsis of some chapters of a forthcoming book entitled "Bharat men Angrezi Rajya" written by Pandit Sunder Lal. This issue of the magazine was however, proscribed on December 10, 1928, under Sec. 199A of the Cr. P.C. The book was nevertheless, published on March 18, 1929. On March 20, 1929 the publisher was informed by the Superintendent of Police at Allahabad that the advertisement had been proscribed and that the book would be published by the publisher at his own risk. The publisher thereupon informed him that the book had already been published two days ago- Then the book itself was proscribed on March 22, 1929 and notifications proscribing the advertisement and the book dated March 15, 1929 and March 22, 1929 appeared simultaneously in the Gazette of March 23, 1929. An application was subsequently made by the publisher to the

High Court at Allahabad for setting aside these proscriptions. The High Court by its judgement on March 5, 1930 set aside the forfeiture regarding the advertisement but confirmed it as regards the book.

In a lengthy note to the Governor on November 1, 1937 Premier Pant observed that "Government as it is at present constituted cannot possibly accept that. In my opinion, there is no justification to maintain the order of forfeiture any longer and I therefore direct that it should be withdrawn. He said that the book professed to be a history of the origin of British rule in India, and the historical narrative terminated with a description of the Indian Mutiny and the subsequent transfer of the Indian administration from the East India Company to the Crown.

The period subsequent to 1858 up to date had not been dealt with, though there was a chapter in which the author attempted to draw a moral from the events of the century ending with 1858. He added that during the last seven years political events in India had moved very fast and what was considered objectionable in 1929 could not possibly be so considered in 1937. He affirmed that attainment of complete independence was the recognised political ideal of the Indian National Congress and any advocacy of that ideal could not be considered to be objectionable; and if a textbook writer sought to draw an inference from past history that also could not be considered to be objectionable.

Most history was partial, he said and the bias of the historian consciously or unconsciously coloured both his narrative and his appreciation of events, and it seemed to him that a book like this, which was heavily priced and which could not possibly be within the means of an ordinary leader, could not, at any rate be proscribed under Sec. 199 A, portions of which had then become out of date. He added that he had no doubt that "if the order of forfeiture is withdrawn both - the writer and the publisher - if they are so minded, will have to bring out another edition and it is quite possible that some portions of the book may have to be rewritten". He emphasised that "condemnation of the East India Company cannot possibly be said to be a condemnation of the Government by law established in British India—at any rate, Government by law as BOW established in these provinces" (The word 'now' underscored by Pantji in his own hand). He also mentioned that the book was hardly distinguishable from Major Basu's *"Rise of Christian Power in India"*, and it was essentially on par with several other works of this type such as R.C. Dutt's *"Economic History of British Rule in India"*, Dadabhai Naoroji's *"Poverty and Unbritish Rule in India"*, Sir William Digby's *"Prosperous India"* and Sir Henry Cotton's *"New India"*.

The Governor in his note of November 3, 1937 recorded that he remembered the case well. The book was at *the* time considered by the local Government to be very objectionable. He referred to the High Court judgement: "The book is not merely a compilation from other books, but contains numerous passages which state the author's own views and his own ideas of the purpose to which Indians of the present day should direct themselves, and of the means by which that purpose, the destruction of the British rule in India, should be carried out." The Governor said that he was anxious that there should be no misunderstanding, but assumed that it was not inconsistent with *the* oath of allegiance to the Crown which had been taken by all Congress Ministers. Expressing his confidence that no Minister of the Crown would wish to express approval of a book the object of which was to advocate the destruction of the British rule in India, he said that he could understand the argument that the present Government did not believe in a policy of preventing expression of opinion, that it was only in extreme cases that they would be prepared to take action against speeches and writings, and that this was not really an extreme case. But he stressed that "I could not understand the argument, and I am sure the Hon'ble Premier does not intend to base himself in any way on such an argument, that revolution is a harmless or even commendable doctrine... because we are not having speeches made in the province of a dangerously revolutionary kind. It may be that in degree they are much worse than anything that is written in this book, but the object appears to be the same, the vilification of the British and their removal from India." He desired the Hon'ble Premier to draw a distinction between such speeches and the book under consideration.

The ban on the book *"Bharat men Angrezi Rajya"* may be removed and necessary notification issued and a letter may also be sent to Pandit Sundar Lal, the author of the book, in reply to his application."

The Governor thereupon was only able to record as follows:

> "I appreciate the Hon'ble Premier's point of view, and I am in full agreement with him that we should confine ourselves to the immediate and practical issues. They are not always easy to resolve *as* I know that H.P. realises. In view of his note I do not wish to offer any further comment."

The ban on the book was ordered to be removed.

Another case related to the adoption of a new Coat of Arms for the United Provinces in place of the existing one under the orders of Premier Pant When samples embossed with coat of arms were put up to him for approval in September 1938, he, after directing certain modifications, ordered that the coat of arms besides being printed on the stationery of Ministers may also appear on the Government gazette and other official publications and suggested giving of sufficient publicity to the change.

When the Governor came to know of this change, he in a note observed that it was unfortunate that this case was not shown to him at a much earlier stage, and that "it was wrong that orders should have been issued before I was even aware that the matter was under consideration." He said that "when we are proposing to replace the Royal Arms, particularly on the Government Gazette which contains the formal expression of the official orders of the provincial government" it is necessary for me to satisfy myself as far as possible how it was that the Royal Arms have been used hitherto and whether any particular significance attaches to this use, or whether it can be declared at our pleasure." Conceding that there may well be no objection to the change, he nevertheless desired that the matters must be enquired into, and "in the meantime I must ask that the order for the change in the form of the Government Gazette and other official publications should be suspended."

When the file was put up to Premier Pant, his indignation on the Governor's note is evident from his following observations:

> "Have we not got full authority in this respect? How does Government of India come in? I think it is the exclusive concern of Provincial Government The symbol for this coat of arms for our province has been duly recognised by a warrant of the College of Arms and may appropriately be used for official purposes. If it is not given place in official publications, it will lose its significance and characteristics. To me the matter looks simple and almost a natural corollary to Provincial Autonomy, but if His Excellency so directs it may be placed before the Cabinet."

Later, on 14 November, 1938, the Governor in a note recorded that according to the information received from the Governor-General, most of the Dominion Governments and a good many of the Provincial Governments in the Dominions used their own arms on their gazettes and also on their note paper. The practice was well established- He therefore, thought that there need be no hesitation about "our carrying out what we wish to do." Premier Pant ordered for issue of a communique about the change in the coat of arms that day itself.

However, the Ministry had been in office hardly for two years till October 27, 1939 when the Congress decided to give up office as a protest against the decision of the British Government to involve India in the Second World War. Pantji was farsighted enough to declare, while moving the resolution on the subject in the U.P. Legislative Assembly that "the freedom of India is bound to come and it must come within a short time." He added in a statesman-like posture.

> "But the question is not only of the freedom of India but of the peace of the world and making the world safe for democracy and saving Great Britain and France and Germany and Italy, the United States and every other country from future temptations which may again upset peace, throw all that may have been achieved through ages into the boiling cauldron. It is for this that we insist on the declaration of Indian independence."

Premier Pant had already put through much needed reforms which greatly benefited the poor and downtrodden masses of the province. The courage with which he overcame the obstacles and the difficulties he faced, marked him out as an able administrator and a great statesman.

During the short period of his premiership various laws were enacted and implemented for the benefit of the farmers, workers and the poorer sections of the society. Among the many achievements of the U.P.'s first popular ministry was the enactment of the U.P. Tenancy Act to free the peasantry from the stranglehold of landed aristocracy. As a pioneering measure of land reforms it gave statutory tenancy rights to the peasants who were previously at the mercy of the landlords.

On his retirement, the U.P. Governor Sir Harry Haig paid a tribute to Pantji's impartial administration and to the manner in which he protected the interests of the minorities.

As Chief Minister of U.P.

When the Congress assumed office again after World War II, Pantji - now 58 - took the reins of administration in U.P. with his old team of six ministers. After Independence in 1947, the state had to encounter the problems bequeathed by the partition of the country. As Chalapathy Rau writes, "his Chief Ministership of the most populous state of the country, in the troubled days of partition, was an assurance of stability and strength. On the conditions in this part of the country depended to a great extent the course of freedom after August Fifteenth, and with his presence of mind, grip over the administration, and shrewdness and wisdom, Pant rode storm after storm successfully". When the provinces of the North Eastern Frontier, Punjab, Bengal and, to a certain extent, even Delhi were in virtual flames with the worst type of communal riots and killings, U.P. remained largely unaffected. Credit for this goes to the deft handling of the situation by the Pant Government. A staunch secularist that he was, Govind Ballabh Pant, along with his illustrious Home Minister, Rafi Ahmed Kidwai took the strongest measures to ensure that there was no communal holocaust in the State. An outstanding achievement of the Pant government was that it not only rehabilitated a large number of refugees who came to U.P. in the wake of partition but also successfully saved the State from communal disharmony and religious fanaticism.

Pantji was the Chief Minister of Uttar Pradesh for nearly 9 years from 1946 to 1954 and during this period, he could provide the State and the people a stable government, efficient in law and order and known for its administrative soundness. An administrator *par excellence,* he believed that administration should always be responsive *to* the call of the times and the changing needs of the people. In his scheme of administration, the human factor always played a pivotal role. As he said once:

> "The problem of administration is not mechanical. It is psychological. Perhaps it is more than that. It is human and unless every one connected with administration is imbibed with sympathy and understanding, it is difficult for administration to yield the results which the people have a right to expect from".

In fact, fair and just dealing was deeply ingrained in the unique administrative style of Pantji. In his judgement one of the gravest faults in a public servant which made him or her unfit to hold public office was insensitivity to fair dealing. He firmly believed that the dull wooden bureaucratic ways which so much disfigure the relations between the public and the public offices actually have their roots in the deadend insensitivity of public servants to standards of fairness and justice. Those who have seen him working closely naturally feel elated in narrating incidents involving his administrative skill. Pantji knew by heart the names not only of all the districts of U.P. perhaps 48 at that time - but also of every single District Magistrate. And, when he visited a District and was received by a District Magistrate, it was not unusual and in fact was most remarkable to hear him call the D.M. by name and ask about the well-being of his family members - parents and children—often by individual names. Who could remain untouched and unmoved by such humane consideration and affection coming from one who was not only the Chief Minister of the biggest State but also a towering national figure.

Pantji was one who believed that the sole goal of government was public good. Man was created not to serve government; rather government was created to serve man, to protect him and safeguard his rights. Speaking on a resolution regarding communal representation in the services in the U.P. Legislative Council on 29 May, 1947, he said:

> "First of all a public servant is meant for the service of the public. He has to forget his caste, his creed and his colour. He must serve all impartially, justly, fairly, without fear and without favour. It will also be conceded, I hope, that every public servant should not only profess but from day to day, from hour to hour and from minute to minute demonstrate his unstinted and unqualified loyalty to the Stale which he is appointed to serve. Loyalty and devotion to the State which maintains public services is the fundamental condition of every public service,, and especially on an occasion like *this* when, we are faced with new problems and when things are going to take shape not only for the present but also for decades or perhaps for centuries."

A secular democrat and socialist to the core, he always strove for a welfare State, He knew fully well that democratic socialism alone could ensure justice for all. The contribution of Pantji's administration and the impact of his personality covered all aspects of development of the State of Uttar Pradesh, ranging from its intricate political webs at one end to the pioneering community development programmes at the other. The agrarian reforms which he had pioneered in the State of Uttar Pradesh speak of his abiding interest in the well-being of the peasantry. Under his stewardship Uttar Pradesh became the first State in India to have successfully abolished the zamindari system. He was conscious that the zamindari system was obstructing the progress of agriculture. He could foresee that the abolition of the system was a prerequisite for the release of the productive forces of the economy. Prior to the abolition of zamindari, the big landlords consisting of only 1.4 per cent of the population owned 57.77 per cent of the agricultural land. And, the top 804 landlords owned one-third land of the State. Naturally, therefore, the poor peasantry deprived of proprietory rights in the land they tilled had lost all incentive to increase agricultural production.

Zamindari had outlived its utility and there was no justification for its existence in free India, Its abolition was necessary for raising agricultural productivity and output, for fair and equitable distribution of agricultural income, to increase employment avenues and to establish social equilibrium.

Pantji set up and himself presided over a committee which prepared a blue print for bringing about the profoundest social and economic change that U.P. had experienced since the first land revenue system was introduced in early fifteenth century. His government took the initiative to pass the U.P. Zamindari Abolition and Land Reforms Act, 1950 and ably faced the problems that followed. There was the question of payment of compensation to the landlords and of a uniform system throughout the State. Pantji activated the adoption of a Constitutional amendment by Parliament which made possible moderating the compensation payable to the landlords. There was confusion about the ultimate form of land tenure. On top of it all, the validity of the Act itself was challenged in the highest court of the land. And when the Act was declared valid by the Supreme Court, the zamindars started leasing out their lands to frustrate the law. To counter this, the Pant government came forward with a new law passed on May 21, 1952 invalidating all such illegal transactions.

The Zamindari Abolition Act was certainly a very complex piece of legislation in as much as it involved so many people covering vast areas of land. But it was a great achievement of his government that such a revolutionary change in the socio-economic sphere could be accomplished peacefully and democratically. With one stroke, the feudal land ownership pattern was unravelled and replaced by the ownership of peasants, and this far-reaching change (the first of its kind in India) was brought about without any sort of violence or conflict As a result, the government could assume effective and direct relations with the peasants in regard to their holdings. Those who saw the impact of this revolutionary measure in the villages would bear witness to the new climate of freedom that seemed to rise from the land in that dawn, Pantji used to travel from district to district in those days to see for himself the preparations for the change-over which, of course, came on the appointed day without any hitch.

Pantji attached the utmost importance to the development of democratic institutions at the grassroots level. He believed in the decentralisation of power. One of the very first acts of Pantji on his taking over as the Chief Minister of U.P. was to declare his faith in the panchayat system. The avowed objective of his government, according to him, was vital for village upliftment. The Panchayats were given a share of land revenue for undertaking welfare work in their villages. Later on Nyaya Panchayats were also established to dispose of petty revenue and civil cases. This saved the villagers much inconvenience, time and expenditure in going to courts at Tehsil and District headquarters.

Village life, however, could not be transformed nor could agricultural production or income of the tillers of the soil increased merely by abolishing zamindari and establishing village Panchayats. Pantji knew it more than anyone else. It was necessary to provide to the farmers improved varieties of seeds, fertilizers, pesticides and modern agricultural implements. Also, necessary coordination between the various departments concerned was necessary so that the farmer did not have to run from office to office. To achieve all these, Pantji embarked upon an ambitious scheme of community development projects.

The Etawah Project, associated with the name of Albert Meyer, which actually became a pace setter for establishment of the community development projects in the country started with his blessings and whole-hearted support- It was a project intended to establish an integrated approach with village level worker as the main instrument of social transformation. Ultimately, it became the prototype for Community Development and National Extension Service in our country.

Pantji can rightly be called the maker of modern Uttar Pradesh. Under his government, the State of U.P. witnessed all-round progress. A few months before he laid down office of Chief Minister in March 1954, Pantji in his address to the U.P. Congress Committee surveyed the working of his Ministry which had faced problems of every sort and magnitude. He said that the partition aftermath, the holocaust that threatened the very stability of the administration, the rehabilitation of huge mass of uprooted humanity, the tendency for the various parts of the country to try to break loose and drift aloof, the scarcity and famine conditions brought about by post-war effects were all met and attention was directed towards *the* attainment of a Welfare State with the utmost speed.

The U.P. Plan of 1950: In the formation of which Pantji had a major role, came much before the Planning Commission was set up. Even though it was a modest one by any modern standards, it laid solid foundations for the economic development of the State. Statistics are revealing. From Rs. 86 *crores,* the allocation of the plan rose to Rs. 132 crores and the State's national income rose from Rs. 1308 crores at the time of Independence to Rs. 1562 crores in 1952. Despite the population increase, the per capita, income also registered a growth from Rs. 218.7 at the time of Independence to Rs. 241.8, five years later. The road construction programme was completed a year ahead of schedule. Considerable progress was achieved in the construction of houses for industrial labour. Intensive work was done under the Community Project Schemes covering more and more areas. The most noticeable advance was however, made in the sphere of agriculture. Pantji visualised that future economic prosperity of the country could be possible only by the development of agriculture and the creation of a network of agro-based industries throughout the length and breadth of the country. The transformation of the Tarai area from a malaria-infested jungle into the most prosperous and fertile land owed its inspiration to Pantji.

Within three years of his taking over as Chief Minister Pantji saw the completion of an important project of Rangawan Dam as also continuing progress on Chandra Prabha, Ahrara and Matateala Dams. A scheme for the Rihand Dam was also worked out These projects were expected to considerably increase food production as also provide electricity to 13 districts of the eastern U.P. This played a significant role in helping the State attain the planned target of additional food production. Uttar Pradesh not only became self-sufficient then but was also able to assist the deficit areas of the country.

The State made considerable progress in the industrial sector also. A cement factory was set up at Churk in Mirzapur district at a cost of Rs. 4.5 crores. A Precision Instruments Factory was set up at Lucknow. To give a boost to the cottage industry a Research Centre was opened at Almora. The handloom sector was also reorganised and the Khadi and Village Industries Board was set up.

Pantji paid special attention to education. His deep-seated and overflowing love for children really made him by instinct an educator. He initiated an innovative reform of education focused in the first instance on 11 to 13 age group deriving its inspiration from Gandhiji's concept of "basic education". Pantji constituted under his chairmanship a high-power interdepartmental committee which monitored the progress of the scheme, meeting almost every month for the purpose. His scheme of education reform, partial though it was, created a new impulse in the education system of the State, which had known no change for decades. With an uncanny touch, Pantji really transformed what would otherwise be just another government-sponsored programme into a people-supported movement for the renovation of education. Members of the legislature, community organisations and political workers were all mobilised to work at the ground level in support of the schools.

Pantji never encouraged political interference in administration. There are numerous instances related by the senior civil servants who had occasion to serve under him to bear testimony to this aspect of his administrative temper. For instance, T.N. Kaul mentions the issue of a circular from Lucknow to the district magistrates to set up district committees for licensing ration shops of essential commodities. The instructions said that local members of the Legislative Assembly (MLAs) should be on the Committee. He found at the very first meeting of the Committee that each MLA was interested in recommending his own protege. They started quarrelling among themselves, even though they belonged to the same Congress Party. Kaul then wrote a personal letter to the Chief Minister, Pandit Pant, pointing out the pros and cons of having the MLAs on the Licensing Committee and, on balance, recommending that they should not be on it They and the party would get a bad name and the administration would lose credibility in the eyes of the public, he said. Pantji saw his point and withdrew the MLAs from the Committee and also sent him a letter of thanks for being frank, honest and constructive.

In another instance, a piece of valuable land adjacent to one of the Central prisons in U.P. and belonging to the Jail Department was promised to be sold to a big local industrialist by a Parliamentary Secretary to the Government. When the matter came to Government for sanction, a senior officer, Shri Govind Narain opposed it vehemently but the Parliamentary Secretary dealing with the Jail Department overruled him and put pressure on the Inspector General of Prisons to give his concurrence. The officer discussed the matter with the Inspector General of Prisons and told him that the piece of land in question might be needed for further expansion of the Prison and that, in any case, there was no point in parting with it at that time. When the matter went again to the Parliamentary Secretary, he again overruled the officer who then decided to refer the matter for consideration of the Chief Minister. Pandit Pant kept the file with him for two or three weeks and then sent it back with a firm order that when the Department did not see any benefit in selling the land, there was no reason why the land should be sold. This was the end of the matter.

Thus from the day Pantji became the premier of the United Provinces to the day he relinquished the office of the Chief Minister of Uttar Pradesh in December, 1954 to join the Union Cabinet, he remained a formidable figure - much feared, loved and respected. His position in U.P. politics remained unchallenged always. The secret behind his ascendency in the party and undisputed leadership throughout the period of his stay in U.P. was perhaps because he always kept himself aloof from conflicts either of principles or personalities. On the other hand, his approach towards the conflicting groups was rather of reconciliation and of himself playing the role of a mediator. In fact he was an expert at political management and utilised this trait in making men work for him. He indeed helped build a powerful organisation of the Congress in U.P. There were of course occasional criticisms, but these took place mostly in the Uttar Pradesh Congress Committee, rather than in the State legislature. After Pandit left Lucknow,

Government and politics in *U.P.* was never the same. His era is important because of the political stability maintained by him in the State till his departure to join the Union Cabinet. He exercised a balancing influence over the various groups and functions in the party and even making enemies work together in a common cause. After his departure the factional rivalries and group politics came to surface disturbing the political stability.

As Union Home Minister

It was Pantji's phenomenal success as the Chief Minister of U.P. and his administrative acumen that prompted Pandit Jawaharlal Nehru to bring him to Delhi in January 1955 as the Union Home Minister after the death of Rafi Ahmed Kidwai. He became in fact "Nehru's conscience keeper" as the *Civil and Military Gazette* of Lahore remarked, adding "As virtual Deputy Prime Minister at the Centre since 1954 he filled the vacuum that had been created by the death of the strong man of the Congress, Sardar Patel." As Home Minister, he grew into a formidable figure and was in fact second Bismarck who successfully handled and completed the task of consolidating the integration of India, the great heritage left behind by Sardar Patel. His outstanding achievement *was* the able and statesman-like manner in which he maintained peace and law and order in the country. The complicated and vital task of the reorganisation of States was accomplished under his Home Ministership. When the partition of U.P. was suggested, Pantji stood like a rock against it and uttered the famous words:

> "No power on earth can divide the land of Rama and Krishna, of Ganga and Jamuna."

His speech held the House spellbound; it was, of course, pure emotions which touched a deep chord in the heart of every member of the august body, whatever his religion or creed. The words echoed throughout the length and breadth of the Stale and we know U.P. remained united and was saved the fate that has befallen Punjab, for example. And, as long as he was alive, there was no question of any one proposing the division of U.P.

Pandit Pant was a practical man and a realist- he himself had said in the Central Assembly in 1935: "So far as I am concerned,

I am neither an idealist nor a materialist; I am a realist" He had foreseen that the reorganisation of States might in initial stages, at any rate, lead to some type of frictions among the States. He therefore, attached special importance to a provision in the States Reorganisation Act for the setting up of Zonal Councils. These Councils were to discuss matters of common interest in the fields of economic and social planning, border disputes, linguistic minorities, inter-State transport, *etc.* Pantji himself used to preside over the meetings of these Councils and direct his efforts towards bringing about greater understanding among the States and a common approach to problems that came tip before them. He in fact built the Zonal Councils into an effective means of national integration.

During his Home Ministership Pantji had to face many problems, each knottier than the other; the mantle of Sardar Patel having fallen on him sometimes he had to pay attention to even the matters raised by the different members of the families of the erstwhile princely States. But because of his administrative skill, power of persuasion and political foresight he handled all problems successfully, be it the demand for a separate Punjabi Suba, or Nagaland or the problem of Pakistani infiltrators in Assam. Punjab presented a serious problem to Pantji. But with his firm determination and strictness he frankly told Master Tara Singh that unity in the border *State* had got to be maintained at all costs and he did not deviate from the policy till the very end.

But perhaps the most important achievement for which he will be remembered was the historic declaration he had made soon after his assumption of office, in the summer of 1955, that many things had happened since India undertook to hold a plebiscite in Kashmir and since Pakistan did not fulfil its commitments, the tide of events in Kashmir could not now be turned back. The statement undoubtedly put an end to the chapter of uncertainty about Kashmir and established him as the "Strong Man of India" in the mould of Sardar Patel, as Shri H.N. Bahuguna once said. Thus *it* may be said that Pandit Pant's firmness of purpose was most evident in reinforcing the Prime Minister's hands directly or indirectly and speaking his mind particularly at times when Pandit Nehru found it inconvenient or embarrassing to do so himself. His firm declaration about Kashmir's accession to India being final was surely to strengthen Nehru's hands in his future dealing with the problem with Pakistan.

Pantji had to bear considerable strain as Home Minister while piloting or dealing with innumberable legislative measures or other problems of great significance in the two Houses of Parliament. Some of the major Bills piloted by him were: Citizenship Bill, Constitution (Fourth Amendment) Bill, Constitution (Eighth *Amendment)* Bill, Dargah Khwaja Sahab Bill, States Reorganisation Bill, Prevention of Corruption (Amendment) Bill, Untouchability (Offences) Bill, Young Persons (Harmful Publications) Bill, Bihar and West Bengal (Transfer of Territories) Bill, Prize Competitions Bill, Central Excise and Salt (Amendment) Bill, Constitution (Ninth Amendment) Bill, Faridabad Development Corporation Bill, Slum Areas (Improvement and Clearance) Bill, Preventive Detention (Continuance) Bill, Probation of Offenders Bill, Armed Forces (Assam and Manipur) Special Powers Bill, Bombay Reorganisation Bill, Delhi (Control of Building Operation) Continuance Bill, Delhi Development Bill, Delhi Municipal Corporation Bill, Delhi Rent Control Bill.

Besides, as Home Minister he had to handle matters of great controversy or of far reaching significance like: President's Rule in Andhra Pradesh, Manipur and Kerala and passing of their budgets and supplementary grants in Parliament. States Reorganisation Commission Report. Emergency recruitment to IAS. Leakage of budget proposals. Memorandum *on* safeguards to Linguistic Minorities. Working of Preventive Detention Act. Sweepers' Strike and Police firing in Delhi. Report of the Official Language Commission. Report of the Commission of Enquiry into the LIC Affairs (the Mundhra case). Report of the Parliamentary Committee on Official Language, and. General strike by Central Government Employees.

Pantji's achievements as the Union Home Minister were in fact more than a happy fulfilment of expectations. He provided a much needed relief to Nehru in running the parliamentary party and was also his great collaborator in all important policies. In terms of power and influence his role undoubtedly became larger than it had been in U.P.

Pantji had complete grasp of details and was an expert at dealing with files. At Committee meetings particularly he was just superb. In the Home Ministry complex service questions were sent to the Minister for his orders. As his erstwhile special Assistant Shri B.D. Jayal who had closely watched him function says, Pantji "could always get at the crux of a problem and was a master of detail as of perceiving the broad implications of decisions and policy measures."

In regard to his stupendous memory, Jayal recalls that before the Lok Sabha debate on the strike by Central Government Employees in 1960 he had handed over to Pantji a statistical abstract of the situation of the strike state-wise and department-wise which ran into three closely typed pages. He went through it quickly and to Shri Jayal's surprise Pantji made use of the statistics during the debate having retained ail in his memory.

Man of Vision

As Chief Minister of U.P. Govind Ballabh Pant strove hard to solve the most elementary needs of the common man. The problem of food, clothing and employment, which worried the common man, received top priority. He declared: "Every man from the cradle to the grave would have freedom from want and fear." For achieving these aims, he had to take several steps. More food had to be produced through better management of agriculture. Canals had to be dug for watering the fields. Industries were to be started. In short, the economy of the state had to be revitalised. It was also necessary to educate the people.

In the first year of his administration in U.P., he planned to open 60,000 schools for the education of the people. Similarly, he opened cooperative societies in two lakh villages of U.P. He also wanted that in every village, a Panchayat should be formed, which will not only resolve disputes among the village people, but also would be responsible for the economic welfare of the community. He wanted every man and woman of the village to feel responsible and contribute to the common good. The country could grow only when one and all worked to increase production.

Under Pant's government there was all around progress. In the field of agriculture much progress was made. The production of rice, wheat, pulses, sugar cane increased.

Japanese method of cultivation for rice production was adopted as an experimental measure in 35,000 acres of land. The production of rice increased from 503 lakh maunds in 1952-53 to 598 lakh maunds in 1953-54. Similar gains were recorded in the production of other crops. To bring about agricultural revolution, he laid the foundation of several irrigation projects. In the first three years, the Rangawan Dam was completed, which irrigated 90,000 acres of land. Similarly, progress was maintained in the construction of four dams in different rivers of U.P. In the eastern U.P. which was generally a poor area, a big project, the Rihand Dam was planned and work was begun.

At the same time, several industries were started. Mills and factories for production of steel, iron and paper, etc. were established. In 1955, the manufacture of cotton cloth reached an all time record. Khadi and cottage industries were given encouragement. A research centre for wool was established at Almora. Also, cement factories were set up in Mirzapur and Lucknow. A precision instruments factory for production of water metres and engineering goods was also established. Electricity production went up appreciably during the period.

The Community Project schemes were strengthened. Provision for better seeds and fertilizers for farmers was made. Thirty-five centres to look after the cattle wealth of U.P. were established. Through exhibitions and demonstrations the farmers were given information on new methods of production in agriculture. And most important of all, zamindaris were abolished on 1 April 1952. As a consequence of this measure, the peasants became owners of the land they cultivated. Henceforth, they could invest more on their lands and work with full freedom to grow better crops.

Under Pant, U.P. became a prosperous state and the future progress was assured. In 1955, when Pant left U.P. to join the Centre as Home Minister under Prime Minister Jawaharlal Nehru, every person of U.P. felt a sense of pride, in having such a great Chief Minister, who worked for the welfare of the people and under whom the state had become stronger economically, socially and politically.

As Home Minister of India, Pant was called upon to carry out the most difficult task, i.e. of reorganisation of states. Fortunately for him, after India became independent, Sardar Patel had already brought about the integration of nearly 600 princely states into India. Yet, these states had to be brought into the fold of an uniform administrative system. After the merger of these states into the Indian Union, it was necessary to reorganise these states on a more scientific and rational basis.

The reorganisation of the States does not in any way involve any separation from India.... Whether a part remains in one State or is transferred to another, is not of such an enormous importance that it should bring about convulsions and controversies... There is no occasion for it. There is none else to determine these things. We have to settle them ourselves. —*19 December 1955*

Secondly, it must be remembered that the British had conquered India bit by bit. As and when the territories came under their possession, the territories were grouped together as provinces. For example, in the beginning Bengal, Bihar and Orissa were formed into one unit as the Bengal Presidency and was ruled by a governor. Later, however, Bengal. Bihar and Orissa were created into three separate provinces. In other parts of India also the position was similar. The British recognised many princely states and created provinces for running the administration smoothly, main function of which was maintenance of law and order. They did not take into account, while creating provinces, considerations of history, traditions, languages, and cultural similarity. Thus, when India became independent, a more rational basis for redrawing of the boundaries of states of India needed to be found.

India is a vast country and people speaking different languages inhabit India. People speaking each language felt that their own mother tongue should be used in all offices and it should be made the medium of instruction at schools and colleges, etc. Each of these groups, claimed a long historical past, with its own language and tradition. Of course, most of these languages originated from the same source, i.e. Sanskrit, yet each had developed its own literature and distinct character, over a long time. The people belonging to each linguistic group, therefore, wanted a state of their own, so that they could use their mother tongue as the medium of instruction as well as for the official work. It was argued, that such states would lead to the preservation and development of their own literary and creative traditions, enriching their own state and India as a whole.

As you know, the Constitution of India has recognised Hindi as the official language for the whole country, but at the same time, other major languages of India were also given recognition in their own state. The mother tongue was made the medium of instruction in the state universities, colleges and schools. It was believed that if states were formed on the basis of one language one state, it would lead to a better government and the state would be more responsive to the wishes of the people. If the states were formed on linguistic basis, it was hoped, there would be homogeneity of interests and each state will be able to render better service, fulfilling the aspirations of the people of that region. Hence, it was thought proper to constitute states on the basis of the wishes of the people and the linguistic unity of the area.

There was general agreement among the Indian people on the question of formation of states on these principles.

As early as 1920, the Indian National Congress, which virtually represented the people of India, had accepted the principle of formation of states on linguistic basis and had declared that the provinces of Andhra Pradesh, Orissa, Sindh, Karnataka would be created soon after India achieved independence, the same principle had been reiterated in 1945.

After independence, people from different parts of the country desired that states should be formed keeping in view, the linguistic and cultural unity of the area. The government of India, therefore, decided to set up a Commission called States Reorganisation Commission under the chairmanship of Justice Fazal Ali in 1953. After a good deal of study, meetings and discussions with leaders, administrators and people from different walks of life, the Commission submitted its report on reorganisation of states in 1955.

The governing principles behind the plan of reorganisation were linguistic unity, cultural oneness of the region, geographical nearness and economic viability. In other words, a certain geographical area inhabited by people speaking, by and large, the same language, was made into a state, provided the area had its own economic resources to efficiently run its government and had the potentialities for future development of the state.

The linguistic redistribution of states, whatever its merits may have been, raised bitter controversies and problems which Pant was expected to resolve. In the Parliament, during debates on States Reorganisation Bill much heat was generated. Pant had to pacify the members and mollify ruffled tempers. He also had to negotiate with leaders of the affected states for an agreement.

It must be remembered that in the border districts and tahsils of adjoining states, people speaking different languages lived. For example, in the northern districts of Karnataka, touching Andhra Pradesh, Telugu speaking people also lived. Similarly, on the northwestern side, there were those who spoke Marathi. Yet, the majority of the total population in these districts spoke Kannada. It was not easy to distribute each village, tahsil or district on the basis of language only.

In Andhra Pradesh, the people of Telengana demanded a separate state. Pant argued that it was irrational for the people of Telengana to demand another state especially when Andhra Pradesh had been created, wherein the majority of the people spoke Telugu.

In Maharashtra, passions and emotions were aroused on the question of Bombay city. Gujarati and Marathi speaking people laid claim on it. At one point of time, it was being argued whether Bombay city should not be kept separate as the centrally administered area. But the Marathi speaking people would have nothing of it. On the issue of Bombay city, even an eminent Minister and highly patriotic Indian like C.D. Deshmukh resigned from the Cabinet. So you can imagine the depth of emotions, the reorganisation of states aroused not only among the ill-informed people but even among the intelligent, educated and rational men and women.

The Marathi speaking people of the erstwhile Central Provinces and Berar demanded a separate state of Vidarbha. However, these areas were finally amalgamated in Maharashtra and Bombay city was also given to Maharashtra after sustained negotiations.

These examples are illustrative of the complexity of the issues which reorganisation process started. However, with untiring effort, tact, spirit of conciliation shown by Govind Ballabh Pant, it was possible to find solutions, and agreement was reached between different groups within the linguistic state and between one state and the other.

Similarly, in the Parliament, Pant displayed great debating skills and negotiating abilities. Above all, he showed a vision of future India. Jawaharlal Nehru had argued on several occasions that the paramount interest of India must prevail; that unity and stability of the country must receive priority over the considerations of language.

As long as he lived, he did not allow Assam, Punjab, Haryana to be made separate states, because he felt that these states were of great strategic importance being border states. And hence, linguistic passions could not be allowed to prevail over national interest. Pant also firmly advocated that the fundamental unity of India must be maintained at all costs and they did not allow linguistic passions to grow.

Pant observed:

> "Language is no doubt a powerful factor. Its importance cannot and need not be minimised. It is not only a means of communication but it reflects the culture and character of people. So, we have to attach sufficient importance to it, but language can also be a dividing factor. If we are cut away from each other and if we think of language alone and not of so many other things in our country, then, instead of serving the cause of unification and advancement, languages become a source of disruption. We have to adjust the claims of language with the needs of national cohesion."

These were words of wisdom indeed, which ring true even today.

During these years of incessant toil and activity Pant showed immense patience and practical wisdom and endeared himself to one and all. He was one of the greatest nation builders of India.

Warm Tributes from Press

National Herald, editorially wrote:

"After a fortnight of farewells, Pandit Pant had laid down the Chief Ministership to take up immense responsibilities in a wider sphere. The whole-hearted and unanimous tribute paid to him in the two houses of the legislature gives him an enduring place as a Chief Minister unrivalled in his popularity and his hold on the people. It was a tribute both of admiration and affection for one whose intellectual qualities were matched by the qualities of his heart.

"The U. P. Congress, whatever its faults, has, in spite of extraordinary strain, shown unity and cohesion. This has been particularly noticeable in the administration, where Pandit Pant's leadership was outstanding."

The Pioneer, Lucknow:

'It has to measure up the exacting standards set up by the Government under the administrative wizard Pt. G. B. Pant who could keep incongruous elements together by his masterful presence.'

Hindustan Times, New Delhi:

"The extraordinary tributes paid to Pandit Pant on laying down his charge as Chief Minister shows what a fund of good-will his successor has inherited and how fortunate the State has been under such a gifted guide for the past 17 years."

Statesman, New Delhi:

"Lucknow has been busy saying farewell to Pandit Pant. The many years that he has devoted to public service span the most critical period in U. P.'s modern history. He has been associated with the U. P. Legislature for over thirty years, starting from a time when the established form of government, over which

> Sir Harcourt Butler had lately presided, was already on the shadow of vast change.

"U.P.'s loss of its Chief Minister will be the Central Cabinet's gain. Pandit Pant's presence will mean help for Pt. Nehru in his many exacting duties. Pt. Pant leaves U.P. in good health. A major political change— there has been effected with apparent smoothness. For that much credit goes to him."

The U.P. Governor speaking at the banquet in honour of the outgoing Chief Minister paid a warm tribute to Pandit Pant when he said:

> "In going to the Centre, he is maintaining the highest tradition of the Gandhian school. He is going there at considerable personal inconvenience, for he has worked in spite of indifferent health to build up U.P. and I can easily realise what he feels in having to leave the great work which he is leaving half done. If Gandhiji taught us one thing—it was to subordinate every inclination to the demands of duty. Like a disciplined soldier at the behest of our great leader, the Prime Minister, he is going to Delhi, setting a splendid example for younger people. Pantji's great experience, his sanity of outlook, his foresight and his constructive statesmanship will lend strength to India as a whole."

Replying to the tributes paid to him Pandit Pant said:

> "I have been overwhelmed by the universal manifestation, altogether spontaneous of the affection and confidence which has been the main feature of the Press as well as of the public since the news of my going to the Centre found its way to the columns of the Press. I have never had any illusions about myself. I know my limitations and I know that with growing age and infirmity, the handicaps are growing perhaps in a geometrical progression. But still all my foibles and shortcomings have been covered by my friends and by those who have readily given me their

best during the last many years that I have been connected, either in public life or in the administration of this great, grand and glorious State.

"The idea of parting from Uttar Pradesh is to me a fantastic one. How can that be possible.? Uttar Pradesh and I have come to form an integrated organism. So, wherever I may be, I will be carrying the message of Uttar Pradesh, and whenever I come to Uttar Pradesh, I shall continue to count upon the munificent kindness, charity and generosity not only of my friend but of the masses along with the classes living in this State with a glorious past and I hope with a still more glorious future.

"I know that I can do but little in another sphere today. But, luckily or unluckily, I still continue to retain the adventurous spirit of youth and with that spirit I go forward to have one more trial and to see whether old men can surpass the young even at this age. That is the only ideal which sustains me and prompts me to go away from a place from which I cannot possibly be separated."

Pandit Pant recalled:

"I remember the day when we first took charge of the administration in July, 1937. Times have changed. It will be difficult for anyone to imagine the circumstances in which we had to function then. We were trying to do our best through what was known as the rigid and unbending steel frame in those times. All the Secretaries at that time, perhaps excepting one, belonged to the alien race. Yet, from the very first day I took charge, I called them and spoke to them and I had little trouble from my Secretaries since that day. But we were in a difficult position because of the anomalous Constitution under which we had to work then. There were many an occasion when we had to wrestle with the Governor. Sometimes we thought it would come to the physical plane, but it did not culminate. I recollect, and recollect with a certain degree of satisfaction, that whenever we had these powers, the Secretaries, the Chief Secretary, in particular, always told me that we were in the right and the Governor was in the wrong. That gave us some moral strength; and he told me that he was not speaking to me in secret but that he had made his views known to the Governor and had told him that he was espousing a wrong cause in a perverse manner.

"Many were again (he occasions when I tendered resignations on my own and my colleague's behalf. At one time the resignations were well-nigh or perhaps finally accepted. But Gandhiji applied his magic wand and the Governor again invited us in a nice way, expressed regret for what had happened, and gave an undertaking for good behaviour in future.

"But those days were really more lively, and in a sense, more exciting too. Everyday there was some problem or other and everyday we were determined to have things our own way and we succeeded in having them our own way. During those days we did what paved the way for our future work. The main pivotal purpose of our activity was achievement of swaraj, and we had to handle affair in such a way as to enlarge the field of our responsibility and to make it impossible for the Governor to get rid of us. But in spite of all that our personal relations with the Governors were perfectly cordial and every Governor treated me with utmost consideration, if not respect. I am an admirer of personal qualities; political differences did not come in the way of our assessment of personal qualities of individuals, and even though as political adversaries we were arrayed against each other, their conduct was honourable."

In the chilly morning of December 30 thousands gathered at the Charbagh railway station, which was tastefully decorated to bid farewell to Pandit Pant. It was Lucknow's memorable farewell to their architect after more than a fortnight of farewell parties, lunches, dinners and at homes. Over 3000 guests were present at the Citizens' At Home and more than 6000 at the Government At Home which was unprecedented in the whole life of this province. Lucknow had not witnessed such a farewell before. Pandit Pant's special saloon was jammed by the pressing crowd. Several thousand people, his Cabinet Colleagues, secretariat and departmental officers, members of the legislature and citizens began assembling at the platform from early morning. We travelled with him in his saloon from Lucknow to Bareilly. At every station during his journey thousands of people from surrounding villages had gathered with Congress flags and flowers at the railway platforms and gave him a great ovation. He had to get down and thank the waiting crowds for their love and assured them that he was with them and he simply was shifting his place of work. He was overwhelmed by this spontaneity of love and affection which was not so witnessed and which was so bountifully showered on him.

The train arrived at Bareilly Station three hours late. About five thousand people, representatives of all shades of opinion, officials, and ladies were waiting at the station in a very orderly form. They all cheered and garlanded him. Pandit Pant was visibly moved by the crowd. He had a very crowded programme for two days. He met practically every one, and everybody was touched. He told us at the Citizens At *Home* that the membership of the Assembly from Bareilly was only of some days more. There was pathetic touch in his words. He spoke at Bareilly Citizens farewell function for more than 50 minutes in a well attended gathering in which more than a dozen farewell addresses were presented by different organisations of the city. His speech was very fine and touching. He was in a reminiscent mood. He fully surveyed his life and his long associations with Bareilly since the days of his student life, when he was in legal profession; his prison days in Bareilly District Jail with Pandit Nehru. Then his associations as their representative in the Central and U. P. Legislative assemblies. He made a significant observation. He said that he was put to a test. He was not afraid of trials. He had always faced them in life with confidence and success. He said it was not an act of wisdom to put oneself on test at this age when his physical qualities were not as good. Some thought that he was fully equipped for the new work. He himself thought otherwise. He welcomed this opportunity of putting him on test. If he failed their misunderstandings would be removed. If he succeeded, his own misunderstanding would be removed. He had never fled from such tests in his life—and also he had never failed. He wanted their good wishes. His speech created a very profound impression. He was so affectionate and so personal. Every one was charmed by its human touch.

In the night of January, 1, 1955, admirers bade farewell to Pandit Pant at Bareilly station. There was a big crowd in that chilly winter night. There were tears in every eye. Pandit Pant stood at the door of his saloon profusely garlanded. It was a difficult scene. He remained at the gate for about seven minutes. In that atmosphere it was difficult to stand. Amidst *Pandit Pant ki Jai* he took leave. The door was closed. After five minutes there was a great pressure from the side of the parting crowd that he should come out. Pandit Pant came out at once again. He stood for a couple of minutes, and then departed. The crowd waited for some time and then dispersed—sad in heart. With his departure one chapter is closed and the other opened with the advent of the New Year.

Next morning hearty welcome was accorded to him at the Delhi Railway Station. In the early hours of chilly fog bound morning hundreds of people had managed to reach the station—and many had gone even to Ghaziabad to welcome him. His saloon was piled with flowers which he received in his constituency town of Bareilly and from the people on his journey.

On January 3, at Rashtrapati Bhawan in the midst of Central Ministers Pandit Pant was sworn in as a Minister of Union Cabinet by the President, his friend and colleague for decades in the Congress Working Committee Dr. Rajendra Prasad.

In the first week of February 1955 Pandit Pant resigned from the membership of U.P. Assembly with which he was associated as a member for the last thirty years. In his formal letter of resignation to Sri A. G. Kher, the Speaker of U.P. Assembly, Pt. Pant wrote:

"I hereby tender my resignation from the membership of the Assembly from Bareilly city constituency. I need not state the circumstances which have impelled me to do so. I am thankful to you and other members of the Assembly for the kindness and consideration which I uniformly received from them all and also from you personally".

We use the language not of flattery but of sincerity and truth when we say that he had maintained the best traditions in law and also in public life. He had no love for money. His outstanding positive quality was his humanism. He possessed the qualities which Mark Antony claimed for Caesar—austerity and an ascetic way of life. The standard which he has all along followed was what he read in his law classes, and which he pleaded in courts—the standard of "Justice, equity, and good conscience."

He was actuated by one desire, one feeling—and one ideal that he should employ himself to do something good, to leave something better than he found it. He works for this noble ideal in the spirit of high idealism and he realises them into realism.

Writing to his life long friend, fellow lawyer and afterwards a colleague, Dr. Kailash Nath Katju he said:

"I do not attach undue importance to life in general and still less to my own. On the other, I do not regard it as a result of evil itself, nor as a punishment. Whether the world is a prison and the cessation of life tantamounts to release from it, I have no knowledge. It is difficult to say exactly what constitutes life or what is its essence; but the negative is certainly true—neither inaction nor inertia is the sign of life. Motion, energy, action are its inseparable threads. I am willing to live so long as I can be of some active service without being too much of a burden on others. I would hate to live merely as a drone or as a parasite, though I am not sure if some would not regard as such even now."

5

Seasoned Parliamentarian

Accomplished Parliamentarian

Pandit Govind Ballabh Pant was without doubt one of the most accomplished parliamentarians of his generation. Not only a skilful debater, he was deeply and devoutly committed to the parliamentary way of life and any discerning observer could see this commitment becoming in later years almost an all-absorbing passion. In fact matters like upholding the authority of Parliament and the Government's accountability to it, strengthening its procedures, maintaining and enhancing the standards of parliamentary debates preoccupied him increasingly in his last years. He may truly be described as a "Parliament's man". He bestowed his closest and most careful attention on everything relating to Parliament, whether it was an unstarred question, or a major debate on a resolution or a Bill.

Ideal Parliamentarian

He was one of the most accomplished Parliamentarians of his age. If there was one man in whom the characteristics features of parliamentary system had found the fullest expression, it was Pandit Pant. He had natural eloquence. His parliamentary talents were remarkable—that it was true of him as of Asquith and Peel that "he can play in the House as an old fiddle." His power of evading or postponing difficulties and of finding solutions to the difficult situations were extraordinary. He had been with Bhullabhai Desai, Satyamurti, Jinnah in the Central Assembly. He would rank among the greatest of our parliamentarians. People had watched the stormy debates when passions loosened. He kept his coolness of temper, never irritated, in sweet and gracious manner gave a thrashing reply. He had thus risen to great heights. No one might provoke him, he had never lost his temper in the house during long years nor used unparliamentary language. His grasp of the English most suited to Parliamentary debate enabled him to attack effectively with a minimum of offence. He was a master of the technique of parliamentary procedure.

Once commenting a Lucknow English daily, the Pioneer, wrote about him:

> "A finished Parliamentarian, he can pulverise, when he chooses his critics with devastating ruthlessness by his sledge hammer oratory. His personal prestige is so great and his personality is so overwhelming that few can stand up to him either in any House or outside. Both as a parliamentarian and debater he stands unexcelled."

When after many years he appeared in the Chamber of the Lok Sabha on February 22, 1955 as Home Minister to answer certain charges levelled by the Communist Party through an adjournment motion in regard to the election then going on in Andhra, a correspondent in a Calcutta daily—Amrita Bazar Patrika thus described:

> "As he entered the House he received great ovation. He was loudly cheered when he rose to state the Government case in relation to the motion. And what an effective speech he made! Some opposition members tried to heckle him in the midst of his statement, but only to receive sharp and quick retorts. Crossing swords with Pandit Pant is no child's play. One by one he took up the allegations made in the adjournment motion, and demonstrated them to be

> utterly lacking in substance or grossly exaggerated. Police versions of incidents do not usually carry conviction with our people, particularly with the opposition. But how masterly and with what parliamentary deftness he used the police version to completely demolish the Communist case without provoking their anger or wounding their susceptibility. It was a treat to hear him deal hard knocks with good humour. His marshalling of facts and arguments were prefaced by some obiter dicta which went home. He was lustily applauded as he resumed his seat."

Thus the very first speech that he as Home Minister made in the Parliament created a deep impression. His second speech was made in the Rajya Sabha three days later in reply to the debate on the President's address. As expected, he won more laurels.

Those who had watched Pandit Pant's performance in the Central Assembly, remarked that with the advance of years the veteran Parliamentarian has lost none of his old fire or gifts but became more seasoned.

The correspondent also observed:

> "A giant among men, able administrator and powerful debater, Pandit Pant has proved a tower of strength to Prime Minister Nehru inside the Cabinet and on the floor of the Parliament."

Pt. Nehru paid a warm tribute to Pandit Pant in the Parliament while speaking on the States Reorganisation Debate. Pandit Pant had participated in the strenuous debates in the Lok Sabha and the Rajya Sabha in-spite of being "acutely unwell and in great pain."

Prime Minister said:

> "I am intervening chiefly because, if I may be quite frank with this House, I do not want my colleague to speak again. As many members of this House might know, he delivered a great and noble speech yesterday in the Lok Sabha (*cheers*). But, perhaps everybody does not know that during these days when he has

been in charge of these two debates, apart from other heavy burdens he carries, he has been acutely unwell and in great pain. Nevertheless, in spite of these, he has discharged this heavy burden with the great ability that he possesses *(cheers)* Obviously I cannot discharge this business of speaking towards the end of this debate with that facility or knowledge that he possesses".

Many Phases of his Career

The Parliamentary career of Pandit Pant had many phases. He was a member of the U.P. Legislative Council from 1924 to 1929, Central Legislative Assembly during 1935-37 and U.P. Legislative Assembly, during March 1937 - October 1939 and again in 1946-54. Simultaneously, he was also a member of the Constituent Assembly of India in 1946-50. Pandit Pant had a rare privilege of first leading the Opposition and then of being a member of Treasury Benches - as Chief Minister of U.P. twice and as Home Minister in the Union Government When finally, he joined the Central Cabinet as Home Minister he became a member of the Rajya Sabha and Leader of the House in 1955 and occupied that position till his death. He had to match himself against other debaters of nationwide reputation but as a leader, pre-eminently suited to parliamentary democracy his stature touched its highest peak in Parliament Pantji was really a colossus who strode amongst the great and contributed much to the development of parliamentary democracy and parliamentary institutions in India. He believed in liberty and equality of all men and women and attached great importance to a free press. He had the highest respect for the opposition and considered its role as an essential ingredient for the successful functioning of parliamentary democracy. "He combined strength with wisdom, and while he could be an orator he was content to be a debater, statesman-like in dealing with a storm and deadly in dealing with Opposition." He possessed a perfect equilibrium of mind and an accommodating spirit with his personal magnetism, so essential in a parliamentarian. He knew how to woo and win. He was a political tactician and possessed an instinct for seizing the opportune moment with an unerring insight.

Pantji's grasp of English was most suited to parliamentary debate and it enabled him to attack effectively with a minimum of offence. As a debater he was formidable and devastating. His opponents simply played into his hands. He was not a very striking speaker, but he had natural eloquence. He delivered his speech rather haltingly, but when his speeches are read in print they are marked for cogent arguments. During the stormy debates when passions were let loose, he kept his cool. He hardly used any harsh or unparliamentary words to silence his rivals and seldom attempted to ridicule them down by the sheer force of facts. In fact as Frank Moraes has said, "Pantji struck decisively, killing without inflicting a wound. In setting the example for tolerance of the opposition, courtesy to members from every side of the House - whether senior or junior -and ability to cast his charm and unmistakable spell over the entire House and all those listening to him, he had no equal.

Pandit Pant possessed almost a photographic memory. He never referred to notes while replying to debates. This was because he prepared himself with the thoroughness of a brilliant lawyer, checking and re-checking all facts and data, scrutinising statistics and referencing supporting documents. He missed no point and gave complete reply from the profundity of his memory and knowledge. While presiding over the sittings of the Joint Committee dealing with the States Reorganisation Bill with several sections and subsections and each subsection with several sub-clauses, he carried no notes and, yet, whenever he intervened in the debate, it was crystal clear that all the sections, subsections and clauses were before his mind's eye. He would in fact, allow no ambiguity, least of all any inaccuracy, to creep into any statement he made in Parliament Remarkably his choice of words and sentences was such that no corrections were indeed required to be made in the proof copies of parliamentary proceedings.

The calm and unruffled manner in which he spoke in Parliament on important occasions showed his mastery over the subject and his ability to present his case with unrivalled skill. Referring to Pantji's performance in the Legislature, the *Pioneer* once commented:

> "A finished Parliamentarian, he can pulverise when he chooses his critics with devastating ruthlessness by Ms sledge hammer oratory. His personal prestige is so great and his personality is so overwhelming that few can stand up to him either in any House or outside. Both as a Parliamentarian and debater he stands excelled."

As a matter of fact, Pandit Pant belonged to the race of Malaviyas and Gokhales whose speeches still shed lustre on the records of the proceedings of the legislatures of those days. They had been brought up in the best traditions of British liberalism and the techniques of Parliamentary debate. But despite their genius, their words had no sanction behind them. In this respect Pandit Pant was most fortunate. Even at the time he made Ms debut in the U.P. Legislative Council in 1924, some elements of democracy had been introduced in the form of dyarchy; with the march of events from 1927 to 1947, the advance towards democratic government, with the rich opportunities it provided for debating skill and the finesse of parliamentary technique, became more rapid and complete.

In U.P. Legislative Council

As a member of the U.P. Legislative Council (of which he was the Leader of the Opposition) and later on as a Member of the Central Legislative Assembly (of which he was the Deputy Leader of the Opposition) through his well reasoned arguments on the floor of the legislature aroused the national and international conscience against imperialistic oppression and exploitation of the people of India. He fully utilised the opportunities offered to him by the Act of 1909, 1919 and 1935 to expose the evils of colonialism and present India's case for self-rule and national unity. The first such opportunity capitalised by him was in April, 1925, when intervening in the discussion on a resolution of Dr. Ganesh Prasad, which opened the most important question of the day—the report of the Reforms Enquiry Committee - he said:

> "I personally think it is not regulations, it is not acts, it is not rules which determine the position of people

> in the race for freedom... The right to freedom is an inherent, an inalienable right and everybody is entitled to rely on that well-recognised principle of self-determination... We are here only to express our conviction that unless and until the Constitution is amended fundamentally and categorically we cannot have anything rational to work through which the need of the country may be fulfilled."

Concluding his speech he remarked:

> "Too late is writ large in the history of this country, and all this bitterness has resulted because Government shadowed and eclipsed by the Bureaucracy, has failed to take notice of the omens betimes and has stupidly opposed popular wishes till the very last. It is time for them to reconsider their position. After all, this calm should not mislead them. Now, we have reached a situation in the country when the limit to tolerance has been reached, if not outstripped and it must think seriously before flouting public opinion now. In this case think before it is too late and save India and save England; and put an end to the bitterness and animosity which will otherwise lead to *the* doom of both countries. There are breakers ahead and if you will cling to your discredited oars, the barge will be foundered and disaster will follow. After all, you have to restore to us what is ours, then why not do so in good grace and good time".

On February 24 and 25, 1928 there was another memorable debate in the U.P. Legislative Council on the Simon Commission. In this historic debate Pandit Pant rose heads and shoulders above all others by his forceful arguments. Delivering his inspiring speech, he reiterated that India stood for self- determination. After narrating the experiences of various Dominions of the British Commonwealth, the Leader of the Opposition observed:

> "History has established two or three principles and they are indisputable. It has been repeatedly proved

> that unless and until a Constitution framed and formulated by the representatives of the people of the country for which the Constitution is intended, is introduced, makeshift contrivances cannot put an end to the struggle for liberty. It is equally clear that whenever efforts have been made to superimpose something from without, it has only added to complications and bitterness and has made things worse."

Quoting from the speech of Sir John Simon made by him in 1921 on the Irish Constitution Bill in which he had pointedly observed that "Constitutions which promote prosperity and loyalty and which have been found to be lasting Constitutions have been framed by those who were to live under them themselves". Pandit Pant wondered as to how Sir Simon should have agreed to be a party to the working of a scheme which went fundamentally against the principles which he enunciated in 1921.

Referring to a sentence from the speech of the Finance Member:

> "In politics the unexpected often happens", Pandit Pant retorted by quoting the case of Ireland when the Government in power in 1920 did not agree to the conferment of Dominion Status on Ireland and within a year of the passage of the Home Rule Act in 1921 the British Parliament had to confer on Ireland a Constitution going far beyond the Dominion Status. "The unexpected happened", said the speaker looking towards the Finance Member, and "it happened within a year. I am not using the language of intimidation. I ask the Government in power here who are in close touch with the state of things in this country, to tell those who are their masters and who have appointed them our masters, that the unexpected may also happen in India".

The U.P. Government having lost the battle of the Simon Commission issue thought of another device. On September 18, 1928 Mr. Lambert the Finance Member on behalf of the Government moved that the Council elect a Committee of seven to cooperate with the Simon Commission. Pandit Pant sought permission to make a few remarks before the Finance Member moved his motion. He said that no alternative course was open to him and his party except to dissociate themselves completely from the motion having regard to their sense of personal decency, national dignity and the honour of the House. He asked for what the legislatures existed, if their verdicts, recorded after careful, elaborate full dress debates were going to be reopened every day, if the executive took it into its head to bring forward the question again. On February 25 a clear, emphatic and definite verdict was recorded by the members of the House. That verdict was not the verdict of any precipitate hurry. After carefully weighing all the pros and cons of the proposition before them they definitely determined that this House would never have anything to do with the Statutory Commission at any stage and in any form. Now they were asked to trample upon that resolution.

Concluding, Pandit Pant said:

> "We feel that in the present circumstances, when all constitutional methods, when everything has been thrown *to* the winds, has been trampled upon, there can be only one goal, that noble goal, that glorious goal of Independence for this great country. We cannot think of anything else. We have to live and to die for that; and for us these little juggleries in the form of commissions and committees, these little devices in one name or another, have little meaning. We must steer clear of them all. We refuse to be deluded, to be misguided by these things."

On November 2, 1929 speaking in the U.P., Council on Bedar's resolution for release of political prisoners, Pandit Pant once again urged the Britishers to leave India in the following words:

> "It is time for England to restore to India what really is her own. We ask for nothing more. We cannot wait for an answer nor can we possibly reconcile ourselves to any progress by stages. We want full freedom. They have to make their choice. So far as we are concerned, there should foe no misunderstanding. We are determined to be free."

In U.P. Legislative Assembly

In the first general elections held under the Government of India Act, 1935 which provided for Provincial Autonomy. Pandit Pant was elected to the U.P. Legislative Assembly on 18 February, 1937. Congress Party secured absolute majority in U. P. as in six other provinces. As was expected Pantji was unanimously elected leader of the Congress Legislature Party in U.P. on 7 March, 1937. After the elections, there was fierce controversy whether to accept office or not and opinions were sharply divided. When the Congress Working Committee met at Wardha to discuss the matter, Gandhiji advised that the Congress should obtain an assurance from the British Government that the special powers of the Governor would not be used and that the Congress Ministers would be given a real chance to do good for the people. Ultimately, in the third week of March a resolution was passed by the All India Congress Committee providing that "the ministership shall not be accepted unless the leader of the Congress Party in the legislature is satisfied and able to state publicly that the Governor will not use his special powers of interference or set aside the office of ministers in regard to their constitutional activities." This however led to a deadlock which was resolved only after the Viceroy's pronouncement on 21 June, 1937 wherein he clarified that he in fact saw no foundation for the Congress apprehensions and *that* the Governor would not seek occasions to interfere with the policies of the Ministers. Thus when on 7 July, the Congress Working Committee decided to permit Congressmen to accept office, the Congress Ministry assumed office in U.P. on 17 July, 1937 under the premiership of Pandit Pant.

The first budget of his Government was presented by Premier Pant, who held the portfolio of Finance also, on 6 September, 1937. The supreme purpose of the financial policy of the Government was enunciated in emphatic language by him in his very first budget statement He said:

> "We hold that Government have no business to exist if they cannot contribute towards the uplift and enrichment of the people whom they have been appointed to serve. It is their essential duty to devise

> necessary ways and means and to frame appropriate plans for social progress and reconstruction."

Referring to the objective he had in view, the Premier observed:

> "The Congress attaches great importance to ameliorating the lot of the rural population. In fact the Congress Government is out for creating a new era for the countryside. We are determined to raise their general level of life. The appalling poverty has so be removed from one hundred and five thousand villages in the province; darkness has to be replaced by light; dull and monotonous drudgery and despair by a little hope, relaxation and good cheer."

The guiding principles were two for Pantji:

> rigid economy in the existing administration and
>
> financing of all nation-building activities. The budgets were framed to better the condition of the poor people. The policy of taxation was simple.

Pantji put it in his inimitable style as follows;

> "It will, however, be our duty to see that full value is restored to the public for their contributions. All that Government collects must bear a rich harvest. In the words of a Sanskrit poet 'just as the sun draws moisture from the earth which ultimately returns to it in much larger quantities in the form of rain, irrigating the soil, giving relief from heat and promoting vegetable growth, so Government should repay to the people in the form of various benefits what they take from them as taxes."

When Europe was engulfed in the Second World War in September 1939, England declared war on Germany on 3 September, and on that very day, the Viceroy, without consulting any of the Indian leaders or legislatures, proclaimed that India too was at war. Later, of course, the Viceroy invited the Indian leaders for consultation. The Congress Working Committee discussed the situation at its meeting at Wardha which was attended by Gandhiji also. In a resolution the Committee declared that it could not associate or offer any cooperation in a war which was conducted on imperialist lines and which was meant to consolidate imperialism in India and elsewhere. It invited the British Government to declare in unequivocal terms their war aims in regard to democracy and imperialism and the new order that was envisaged. The Working Committee's statement was discussed at the A.I.C.C. meeting at Wardha on 9 October. The A.I.C.C. took the stand that "India must be declared an independent nation". Meanwhile, the British Parliament amended the Government of India Act, 1935 encroaching upon the autonomous powers of the provincial governments.

Premier Pant moving a resolution in the U.P. Legislative Assembly on 27 October said that his Government could not associate itself with the British policy. His speech on that occasion was truly that of a staunch patriot and a seasoned statesman. He said:

> "When, therefore, we ask for a declaration and recognition of the principle of Indian independence we are neither bargaining nor seeking any selfish advantage. We are as much interested as any other country in the peace and happiness of humanity and it is as much our right as our duty to see to it that the sacrifices which unsophisticated people are asked to make bear rich fruit and the noble and inspiring slogans, which experienced politicians employ to secure the cooperation of the general public are fully respected. If violence has to be tolerated and to be resorted to, it can be only on the clear understanding that there will be no recrudescence of it hereafter, that men will live as brothers and that while every man will be free to serve his neighbour and his country, he will also be a citizen of the world. Unless the political and social order is recognised and security established on a fundamentally moral basis there can be no peace or freedom. If we have the courage of our convictions, if we are honest and if we sincerely realise and appreciate *the* demands of the times we should

> unhesitatingly accept the principles of democracy and freedom for all alike, and should see to it that none will hereafter be placed under subjection simply because he had to yield in the past to superior physical force and violence."

When Pantji again assumed office of Premier of U.P. on 1 April, 1946, the province was overwhelmed with the problems of Partition particularly of rehabilitating the refugees; as well as of food scarcity. However, speaking on a resolution in the U.P. Assembly on the food situation in the province, he said:

> "I must tell honourable members that, so far as I am concerned, I do not see any room for panic or alarm. I still believe that with what we have and what we are expecting to get from the Government of India we can tide over the present difficult times, but we can do so only if we all put our shoulders to the wheel and if everyone is prepared to do his part well and honourably and sympathetically and in a manly and humane manner. There is a tendency in certain quarters to pander to the whims of simpletons. That is not the way of the robust to manage affairs. We must be able to handle things well and rightly and do the right thing. After all, wisdom lies *in* keeping an eye on the future and not to be entrapped in the present. So we must see what will be the consequences of the course that we decide to follow."

Of course, Pantji had a soft corner for the villagers. He said:

> "It is our aspiration to serve all classes of the community in all places. In fact, we are more anxious to do what we can for the villagers than for the townsmen, because people in the towns are better educated, they are more conscious and they are more vociferous than the people in the villages. The villager has always attracted -our greater attention and honourable members are aware we have given him the first place in all our things and in all our actions.

Soon Pantji also took some concerted steps for abolition of the zamindari system which had assumed the shape of a cancerous growth in the body politic of the province. On 7 August, 1946 speaking on a resolution in the U.P. Assembly seeking abolition of the zamindari, he said that the heart-rendering condition of the 80-90 per cent of the rural population of the province who were not able to make two ends meet in spite of working hard in the sun, rain and cold, was really pitiable. Their education was negligible, they neither had sufficient clothing to cover their bare bodies nor enough to fill their bellies and had been reduced to skeletons. On the other hand, there were only 5000 zamindars. Should the progress of the province and the welfare of five crores of people be stalled for the sake of these 5000 zamindars, he asked. Pointing out that even the Muslim League government *in* Bengal favoured zamindari abolition, he said that the zamindars had unfortunately become an appendix for the people whose sole purpose was to create appendicitis in the body politic. He further said that the zamindars could not be compared with the industrialists who in fact constituted the fourth wheel in the carriage, without whom progress was not possible.

Speaking on the Zamindari Abolition Bill in the Assembly on 13 July, 1949, Pantji said that the greatest problem in the province was of an unbalanced economy. In his view there was dire need of industrialisation of the rural area in the natural way. So, if money could be saved out of the payments received from the cultivators, it could be utilised for providing electricity in the rural areas. He hoped that through the Bill a new social, spiritual and economic order would be established in the country.

When the Bill as reported by the Joint Select Committee — the first such exercise in the history of the U.P. Legislature — was brought before the Assembly on 16 January, 1950 for consideration, Pandit Pant declared that the Bill was no ordinary Bill; it was in fact intended to bring about a peaceful revolution and also to completely change the social structure in the province. Speaking with a sense of pride he said that no other government or legislature in the country and perhaps only a few elsewhere had the good fortune and privilege to bring forward such a Bill, When the Bill finally came of before the Assembly for passing on 10 January,

1951, Pantji referring to the zamindars said that he sympathised with them as they were being deprived of the privileges they had enjoyed for a long time. But he requested them to live amicably with the cultivators as before. Both had a long chain of close relationship. On the occasion of a good work therefore, the zamindars should instead of opposing the measure derive spiritual benefit and the goodwill of the people by supporting it In his own words:

> "Abolition of Zamindari has not been prompted by any ill-will against any class. Many zamindars have been in the vanguard of the struggle and have worked valiantly in order to make our peasantry bold and place them firmly on the right road. Let there be no distinction and *no* trace of bitterness anywhere. There will be no classes in our rural parts now and all will form a healthy team and live in a friendly atmosphere of fellowship and comradeship each regarding himself as the custodian and trustee of the honour and welfare of every other.

Pantji was a great optimist Once he took reins of the government in his hands, there was nothing else for him but to sec that the country progressed further and the material and moral standard of her people was raised. In his reply to the discussion on the enhanced irrigation rates in the U.P. Legislative Assembly, he said:

> "There is little meaning in looking backwards; we should look forward This country has to be built and all its troubles eradicated. Our past has been one of hardships and now is the period of their eradication....
>
> "I want to emphasise that we should look at these grave problems from the point of view of the good of the people. Jugglery of figures can deceive those who do not have a complete picture before them but those who have it, cannot be misled."

When Mahatma Gandhi fell to the bullets of his assassin, Pantji paid eloquent tributes to his leadership which indeed transcended the boundaries of India, Speaking in the U.P. Legislative Assembly on 16 February, 1948, he said:

> "Mahatmaji was not just an Indian, though in India's national struggle and in her liberation he took the fullest part and was always in the forefront. True it is that in her moral uplift, in improving the condition of her people, in helping the fallen to rise up, in getting food for the hungry and raiment for the naked and in bringing back to life her suppressed people Mahatmaji alone was responsible, but his soul *and* spirit were not confined merely to India's national boundaries. He was a great man of the world. His yearning to liberate the world's suppressed and dependent peoples was as acute as it was for the liberation of the people of India. But he always realised that his sphere of action was the area where he was and it was there that he had to work. He did his duty by the world also for his movement awakened the people of all downtrodden countries, gave them life and self-confidence and spread among them the feeling that they could also rise and become free and there was a place of respect for them in the world. And actually it so happened that side by side with the liberation of India whole Asia became free and secured a respectable place for herself in the comity of nations."

On 10 October, 1952 a resolution regarding raising of the moral standard of the people was brought before the Legislative Assembly, Pantji observed that there could be no two opinions on the basic tenets of the resolution. He conceded that morality had suffered a decline all over the world after the Second World War. But they were trying to give a new shape to the society and in this process certain changes were necessary whether one liked them or not So what he would foremost like to have in the country was that there should be life, there should be manliness and what is important, there should be a burning desire in the people for spiritual and social upliftment Everyone should, keeping his head high, be able to march forward *in* different directions and be always prepared to derive benefit of the universal human rights.

In Central Legislative Assembly

Pantji's term as member of the Central Legislative Assembly daring 1935-37 may be regarded as the best period of his parliamentary career. He shone there in all his brightness. As Deputy Leader of the Congress Party in the Central Assembly, he made a mark as a seasoned parliamentarian par excellence. Suave, but vigorous, he put the Treasury Benches often at their wit's end during the debates by his well-informed and positive criticism. He was soon an acknowledged authority on economic and financial matters. Sir Henry Craik and Sir James Grigg, the Home and Finance Members of the Government of India at that time showed Pantji utmost respect because they found in him more than a match for them. He was the 'Big Bertha' of the Congress Party in the House as one distinguished observer remarked. Many an Executive Councillor admitted, "it is difficult to say who is more fearful than whom, between Bhulabhai, Satyamurti and Pant, each one in his own way is terrible but the elephant-like trumpeting and treading we get from Pant stampedes all our frontage and prestige."

On the very first day of his taking seat in the House on January 21, 1935, there was a 'Motion for adjournment' intended to censure the Government for the issue of a confidential circular to the local authorities calling their attention to the probable implications of the 'new deal' of Gandhiji in the form of Bombay Congress resolution to organise a village industries association. It evoked a great fear in their minds as it might prove to be of far-reaching political importance. The Government wanted to forestall Congress activities in the village service prescribed by public men in this country, howsoever wholesome and promising it be, should be opposed, and they should fight shy of it and they should obstruct its progress because it is likely to result in strengthening *the* position of those who will perform such service?"

A major issue, apart from the Budgets was the Indo-British Trade Agreement of 1935. From 1927 onwards, the Government of India, obviously prompted by their British interests, had so devised the Indian Tariff system as to give British products, in effect, a competitive advantage over both non-Empire and Indian products in the Indian market. This was epitomised in the principle of Imperial Preference under the Ottawa Trade Agreement. Thus, just on the eve of the inauguration of the new Legislative Assembly, the Government of India entered into an Agreement with the British Government embodying and expanding the Ottawa Agreement to widen the system of Imperial Preference. Indian political and economic interests however converged to put up a stiff fight to this imperialist imposition.

On 29 January, 1935 Commerce Member Sir Joseph Bhore moved in the Assembly that the Agreement signed on 9 January be taken into consideration. After a very interesting two-day debate, the Assembly rejected the Agreement. Pandit Pant who participated in the discussion contended that the Imperial Preference accepted under the Ottawa Agreement had been of no use to India. He said:

> "It is absolutely true that the policy of Imperial Preference imposes additional burden on the consumer and makes his lot worse. We are told that Indian exports *to* England have increased — I admit the correctness of the statement, and there are many reasons for this increase on which I have not time to dwell at present, but this important fact remains and the House will, I hope, bear it in mind, that the increase in the case of preferential goods has bean about 20 per cent, while in the case of non-preferential goods, it has been about 50 per cent. *This* clearly proves that preference has nothing to do with *this* rise. The imports into India of United Kingdom goods have gone up by several crores in those articles in which England gets preference."

An interesting debate on the subject took place in the Assembly in September 1936 when the Government of India announced 5 per cent reduction of duty on British textiles without consulting the Assembly. T.S. Avinashlingam Chettiar moved an adjournment motion in the Assembly on 2 September, 1936 to discuss the above action of the Government. Pandit Pant who also participated in the discussion expressed surprise that after an elaborate enquiry, the *ad hoc* Tariff Board should come exactly to the same conclusion which the abortive Indo-British Trade Agreement had come to, about two years ago, i.e. the reduction of *ad valorem* duty from 25 to 20 per cent. "It is rather suspicious and amazing how the prophet could have foretold the decisions of the Tariff Board about two years before its appointment. It is a genuine case of inspiration", he said. Concluding his speech, he pointed out

> "While the import duty on imports from other countries stood at 50 per cent, on British textiles this import duty did not go beyond 25 per cent, and England was enjoying an advantage of 50 per cent, as against other countries even before the reduction; and even that was not considered enough. Why should we *go* on giving fresh advantages? If the Government of India were candid and told us that they are only a subordinate wheel in the mill, and, as such cannot do anything better, it would be intelligible, but they lack candour and honesty, and in trying to defend the indefensible look ridiculous. Sir, the attitude the Government of India have adopted in this matter is not only anti-national and detrimental to the interests of this country, but amounts to a distinct breach of faith."

In February, 1935, there was a well-dressed memorable debate for three days on the report of the Joint Parliamentary Committee on Constitutional Reform. In a magnificent speech delivered in the House, Pandit Pant after referring to the course of events declared that the Joint Parliamentary Committee Scheme did in no way satisfy the self-respect and the national pride of the people of India and rather "from whatever point of view we may look at it, the scheme is a monstrosity; and I submit that such a disingenuous fraud has never been committed in the name of constitutional advance in any country before". Elaborating his point of view, he added:

> "In this Joint Parliamentary Committee scheme, there is not the least iota of advance. In fact, it goes back *upon* all the previous promises. We have been asked *to* trust to the goodness of those who will administer this Act. If we could assume that reasonable men will act reasonably in all times, then the very need for Government would cease. If men could always be

> reasonable, then there would be no need for any restraint much less for organised Government."

During the period of his membership of the Central Legislative Assembly, Pandit Pant had been a nominated Member of the Panel of Chairmen in 1935 and 1936, He had also been Member of the Committee on Petitions in 1935, besides being a Member of the Standing Finance Committee for three years consecutively, i.e. 1934-35, 1935-36 and 1936-37. By his learned speeches and studied comments on Budget proposals, Pandit Pant came to be recognised as an expert on questions of public finance and economics. He showed good grasp particularly of financial problems. If a budget speech was to be dissected, it was invariably Pantji who spoke for the Congress Party. His deep study and his resourceful mind were capable of meeting any situation. After he had spoken, there was little the Government could do to retrieve the situation.

During his speech on the "General Budget - General Discussion" on March 4, 1936, Pandit Pant pointed out a number of loopholes in the Budget:

> I should like to invite the attention of the Honourable the Finance Mamber to two other aspects of the accounts that are before us. He knows, I think better than anyone of us here, that his control over expenditure today, even as the officer in charge of the Finance Department, is not as complete as it ought to be. He knows much better than I do perhaps that, from year to year, allotments have remained in part unappropriated. There has been over-budgeting in a number of Departments. He also knows that from year to year a number of supplementary demands have been made and approved by this House which have not been utilised at all. I would ask him whether, in these circumstances, it is not necessary to overhaul the machinery which regulates the expenditure. I wonder if it is not possible to introduce a system of pre-audit accounting... whether it is not time for him to consider some method of what might be succinctly called Efficiency Audit.

The Honourable Finance Member or the Government had no authority whatsoever to make grants out of rural development fund without the sanction of the Finance Committee. In so far as he has done so, he has gone against the policy that was accepted by the Government and that was approved by the House and that forms past of the records of the Assembly. His grants were unconstitutional, if not illegal. I hope he will take great care hereafter to treat the Finance Committee with greater respect, I do not say with greater indulgence, as, so long as I am there. I do not want any concession, I will, however, insist on and safeguard its rights and privileges. The Honourable the Finance Member has not shown any respect for the decisions of the Finance Committee.

On March 25, 1936, Pantji through a motion to reduce Supplementary Demands in respect of "Taxes on Income", pointed out that it was one more illustration of the arbitrary, autocratic and unconstitutional ways of the present Government of India", He reiterated that under the rules government supplementary estimates, the financial proposals of the Government must be laid before the Standing Finance Committee before they were actually placed before the House. But this particular proposal had never been placed before that Committee. He observed:

> "It involves an inroad on the recognised privileges of this House. The Government have been dealing with this House in a very unconstitutional and arbitrary manner. In other cases they have gone against the principles that are involved in constitutional and representative Government, but in this particular case they have even violated the rules and the Resolutions laid down by this House and accepted by the Government and also by the Auditor-General."

The Finance Member, James Grigg intervening in the discussion admitted that "it is true this case appears to be one which ought to be put to the Standing Finance Committee in this case there has been a slip.... To that extent, my Honourable friend has a genuine grievance."

Stressing the need for showing proper respect to the Committees of Parliament, Pandit Pant observed:

> ".... I ask Honourable Members whether it is fair that, where a Committee has been formed by them, by means of election with the vote of every single Member of this House and with the additional safe guard of the single transferable vote, that the decisions of such a Committee, which seldom rejected the proposals of the Government, should be disregarded and thrown overboard. The Honourable the Finance Member tells us that it is only an Advisory Committee. Well, all Cabinets in the world are advisory bodies. All the Ministers in the House of Commons held the position of no more than advisers to the King, and here the Honourable Members on the Treasury Benches are perhaps no better than constitutional adviser to the Governor-General. If the decisions of those advisory bodies like the Cabinets or like the Ministers were upset all the world over, because they are advisory bodies, then constitutional Government would lose all its force and its significance and meaning."

The ill-treatment of Indians abroad had always been one of the issues of national agitation inside and outside the Legislature. The condition of the Indians abroad became the subject of discussion on several occasions in the Assembly. Pandit Govind Ballabh Pant moved a resolution on September 18, 1935 recommending to the Governor-General in Council to take all effective steps in the interests and to vindicate the position of Indian nationals settled in Zanzibar. After deliberations the resolution was adopted by the House, Perhaps Pantji was aware of the hardship and indignity suffered by Indians who went to foreign lands. What he then said in the Assembly seems to have remarkable validity in the present circumstances too wherever the Indians may be abroad. Pleading for the cause of Indians in Zanzibar, Pandit Pant said:

> "The migration of Indians to Zanzibar was not due to any predatory instincts, but to their response to the earnest Invitations coupled with assurances of the Sultans of Zanzibar. What I am saying is supported by historians, mainly British historians... In these

circumstances, it is atrocious that the descendants of those very people who were invited in this manner should be treated in such an invidious way with a deliberate design to squeeze them out of the islands, which is the real objective of the decrees that were introduced by the Resident of Zanzibar in June, 1934. Sir, that is one fact that I wish to impress with all the emphasis that I am capable of on the people who are now concerned in or connected with these affairs. There is another fact which I would like to impress upon the Government of India and it is this that they were active agents in sending Indians abroad to these foreign countries. It was with their active assistance, with their cooperation, at their instance and on the basis of the guarantees given by them that Indians migrated to these foreign States. In the circumstances, there is a special responsibility attaching to the Government of India and they will be guilty of breach of faith if they do not do their utmost to save Indians from this bad predicament."

In Parliament

During debates in Parliament Pantji used to listen to the various speakers very attentively and seldom made notes of what the other speakers said. He retained all these in his memory and would answer to the points made by each speaker. Once when on the debate on the Continuance of the Preventive Detention Act, a yound member denounced the Act as "even worse than the Rowlatt Act", Pantji dwelt at length on the differences between the two and added that the member had evidently been too young at the time of the Rowlatt Act to know of its provisions and the way it was implemented.

Pandit Jawaharlal Nehru with his characteristic generosity of heart often recognised with pleasure and pride the unique position which Pantji occupied as a parliamentarian in the debates in the Legislative chamber. Indeed as a parliamentarian, he had few parallels. The dexterity and skill with which he took part in parliamentary debates was remarkable. He was an excellent orator who could marshal facts most vehemently and formidably. In an easy-flowing style, without any bitterness or rancour, he could always successfully meet the arguments of his opponents. He was invincible in his arguments and this made even the Opposition to develop the highest regard and respect for him. Be it in the State Legislature or in Parliament, he was some kind of a guide to all and naturally on vital matters, he was consulted and his guidance sought as much by opposition members as by Congressmen.

Pantji had an admirably sweet style of disarming his critics by first appearing to agree with them, even showering praise on them and then gradually demolishing most devastatingly and convincingly everyone of their arguments. Defeat at the hands of this great parliamentarian was considered a privilege by his opponents.

Pantji's Home Ministership was marked for various achievements including redrawing the map of India in the light of the recommendations of the States Reorganisation Commission, in piloting the necessary legislation through the Parliament and in maintaining the unity of the country when many forces of disintegration threatened to destroy it. As a matter of fact the basis of linguistic identity for the formation of States was the pioneering idea promoted by Pandit Pant.

When Pantji piloted the most controversial piece of legislation that had ever come before Parliament—the States Reorganisation Bill there was stormy debate in Parliament and the Bill was fiercely attacked by many members of the House from divergent points of view right from the introduction stage to its final adoption. On each such occasion, Pantji delivered his speech in his characteristic style, unruffled, calm and quiet, and put forward the Government's case with matchless effectiveness.

At the introduction stage, the Bill was opposed by a Member of Opposition on the ground that the Travancore-Cochin Legislature (dissolved with the imposition of President's rule in that State) had not been consulted. Dealing with the objection, Pandit Pant maintaining that it had no validity in law, observed that "when the President's proclamation taking over the administration of Travancore-Cochin was issued, the proviso to article 3 of the Constitution which required a reference to be made to the State concerned was, I think, suspended. Apart from that, the powers of the Legislature then vested in Parliament, therefore, could deal with all matters which would otherwise have come within the purview of the State Legislatures. There could be no exception in the case of the reorganisation of States". He further added:

> "Suppose a State cannot possibly function under circumstances which are beyond the control of anybody when we, all of us, may be unanimous about the incapacity and inability of the State to function under particular circumstances and the remedy may lie in adjusting the boundaries, then certainly it will be open to Parliament to exercise the authority vested in it for changing the boundaries. Besides, literally speaking, the Bill was referred to the Travancore-Cochin Government and Legislature on the 16th of last month when it was functioning. So 30 days have passed since it was referred. Whatever might be the causes which have stood in the way of submitting its views to us, it does not in any way affect the legal position. The provisions of Article 3 have been carried out. Even if that Article was 'alive' even if those objections were still binding, nobody can raise an objection on the ground that there had been no compliance with the provisions of that Article."

On April 26, 1956, replying to the three-day debate on a motion of reference of the Bill to a Joint Committee, Pandit Pant said that most of the controversy had centred round the city of Bombay:

> "If you leave aside that problem of Bombay, which has become almost baffling and to which the solutions proposed so far have not appeared at least to some of the members and to certain sections of oar people as satisfactory and conducive, that question of Bombay still continues to loom large. But if for the time being, we put it out of the way, then we find that the proposals contained in the Bill have the general support of this House."

Referring to the observation that it would have been safer that the Government had adhered mechanically to the recommendations of the States Reorganisation Commission, he said: "I stand for it, but not at the cost of public weal and the general good of the people". Justifying the departures made from the Commission's recommendations, he said that he had expressed his view more than once about the Commission's proposal for a bilingual State of Bombay. But, friends from Maharashtra not only did not like that proposal but would not look at it. They had almost an unbounded aversion for it In the circumstances, to impose it and to stick to it would have been hardly wise, useful or helpful. That had to be discarded. It was replaced by the suggestions for the formation of the State of Maharashtra with Vidarbha, the State of Gujarat and Centrally-administered Bombay.

Pantji therefore, added:

> "We would have been glad if we had succeeded in having a bigger bilingual Stale of Bombay and Maharashtra and Gujarat That would have fulfilled the dream of some of the visionaries. Besides, it would have brought the day of fruition and fulfilment nearer in other States also, but so far we have not succeeded."

When the debate came to an end and It was necessary to give a reply on behalf of the Government, Pandit Nehru intervened just to pay tribute to Pantji. This is what he said:

> "I am intervening chiefly because, if I may be quite frank with this House, I do not want my colleague to speak again. As many members of this House might know he delivered a great and noble speech yesterday in the Lok Sabha. But, perhaps everybody does not know that during these days when he had been in charge of these two debates, apart from other heavy burdens he carries, he has been acutely unwell and in great pain. Nevertheless, in spite of these, he has discharged this heavy burden with the great ability that he possesses. Obviously I cannot discharge this business of speaking towards the end of this debate with that facility or knowledge that he possesses."

Another memorable occasion was the debate on the famous "Mundhra affair" in Parliament which led to the resignation of the Finance Minister T.T. Krishnamachari Pantji's stand was clear; T.T. Krishnamachari's resignation was in the highest parliamentary tradition of ministerial responsibility. In one of the profoundest statements he upheld T.T. Krishnamachari's decision "while cleansing it of any innuendo of wrong doing." He said in the Rajya Sabha:

> "I should think that except where a Minister is not concerned in any way with an act or with an omission which reflects on the administration he should assume responsibility. The field of responsibility should be larger. Responsibility should be interpreted not in strict but in liberal terms. Especially when we are starting on this period of parliamentary administration and are trying to build parliamentary system it is necessary that the Ministers should assume responsibility, except where it is obvious that they are not, *in* any way, answerable directly or indirectly."

6

A Constitution Maker

Expert on Constitutional Matters

Pandit Govind Ballabh Pant was essentially a man of learning and fully knew the value of constitutionalism. It is often said that those who are very much engrossed in constitutional technicalities and intricacies lose the revolutionary fervour and develop a dislike for any kind of struggle. But this was not tree of Pantji. There was hardly any instance when he did not participate in a movement or opposed it. He gave all importance to constitutionalism but he was fully aware of the fact that at times it became meaningless and a revolutionary programme was the only choice. It was always a delightful experience to see him unravel the constitutional intricacies and overwhelm his opponent with brilliant arguments and advocacy. When the Congress accepted office in the provinces in 1937, under the Government of India Act; 1935, he came to be looked upon even by the British as one who believed firmly in constitutional methods and who held an abiding faith in the parliamentary system.

Right from the beginning of his legislative career Pantji used to take keen interest in debates on constitutional matters. This Interest was later to pot him among the founding fathers of the Constitution of independent India.

Demand for Constituent Assembly

Pandit Pant had daring his premiership got introduced in the U.P. Legislative Assembly a resolution demanding setting up of a Constituent Assembly for India. The resolution moved by Smt. Vijay Laxmi Pandit, Minister for Local Self-Government was adopted by the House. Winding up the discussion on the resolution, the Premier in the course of an elaborate speech said that when they asked for a Constituent Assembly, they asked only for the practical application and adoption of the principle of self-determination. Referring to the fear of a revolution taking place in connection with the Constituent Assembly he pointed out that so far as the Congress, the attitude of the people of India, and the native genius of their country were concerned, it did not involve idea of violence or bloodshed.

Important Role

As a member of the Constituent Assembly, Pandit Pant played an important role in the formulation of the Constitution and guided its course on some very vital subjects. He was a member of its various important Committees and Sub-Committees - Advisory Committee on Fundamental Rights and Minorities, Union Constitution Committee, Minorities Sub-Committee and Sub-Committee to report on the position of Anglo-Indians in certain services. Pantji also appeared to have become "the unofficial spokesman of the provincial premiers in the Assembly". His contribution to the framing of the federal provisions and to a lesser extent in the language and due process controversies was substantial.

On January 24, 1947, Pandit Pant moved an important resolution about the Constitution of "Advisory Committee on Fundamental Rights and Minorities". After giving factual narration, analysis and a certain degree of elucidation of the resolution Pandit Pant with his natural eloquence pleaded in a moving speech that the importance of fundamental rights on the proper application of which depended the "progress of humanity" could be better understood and appreciated, if one realised the importance and the sanctity of the individual citizen. "It is the citizen", he said, "that forms *the* base as well as the summit of the social pyramid and his importance, his dignity and his sanctity, should always be remembered. If you bear this in mind. I think we should understand and appreciate the importance of Fundamental Rights." Deploring the morbid tendency of undermining the individual in the context of community, he observed:

> "The individual citizen who is really the backbone of the State, the pivot, the cardinal centre of all social activity, and whose happiness and satisfaction should be the goal of every social mechanism, has been lost here in that indiscriminate body known as the community.. We have even forgotten that citizen exists as such. There is the unwholesome and to some extent a degrading habit of thinking always in terms of communities and never in terms of citizens."

He was equally conscious that in large measures of social reform, it was the welfare of the entire State and the entire community that had to be borne in mind, and he laid special emphasis on this in dealing with his first-hand knowledge of the functioning of the Zamindari system in Uttar Pradesh. He was fully aware how the landed gentry exploited the actual tiller of the soil for their personal benefit.

Pandit Pant dwelt upon the question of minorities and said "this question everywhere looms large in constitutional discussions and many a Constitution has foundered on this rock." Referring to the position then obtaining in India he said:

> "It has been used so far for creating strife, distrust and cleavage between the different sections of the Indian nation. Imperialism thrives on such strifes. It is interested in fomenting such tendencies. So far, the minorities have been incited and have been influenced in a manner which has hampered the growth of cohesion and unity."

Statesman-like Posture

In a statesman-like posture he urged that it was necessary that a new chapter should start and "we should all realise our responsibility. Unless the minorities are fully satisfied, we cannot make any progress; we cannot make peace in an undisturbed manner". He hoped that a satisfactory solution of the question pertaining to the minorities would ensure the health, vitality and strength of the free state of India that would come into existence as a result of discussions in the Constituent Assembly.

When the Constituent Assembly met in December, 1946, the Muslim League had boycotted it and did not send any representatives to it The prevalent feeling among the members present in the Assembly was however that notwithstanding their absence, the Assembly and its Committees should proceed with their respective tasks ensuring at the same time that the Muslim League was also given the fullest opportunity effectively to participate in the framing of the Constitution should it decide at any stage to join the Assembly and its committees. There was also the further anxiety to ensure that the Advisory Committee should be so constituted as to ensure full discussion of the claims of all minorities, irrespective of their numerical strength.

Keeping these objects in view the resolution for the Constitution of the Committee was moved by Pantji explaining that each of the minorities had been consulted and had agreed to the composition of the Committee. He added:

> "The voice of the minorities and the representatives of the excluded and tribal areas will preponderate in this committee. They will be in a position to record their decisions and no section will be in a majority. So this committee will fully reflect the opinion of the minorities and the backward tracts and will, I hope, be able to reach decisions which will fully secure their position and *ensure* the protection of their rights."

When B. Pocker, a Muslim League member from South India, moved an amendment in the Assembly for continuing separate electorates for the Muslim community, with the support of Khaliquzzaman, Pantji strongly opposed the proposal as suicidal for the minorities themselves. He warned them:

> "If you have separate electorates for the minorities, the inevitable. C.A. Debates, result is that the majority becomes isolated from the minorities, and being thus

> cut off from the minorities, it can ride roughshod upon them."

In the Advisory Committee, Pandit Pant in the face of persistent demand for reservation of seats for the Anglo-Indian community succeeded in getting the following motion relating to the representation of Anglo-Indian community in the Union Parliament and State Legislatures unanimously adopted:

> "There shall be no reservation of seats for the Anglo-Indians, but the President of the Union or the Governor of the State shall have power to nominate representatives of the minorities in the Centre and in the Provinces, if they fail to secure representation in the Legislatures as a result of the General election."

During the discussions in a meeting of the Advisory Committee on Fundamental Rights, and Minorities, Pantji dwelling on the nature of fundamental rights observed:

> "I want the committee to be clear about certain fundamental matters while dealing with these fundamental rights. We are in a way framing *smrithis* that every commentator will thereafter try to get over by introducing some sort of subterfuge or other. It is only to put up some sort of impediment in the way of the advancing tide of public opinion, which you cannot possibly in any way circumvent or guard against. Whatever precautions you introduce are bound to be blown away. Only you make things more difficult. In framing these fundamental rights, you must try to make them clear and simple and not try to put something in one sentence and then to follow it with three provisions which will only make the whole thing unworkable."

On 'Due Process' Clause: On 21 April, the Advisory Committee considered the "due process" clause. Early in the discussion Pandit Pant giving his opinion said that due process would be understood only in a procedural sense. When he was contradicted by Alladi Krishnaswami Ayyar, Pantji firing a volley of questions asked: Will it be open to the legislature under this to empower the executive authority to detain a person for, say, under six months without any trial being held in any court? Will it be open under this clause for any legislature to pass a law that certain property will be acquired for public purposes for ten times its rental value while the market value is 30 times? Will it be open to the court under this clause to hold that a person who is entitled to eject a tenant at will not be allowed to do so hereafter? He concluded:

> "It comes to this. The future of this country is to be determined not by the collective wisdom of the representatives of the people, but by the fiats of those elevated to the judiciary. If this is the case, then I strongly oppose it. The words 'due process of law' should be altered. The language should be foolproof so that every judge may be expected to give the same sort of ruling. We should not put in words which give rise to controversies... To fetter the discretion of the legislature would lead to anarchy. It will lead to a great deal of trouble. Do you agree that in your province people who are creating all sorts of troubles should be tried in a court before they are prevented from committing mischief which leads to communal disorders? If you insist on that, there is no end to these communal disorders. I do not want words to be *used* here which will be the subject of controversy, and which will place the fate of the people of this country on the whims and vagaries of the judges. Your language should be foolproof. If you intend that there should be no detention, it should be clear."

In the end, Pantji warned:

> "We are leaving the fate of the country in the hands of the lawyers who will be raised to the bench and they will have to interpret this law. We should not make it possible for them to interpret it in different ways. We must have foolproof language, if I may say so. We must be quite clear in our minds what we intend to have. It is not good to somehow skip over this point. As its now is, it seems to be wisdom proof,

> that is what it looks like. In our province we are contemplating the abolition of zamindaries and it *is* just possible that there may be a law to the effect that the bigger zamindars may be paid compensation at the rate of ten times their annual value and the smaller ones at forty times. These zamindars may go to the court and say that payment must be on the basis of the market rate and the law may hang on for seven years for the Supreme Court to give a decision. We do not want such a thing to happen. If you say that zamindaries should not be abolished, that private rights should not be touched, I can understand that. But to put in a law which can be interpreted by different people in different ways is to stop all social progress. It is unfair not for a day or two but for generations. I would certainly oppose such a thing and I would expect the House to support me. To allow the court to sit in judgement over the legislature itself and to say that a law will not be valid unless it is declared to be so by a single individual sitting in the Supreme Court is extremely risky and I cannot subscribe to that proposition.

Due Process and Property: On 22 April the Advisory Committee took up the Rights Sub-Committee's draft clause that property could be acquired for public use only on the payment of just compensation—'just' being the word that clearly left the provision open to judicial interpretation. Opening the meeting, Pantji asked if 'public use' meant tenancy legislation. He later said: "Suppose the Government acquires zamindari rights and then abolishes them. Or what if the Government takes over Connaught Place (the central shopping and office area of New Delhi) and then redistributes the buildings to the tenants? The first stage is acquisition. Does that come under this clause?" He opposed the wording if it meant that the Government would not be free to determine the compensation it would have to pay. Expressing his belief that if this covered acquisition for social purposes, "then I submit payment of compensation should not even be compulsory" And, through an amendment he wanted to leave "the mode and manner of compensation entirely to the discretion of the legislatures concerned" which evoked some controversy. It raised the issue not only of the reasonableness of compensation but also a federal question: Should the states of the new India have unfettered discretion over all forms of expropriation? And if such was to be the case, was there, indeed, any reason to include the right to property among the Fundamental Rights? Pantji was however, aiming at zamindars, and, particularly, he must have been trying *to* create a situation in which his own pet anti-zamindari Bill in the United Provinces Legislature could not be tampered with by the Union Government.

On Acquisition of Property: When the draft article pertaining to payment of compensation for acquisition of private property was taken up by the Constituent Assembly, Pantji made a strong plea in defence of clause (4) and the United Provinces Zamindari Abolition and Land Reforms Bill which that article was designed to save from being challenged on the ground of contravention of clause (2). Although the U.P. Bill did in fact provide for equitable compensation to the zamindars, it became necessary to have clause (4) because of what he called the last for litigation of the zamindars and taluqdars. He added, however, that "equity" or "equitable compensation" could not be defined in terms of any yardstick and what was equitable could be determined only in the light of all the relevant factors. Thus, in the case of a large measure of social reforms it was the welfare of the entire State and the entire community that had to be borne in mind.

Further, in an obvious reference to clause (2) and criticisms directed against that clause, Pantji saw absolutely no reason why the article should give the investors any cause for misgivings when they had no such apprehensions with regard to section 299 of the Government of India Act of 1935. The provisions of the article went much further than section 299 in protecting the interests of property-holders; section 299 dealt only with compulsory acquisition of property, while the protection given by the article extended not only to "compulsory acquisition" but also to "taking into possession" of property for public purposes.

On the issue as to whether or to what *extent* compensation under clause (2) was a justiciable matter. Pantji agreed with Alladi

Krishnaswami Ayyar's view that the principles of compensation laid down by the Legislature would be invulnerable in any court unless they amounted to a fraud on the Constitution. Replying to the socialists objection to the article, he pointed out that they had also agreed that there should be no acquisition without compensation,, and that the quantum of compensation would be decided by the Legislature with due regard to the purpose for which the property was acquired and the circumstances in which it was acquired.

On Elections as Fundamental Rights: In a meeting of the Advisory Committee difference of opinion cropped up on whether the provisions relating to adult suffrage, free elections and secrecy of voting should be included in the Constitution as a fundamental right While C. Rajagopalachari argued that it would not be proper to do so, Dr. Ambedkar expressed his fear that If the Committee's report went to the Constituent Assembly without including in It this fundamental right, it might be later argued that this particular right was either condemned or was not approved by the Committee. Pantji then observed:

> "Will it not serve your purpose if this very clause Is sent to the Constituent Assembly, not as part of these fundamental rights, but included in the letter of the Chairman to the effect that we recommend to the Constituent Assembly the following principles in regard to the framing of the Constitution, keeping the text as it is?... The only apprehension is that some people belonging to the States may prick the bubble and say that their rights have been interfered with and so on. They may not be represented. We will have what we desire."

Eventually, the compromise solution suggested by Pantji was adopted and it was decided that the recommendations need not go as part of the clauses on fundamental rights; but that in the letter forwarding the report of the Advisory Committee the Chairman should it clear that the committee recommended the adoption of those proposals.

On Forced Labour: When the clause providing for compulsory military training was taken up by the Subcommittee on Fundamental Rights, there was opposition to the move. Its report simply permitted "compulsory service under any general scheme of education." Not satisfied, the Advisory Committee thereupon appointed several subcommittees to scrutinise it One of them comprising Pantji, C. Rajagopalachari and Mrs. Hansa Mehta redrafted the provision reversing the stand of the subcommittee. The new wording provided that nothing in the forced labour clause should "prevent *the* State from imposing compulsory service for public purposes" - essentially the form in which the provision appeared in the Constitution."

On Secrecy of Correspondence: One of the rights deleted by the Advisory Committee from the list submitted by the Sub-Committee was one providing for secrecy of correspondence and for security of person and dwellings from unreasonable searches and seizures. K.M. Panikkar, A.K. Ayyar, C. Rajagopalachari, B.N. Rau and Patel led by Pandit Pant opposed the inclusion of this right on the plea that providing for the secrecy of correspondence might aid spies and criminals which would impair the working of the Indian Evidence Act, 1872. They feared the clause to be dangerous and helpful to no one but lawyers.

On Official Language: The question of official language naturally evoked considerable controversy in the Assembly and various amendments were proposed -some proposing Hindustani and the Devanagri and Persian scripts, while others laying down different transitional periods. Outside the Assembly also discussions and consultations continued within the Congress Party at various levels to arrive at a solution acceptable to all shades of opinion. While Hindi had been generally accepted, the main point of controversy centred round the length of the transitional period and the continuance of English with the full status of an official language during that period. Pandit Pant then made the remarkable suggestion. He said that the question of prescribing a time limit for doing away with English should be left to the verdict of the non-Hindi speaking people. And, it was this very assurance which found expression through Nehru in Parliament in 1963 and which continues to this day as a sacrosanct testament.

On Linguistic Minorities: Intervening in the discussion on the question of fundamental rights of the linguistic minorities insofar as primary education was concerned, Pantji emphasised that primary education, in the event of its being made universal, would cost heavily and it was necessary that the maximum possible use was made of the limited resources available and as a first step attempts made to extend primary education to the vast numbers of illiterate persons in the country. He said:

> "If every school should have two or three sets of teachers... we would not be able to introduce universal primary education - not to talk of compulsory primary education - till doomsday."

Pantji emphatically deprecated the tendency to link the question of the language or the medium of instruction at the primary stage with the different communities and asserted that there was no particular language attached to the followers of any particular religion. It would never be a communal or a minority problem. As for the facilities for primary education through the mother tongue of any particular section of the people, he pointed out that adequate arrangements would be made for the purpose at all places where students were available in a substantial number.

On Federal Set-up: Pandit Pane was a vigorous advocate of full autonomy for the States with the spheres allowed to them under the Constitution. However, at the same time, he held the definite view that there should be a strong federal Centre capable of maintaining unimpaired the unity and integrity of the country. Realising the States' primary responsibility for providing social services in the widest possible measure he supported their case for generation of adequate resources through the powers vested *in* them. On basic issues concerning the powers of the States, he would not admit of any compromise. He was outspoken in regard to the suggestion for putting health and *education in the* Concurrent List. He pointed out that if the object was to have a federal set-up and the concept of "provincial autonomy" was to have any validity, the Stales most have exclusive control over certain subjects and at least over such "elementary matters" as health and education which affected the everyday life of the citizens. The question of distribution of powers between the Union and the States gave rise to some keen controversy as some Provincial Governments favoured changes in the allocation of powers in such a manner as to secure increased powers for the States. The Drafting Committee thereupon considered It proper that it should consult the Provincial Governments as also the governments of some of the Indian States on matters which affected Union - State relationship, *under* the new Constitution. Accordingly, a conference of the Premiers and Finance Ministers of the Provinces and of some of the Indian States was convened in July, 1947, and at this conference various issues relating to the distribution of revenue between the Centre and the States, the assumption of plenary powers by the Union in circumstances of emergency, the suggestions made in regard to the legislative lists and oilier cognate matters were discussed.

Meanwhile, some of the changes suggested gave rise to keen controversy. An amendment had been suggested by the Ministry of Education, which sought to add to the Union List a new entry dealing with supervisory control of post-secondary educational, scientific and technical institutions for the purpose of coordination and maintenance of standards. Pandit Govind Ballabh Pant, the United Provinces Premier, urged that it was not a sound proposition to empower the Centre to prescribe the standards of higher education and to place on the units the responsibility of meeting the necessary expenditure. But opinion generally was in favour of letting the Centre have a say in regard to the coordination and maintenance of standards of higher education. Nehru pleaded forcefully that some such provision was indispensable to check the growing tendency towards a lowering of the standards of university education which was already discernible in certain parts of the country. The Mysore Premier (K.C. Reddy) felt that the proposed provision was unexceptionable but for the use of the words "supervisory control" which might lead to the impression that the provision was intended to include "administration" also and not merely the maintenance of standards. Ultimately, it was agreed to recast the entry as "Coordination and maintenance of standards of higher educational, scientific and technical institutions".

A more keenly debated subject was whether, as suggested by the Ministry of Industry and Supply, a new entry relating to trade and commerce in, and the production, supply and distribution of, any goods the control of which by the Union was declared by Parliament to be expedient in the public interest, should be added in the Union List Opposing the suggestion, Pandit Pant emphasised that distribution, trade and commerce were in form and practice mostly controlled by the Provinces and that it would be unworkable to leave all these matters to the exclusive control of the Centre. The Premier of the Central Provinces (Ravi Shankar Shukla) also questioned the need for the provision. Eventually, in view of the opposition it was agreed to place the proposed entry in the Concurrent List.

Then there was an amendment, jointly sponsored by the Ministries of Health and Home Affairs which aimed at taking away "Public health and sanitation" from the State List (entry 15) and placing this matter along with "Vital statistics including registration of births and deaths" in the Concurrent List. The proposal sparked off a heated controversy in which many Central Ministers and Premiers of Provinces participated. Commending the amendment, Munshi said that Central legislation on the subject of public health and sanitation would be necessary to prevent the spread of diseases from one Province to another and also for the purpose of setting up common standards. Further, with the obvious object of making the change more acceptable to the representatives of the Provinces and the Indian States, both he and Ambedkar stressed the fact that Central legislation on a concurrent subject would not normally - that is, unless Parliament expressly reserved the administrative power to the Centre - take away from the units the right to administer the subject. Most of the Premiers were firmly opposed to the proposal. Pantji, a zealous champion of the provinces, said that public health and sanitation had always been exclusively the charge of the Provinces, Moreover, as these subjects were dealt with mostly by local bodies, transferring them to the Concurrent List would mean that the Provincial Governments would be subject to the control of the Centre even in matters which were purely of a regional nature. He complained that from the way the question of distribution of powers was being approached, the States would have under the Constitution less power than municipal boards. He could have no objection to such a course being adopted, if the country as a whole was to be treated more or less as centrally administered area and the State Governments were to be just agencies for administering Central laws. He warned that including everything in the Concurrent List would not only increase occasions for friction between the Union and the States - especially, if, as was quite likely in the future, the State Governments were not of the same political complexion as the Government at the Centre - but would also greatly impair the sense of responsibility of the State administrations.

These arguments however, failed to carry conviction with Nehru who supported the change proposed by the Central Ministries of Home Affairs and Health. He said that disease was not a local thing. In fact, it was being tackled increasingly at an international level and becoming progressively subject to international regulations. It was Pantji's contention that each State should be free to agree or not to agree to international regulation. Still unconvinced, he replied that international regulations presented no insuperable difficulty and could be dealt with effectively by mutual consultations between the Central and State Governments. In any case, the little advantage that might be gained by transferring the subject to the Concurrent List would be far outweighed by the disadvantages he had pointed out. Ultimately Pantji's views were vindicated.

Thus Pantji played a very significant role as one of the founding fathers of India's Constitution and his contributions will live and guide the people of India for many many years.

7

Character and Personality

Many Faceted Personality

Pantji's was really a many-splendoured personality. He was a great humanist, lawyer, legislator, organiser, constitutionalist and administrator. His eminent role and contribution in all these facets shall always be remembered by a grateful nation. In whatever capacity he functioned, whether as a soldier in India's march towards freedom, or in the legislature, or in government, his sole objective was the good of India and the well-being of her people. In fact Pant the man and Pant the politician were so intermingled and complexly inter-twined that either one loved this person and his politics both or he must disown him altogether and in every respect But as Paripurnanand Verma has said, "I have yet to meet a sane person, who can, with conscientious arrogance, refuse to love, admire or embellish the sweet, suave, genial Pantji." He inspired confidence in his colleagues in the party and enjoyed respect of his opponents.

The Secretariat Pandits found in him a super-pundit and admitted his high calibre. The legislators found him more skilful than any in their ranks. Congress workers found it a pleasure to work under the direction of one who could not be deflected from the path of duty.

One thing which greatly impressed Pantji's admirers was his love for the poor. He was essentially a people's man; the tiller of the soil and the worker in the factories had in him a warm friend. He was a 'Messiah of Harijans'. He took an active part in the Harijan uplift movement launched by Gandhiji in 1930. It was at his initiative that a social reform conference for eradication of untouchability was convened in Almora as early as 1932 which was attended by almost all the prominent leaders and social reformers of the Kumaon division. The conference after discussing the problem threadbare for ten days ultimately called upon all the participants to visit Harijan bastis and accept drinking water offered by the Harijans in order to inculcate *in* them the feeling of oneness and promote emotional integration with other sections of society. The decision was implemented the next day when a group of about 100 Brahmins, Kshatriyas and Vaishyas went to a Harijan colony and took water from the village 'Naula'. It was indeed a historic event in Almora's public life. Then the two notable steps, taken under his stewardship as Chief Minister of U.P., *viz.* abolition of zamindari and inauguration of panchayati raj were aimed at raising the living standards of the oppressed and the weaker sections.

Pantji never confused party politics with patriotism. Men of all parties—whether in the ruling party or in the Opposition - found in him a perfect gentleman, a helpful politician and a picture of dignity. He worked hard in life and work alone was his rest and relaxation. He was thorough and precise and had a supreme knack of choosing the right men for the jobs he wanted to be done. He combined in him the best of the ancient and the modern. He was a forward looking man and had respect for all religions. His nobility of mind and sweetness of temper charmed his friends and foes alike. In the words of the veteran Parliamentarian Prof. N.G. Ranga, "Bhisma of Kurus was one such statesman, as pictured by Veda Vyas through that great epic of the Mahabharata, and it is only with very rare exceptions like Kautilya of Charidragupta and Timmarasu of Krishnadevaraya, that Indian history has witnessed his likes".

The country benefited immensely by the sagacity, wisdom and self-sacrifice of such a person. Chalapathy Rau also writing in the same vein puts it in these words:

"The qualities which made him an asset to the nation, to the Congress, to the administration, and to Nehru were widely known; wide comprehension, correct judgement of men and matters, tolerance that did not recognise *narrow* division, patience that was monumental, sagacity, imperturbability, tact, firmness, mastery of detail dexterity in debate and an unfailing sense of humour."

A remarkable portrayal of Pantji's personality was done by Pattabhi Sitaramayya when both of them were imprisoned *in* the Ahmednagar fort in 1942 alongwith other eminent leaders like Nehru and Azad, after arrest in the wake of the Quit India Movement. He then wrote:

"Pant's towering personality is quite familiar to the Indian public. He is a statuesque figure in intellect as in stature. His studious habits belie any report of ill-health. His intellect is as keen as his memory is retentive. As things are *in* the world, flashy intelligence and shallow minds generally go together in life while the quality of thoroughness is generally associated with dullness of undemanding and slowness of cerebration. Pant is a complete exception to this rule. He is quick of perception, sharp in debate, and thorough in understanding. His presentation of resolutions at Congress sessions has always been remarkably alive for lucidity and eloquence white his balanced mind and self-confident temperament give him an advantage rarely possessed by Congress speakers. It is the habit of the legal profession which serves the politician in good stead to be able to think while on legs, and therefore, more easily while seated, to develop a theme in all its vividness and carry conviction to the judges and the audience. Pain's interests are as varied as his talents are versatile. He can hold a conversation on the latest development in medicine and science, while he can enliven a talk on Socrates or Voltaire. The gift of side reading is possessed by many, bet many shuffle it off like the

> horse and few chew to the end like the cow. Dharma and Manana are the two great assets of a successful scholar according to Indian psychology and these Pant possesses in abundance. He is fastidious in his tastes, has a meticulous sense of cleanliness as well as neatness, is assertive in temperament and sustained in debate. No wonder that he had been selected to lead the ministry in U.P.

The great historian, Dr. Ishwari Prasad very aptly summed up the personality of Pantji in the following words:

> "More than a parliamentarian, more than a statesman, more than a councillor, and more than a minister, he shines as a man. As a man he is greater than anybody else. Sweet and reasonable, amiable in temper he is always accessible. You may go to him at any time. He is always full of the milk of human kindness. He is always good, he is always gentle; he is always generous."

The country's highest honour "Bharat Ratna" was conferred on Pandit Pant on 26 January, 1957.

A Great Humanist

Dr. Radhakrishnan had once said, Pantji "was human, humane and always anxious to find fault with himself more than with others". He possessed a wonderful understanding of the human mind and knew man's weaknesses and their strong points. His letters to his children from the Ahmednagar jail indicate how intensely human he was. He had tremendous patience and never easily lost his balance. His one great virtue was his poise; his absolute freedom from worry; and the sense of comfort and repose he always seemed to have - however trying the circumstances and however heavy the work may be. And all who came in touch with him were bound to be impressed by this trait of his character. Once one of his friends from the hills and a relation went to meet him. He happened to be terribly angry with Pantji over some matters and denounced him for quite some time. Pantji listened to him patiently and when the man stopped, he quietly enquired, "Is it all or anything more?" The man was aghast at Pantji's sweet and sympathetic tone and left the place much impressed. Later he told his friends, "How can you fight such a man who under severe provocation does not say even one harsh word to you?"

Pandit Pant was a religious person in private life but he was a great liberal or even radical in political ideology. He was neither rightist nor leftist but a straight forward humanist. His ideology revolved round 'human dignity'. He would revolt against anything that went against human dignity. Thus, the zamindari system, prostitution, intoxication and traffic in minor girls became the targets of his anguish and anger and he raised his voice for their abolition or reform right from the beginning of his legislative career or even earlier.

Pantji's hospitality was proverbial; he entertained the biggest and the smallest ones at his house with equal warmth and politeness. P.D. Tandon relates an incident when Pantji invited the President of India, the Governor of U.P. and members of the Council of Ministers of U.P. besides others for lunch at his residence in Nainital. Obviously the party consisted largely of eminent persons, but there were a few small fry too. But remarkably Pantji took more care of the ordinary guests than of the bigwigs for he felt that the former were feeling a little embarrassed in that distinguished gathering. It was this warmth of his heart and his charming manners that endeared him to the people. His depth and nobility of character, as well as his capacity for patience and tolerance made profound impression on whoever met him. His immeasurable restraint was more striking than his other qualities.

Like Pandit Nehru, Maulana Azad and Sardar Patel, Pantji was heads and shoulders above many of his contemporaries who themselves belonged to a unique galaxy of great men - each one fit to lead a nation. Apart from all his work and achievements in public life, Pantji was known for his intensely humane qualities which endeared him to every Indian. As Pandit Jawaharlal Nehru said:

> "Govind Ballabh Pant is a big man, tall and heavy of body and slow of movement. He is a son of our mountains and carries something of their imperturbability about him. I had sometimes seen him irritated and angry, *but* I have never seen him

lose his temper. He and I had shared together lathi blows of the police in 1928 and we had also had adjoining cells in prison. A man of outstanding ability, he was the obvious leader of the Congress Party in our province. It was an aggressive party, more so than in any other province, and not easy to manage. But by his unfailing good humour and tact and his amazing patience, he surmounted every obstacle and was liked even by his critics and opponents. He is not a revolutionary type and his whole bent is towards constitutional activity. But, like so many others in India, circumstances have compelled him to other causes- The chief criticism made of him, has been that he is too good, too soft He is indeed the perfect gentleman.".

Yes, Nehruji was unquestionably right It was these qualities of leadership and tremendous human dimension of Pantji's personality which gave a distinctiveness to his government and to politics in U.P. during his Chief Ministership and to the office of Home Minister he held at the Centre till his death.

Great Advocate of Democracy

He was a great advocate of democracy. Never was a man in the history of government, more amenable to argument, more ready to adjust and always open to man in the history of government, more amenable to argument, more ready to adjust, and always open to conviction.

To him democracy was not the rule of the majority or of the minority but the rule of the right. His heart was the largest and his mind was the widest. He emphasised on right means. He never hesitates to adopt the right course and was always ready to make adjustments at the last moment. Temperamentally he was an idealist. By training he was a lawyer. So balanced was his mind; so serene was his nature; and so vivid and lasting was his memory.

He had correct appreciation of the coming events. He had rightly been described as an ambassador of peace. He had prevented quarrels. He was a powerful unifying force. During some of the most acrimonious debates at Congress sessions he was entrusted with the task of bringing about settlement between various groups and persons in the welter of different points of view. Gandhiji used him as a fire brigade to extinguish the fire of party politics and bitter controversies. Several times he was asked by Pandit Nehru for settling disputes of wide divergencies.

No statesman possessed such power to reconcile the irreconcible and unite divergent interests as Pandit Pant. He was impatiently patient and has capacity to handle delicate and complicated issues. He had successfully mediated between conflicting claims. With equal acumen he perceived the opponents weakness and confronts contradictions. He had the eye of a hawk. In a most charming way he would ask a most deadly question with an agreeable smile. He was an assiduous fact finder and had searching analytical faculty. He was anxious to know all sides of every question. He was a good listener. Nothing would ruffle him, no one might provoke him, not even the attacks often vitriolic. He would squeeze every bit of information he wanted from a casual visitor by his searching questions. He would try to find common ground rather than points of disagreements.

He had placed too high a value on party unity. He conciliated the views of the different sections of the party with admirable success and thus kept together the discontented elements. He had shown exemplary tolerance in his conduct of public business and private dealings. If Uttar Pradesh had a smooth sailing in spite of divergent views, it was because Pandit Pant was able to hold together the discordant elements for such a long period.

Thus commented the National Herald:

> "The U.P. Premier (Pandit Pant) is a supreme smoother. Nobody else could have met effrontery with such conciliation, and petty bickerings with such understanding." (24 May, '47).

He possessed an unrivalled talent in balancing opposites inside the party or the administration. "The whole art of statesmanship," wrote Woodrow Wilson, "is the art of bringing several parts of government into effective cooperation for the accomplishment of common objects."

Pandit Pant was a supremely gifted politician. Politics could not properly be regarded as a branch of virtuous conduct. The prime motive of the politician was not to do good to humanity but simply to gain power for himself. It was a game of intrigues and manoeuvres. Men climb to the topmost place in politics on the bodies of their comrades and friends. Pandit Pant practised purity in politics. He believed that humanity was greater than politics. He abhorred such politics which was based on intrigue. He believed what Disraeli said that the world was never conquered by intrigue, it was conquered by faith. He had full faith in himself, in his powers of persuation and advocacy. He would go alone to an adverse, excited assembly and would convert it to his views singly. His direst political opponents and critics had admitted with great admiration that he never employed such ignoble methods against any one even in thought.

He had elevated political life to a higher plane, to a loftier standard. He was upright in his dealings. He combined the moral qualities of a statesman with the intellectual qualities of a politician. His success in Indian politics was due mainly to his high character, superb courage and virtuous conduct. He realised rightly that politics ought to be adjusted not to human reasoning alone but to human nature also. Personal relationship, which was the source of his strength, was one of the most potent single factors for his success. His greatness was that he was intensely human. The essence of his power was personal. He was most generous and forgiving about human weakness. It was difficult to wield power with equity and equimanity. It was a great tribute to him that he had wielded immense power and he had not abused it. Throughout his long public career one thing had struck us greatly. He never used unfair, untruthful means and he considered himself a trustee of public funds. In England, which was a home of parliamentary democracy the Prime Ministers were reported to possess huge funds and patronage at their disposal to use them to remain in power. Sir Edward Cook, the biographer of "Delane of the Times" referring to the tendencies observed in politicians wrote:

> "When men have first seated themselves on the Treasury Benches, the attachment *to* power grows so strong that almost everything is sacrificed to the cravings of its almost irresistable passion."

For all intents and purposes Pt. Pant was a socialist; though he did not pretend to be so. In its benign form, socialism was less dogma than habit of mind. His approach, his outlook of mind, his philosophy of life are socialistic. He felt that the capitalist system had failed to utilise and organise natural resources for the benefit of the masses. He believed in the democratic socialist state, which would ensure social justice for all. Millions of our people were steeped in poverty and ignorance. His emphasis in the present stage of the country's economic development was on full production, to raise the standard of living of the masses and to abolish poverty. By abolishing Zamindari he had achieved agrarian socialism by bloodless revolution. This was his great contribution to enable the vast masses of farmers and peasants to lead a better life, to develop a true sense of social responsibility and to regain the lost sense of community spirit without which democracy, whether political or economic, cannot blossom fully.

He was irrepressible optimist and even in times when horizon appeared to be black, he saw a ray of hope. He saw things far ahead. When he was released in 1945 after three years detention there was much frustration and despair in the country. He addressed a workers meeting in Gandhi Ashram, Delhi and also a press-conference. We happened to be present there. To the surprise of all he said that they were on the threshold of their independence and that they would soon be free, though many of them did not expect. People there looked askance. One journalist friend asked us whether Pandit Pant really meant that, or it was merely to enthuse people. During the next year in the course of his extensive election speeches Pandit Pant struck the same optimistic note. On becoming the Premier, and speaking in U.P. Assembly on July 31, 1946, he said in a spirit of great optimism that the country was on the threshold of independence in spite of all the trials and tribulations that might be before them. He had absolutely no doubt in his mind that "this great country is going to be free in the fullest sense of term within a few months."

The words had proved prophetic, and really after a short time, on August 15, 1947, India achieved independence.

Pandit Pant had the gift of speech. He was a great speaker. He spoke with admirable lucidly. His speeches which possessed miraculous charm stir the hearts of the people, and had the power of controlling their minds. After hearing his convincing arguments there remained no doubt in the mind of the hearer that his approach was the right one. He had not only ability and lucidity but extensive knowledge of the administrative problems. One of the secrets of his success in public life was his command over the spoken word, his unrivalled mastery of language; clear, compact and dignified. He knew when the heat was more essential than light; emotion more convincing than logic. He pictured the situation very clearly and adjusts it according to the audience and always gave a human touch. His power of inspiration and the quick adaptability were the secrets of his power over crowd. He would come forward singly, and face even the most hostile audience with confidence that he would be able to persuade even his bitterest critics by his sweet reasonableness. His arguments were well marshalled and he handles figures which carry conviction.

He detested making written speeches. He never referred to single notes. In debates he would give complete reply from the profundity of his memory and knowledge. He would always speak in clear, confident and persuasive tone; lucid in expression, calm in presentation. We remember his one exquisite exuberance which captivated the audience. It was poetry in words. In music it was measureless. Shrimati M. S. Subbalakshmi, the noted Indian musician paid a visit to Lucknow in October 1950. A music performance was arranged at his residence before a large, distinguished gathering. After the conclusion of her concert Pandit Pant stood to offer thanks and paid a tribute to Subbalakshmi in the following words:

> "Ladies and gentlemen, I would have myself preferred your leaving this place with an abiding memory of the sweet moments that you and I had the pleasure and the privilege of spending here this evening without any interruption on my part, but I would be failing in my duty if I do not offer most sincere thanks to Sada Shivaji, Shrimati Subbalakshmi and Radha for the exquisite performance they have given us. The memory of it will, I hope, last for the remaining years of the lives of several of us. So far as I am concerned

I will cherish it tenderly and recall the enchanting events of this evening in my moments of leisure and whenever I have to look for inspiration. For us who are enveloped in the dust and smoke of controversy and absorbed in the humdrum affairs of State such moments are rare. I feel as though I have at least for a little while recovered my lost soul. It was not mere music; it was not merely a series of celestial songs; it looked like a perennial fountain pouring forth most delicious nectar in a melodious, noiseless and charming manner with mellowed grace filling the entire space with its fragrance—fragrance which will last for ever and which will sweeten everything by the memory which will be associated with it and which we will cherish for ever. I wish Shri Sada Shivaji, Subbalakshmi and Radha many, many years of equally purposeful and useful life. May they continue to give to the world the best that our art has developed and which it still retains. Lucknow will look forward to their return with hope, with interest and in the expectation that they will not forget us. So far as we are concerned it is impossible for us to forget these unforgettable moments."

Good Parliamentarian

He also proved to be a good parliamentarian. He was elected to the U.P. Legislative Council in 1924. In 1926, he was re-elected to the Council and became the leader of opposition, representing Swaraj Party of the Indian National Congress in the Council.

It is important to remember that between 1919 and 1935, what was called a dyarchical form of government existed in the provinces. According to this scheme, the Governor of the province was assisted by an Executive Council and Council of Ministers. The Executive Council was in charge of the Reserved Subjects and the Council of Ministers of the Transferred Subjects. All important matters relating to administration of the provinces like land revenue, finance, law and order were Reserved Subjects, which were under the control of the Executive Council, consisting of

British officials of the government. The Transferred Subjects were under ministers, most of whom were Indians. They were members of the Provincial Legislature, but they were not responsible to the Legislature. They functioned as ministers at the pleasure of the Governor, who was an Englishman. This system of government did not promote responsible government.

There were also a number of shortcomings in the composition and working of the legislature. The majority in the legislature belonged to the British officials and their supporters, most of whom were elected from communal and class electorates. You know, the British had decided to grant separate electorates on the basis of religion and property qualifications. As a result, landlords, orthodox people, etc. were elected to the Council. The Congress had opposed the principle of separate electorates on the ground that India was one country and divisions on the basis of community, class and religion should not be recognised.

Under the circumstances, the legislatures were not truly representative of the people. The role of the Indian representatives as Swaraj Party members, therefore, became limited. The Indian National Congress under the Non-cooperation programme had boycotted these elections. But, after the withdrawal of the movement in 1922 by Gandhiji, a section of the Congress under the leadership of Motilal Nehru and C.R. Das, decided to fight the election so that they could defeat the representatives of the British government and their programmes in the Legislature. This section of the Congress was called the Swaraj Party. The representatives of the Swaraj Party swept the polls in 1924. That is how Govind Ballabh Pant was elected to U.P. Legislative Council from Kumaon.

The Swaraj Party had decided to enter the Council also with a view to what they called "wrecking the government from within". They knew well that their ideas, views and opinions expressed on the floor of the Legislature will not prevail since the majority in the Legislature lay with the officials and the government. Still they thought by their opposition to the government and their measures from inside the Legislature, they would impress upon them that the British were ruling India against the wishes of Indians. They also wanted to impress the British government and the British Parliament that Indians were capable and extremely well-versed in parliamentary system of government and that they should be granted independence at the earliest.

From the start, Govind Ballabh Pant showed complete command over parliamentary practice and procedure and the government had to face delicate situation whenever he intervened in the debates or spoke on any bill at the Council. He studied the bills and resolutions of the government with care and thoroughness. Through excellent debating skills he was able to put forward the point of view of the Congress and his own with great authority. He also scored many points against the government. The government benches recognised Pant's command over facts and figures and his mastery on financial bills, tenancy laws and other matters relating to administration in general. In addition to his oratorical accomplishments, he proved to be persuasive in his arguments, logical in his reasoning and constructive in his suggestions. His command over English and legal subtleties truly amazed his opponents, both British and Indians alike. Many of them inwardly agreed with his viewpoints, but would not openly support him on the floor of the House as they said so later.

As long as he was in the Legislative Council, he was the most eloquent and effective leader of the opposition. In 1934, he was elected to the Central Legislative Assembly, and in 1935 was elected deputy leader of the Congress Party in the Central Assembly. Both at the central and the provincial legislatures he came out in flying colours as a parliamentarian. He stoutly championed the cause of India, opposed the government policy of dividing Indians on communal lines, exposed the weaknesses of the government's economic policy, which led to exploitation of Indians as a whole and the weaker sections of Indian people in particular.

Champion of Education

Pantji used to take keen interest in education. He was instrumental in the establishment of the Udairaj High School at Kashipur in 1914. When he became a member of the Kashipur Notified Area Committee he was nominated a member of its education committee. When he again became Chairman of the Notified Area *Committee* in June 1921, he got a resolution passed providing for free compulsory primary education.

During his premiership of U.P. he appointed an important committee under the chairmanship of Acharya Narendra Dev, which included not only Congressmen *but* also the Secretary of the Muslim Education Conference, President of the U.P. Muslim League and several prominent educationists, like Dr. Zakir Hussain, Chairman of the Wardha Basic Scheme Committee. The Committee pointed out that education should, as far as possible, be carried on through concrete life situations and should be co-related with one or more forms of manual and productive work and with the social and physical environment of the child. The choice of the craft or crafts should be made with due regard to their educational value and to the environment of the child. The Government accepted the recommendations of the Committee and set about implementing them. Then a strong Universities Committee was appointed in May 1938 under the chairmanship of the Education Minister Sampurnanand. Addressing the first meeting of the Committee Premier Pant said:

> "I personally feel that in our system of education we have perhaps laid greater stress on the formal than on the real, on what we suppose to be the intellect and the brain than on the heart and character. I think what really forms the backbone of society is character, and our system should devote creator attention to the building up of the right type of character."

But before the Government could consider and implement the Committee's recommendations, the Ministry resigned in 1939. During his Chief Ministership (1946-54) Pantji's thoughts again turned to bring about reforms in education. He initiated an innovative reform of the educational system focusing in the first instance on 11-13 age group, deriving its inspiration from Gandhiji's concept of basic education. He constituted a high- powered interdepartmental committee under his chairmanship to monitor the progress of the scheme.

Pandit Pant was very *clear* in his mind about the aims and objects of education which are right ideals of living. While moving a resolution in the Uttar Pradesh Legislative Council on 28 February. 1925, Pantji said:

"Unless and until nationalism is given a proper place, an adequate place, a prominent place, an all-absorbing place in the system of education, the purpose of eduction, which is service of the community through the individual, the attainment of self fulfilment for the country through the actions of the individual, will not be attained, and if that object is not attained then all effort is vain. You may make men better animals, but that is not the object for which humanity exists. If education does not in any way inspire in us a longing for a higher life, a desire to live for our country, a desire to die for our *country*, it is education that has lost its main object. I submit that it is in that sense I am using the word nationalism.

"Then, Sir, education has another aspect about it, and that is the fire, the flame to be free. A self-centred secular system of education makes the people so very cowardly and so very timid. Where self-reliance is lacking in everything, there can be no enterprise and no manly cooperation; these things come out of men who are born with a sense of national dignity, with a sense of national self-respect, with a faith in their national glory and in their future and with reverence for the past; when none of these exists how can you expect that spirit of enterprise, how can you expect that backbone on which alone national life grows? If education has any use it is to create those ideals for which humanity, for which man, should exist, and one of the noblest of those ideals is freedom for the country, the desire to live in a free country. If education in a way leads us to conceal our little life under the shell, to acquire the habit of concealing the truth and not telling that which we feel, how can you expect that education to solve the larger problem which humanity expects from every individual? Education has its object, and that object is the promulgation of right ideals of living. With that object is needed the real, genuine ideal of freedom for the country, the emancipation of the land. Those who have read the history of France must have noticed the nationalism as it existed in that country after the year 1870, that nationalism which does not acquiesce in foreign rule, which burns out of education -I do not say it should lead to a conflagration, but it should lead to a constructive, and selfless effort to be in one's land what others are in theirs: it should lead to the desire to attain one's full stature in one's own country; it should resent every obstacle, everything that is done to put down man from attaining the highest position in the land; it is that which can inflame an Indian to be a Napoleon Bonaparte; it is that which can inflame an Indian to be in his own country what the greatest statesmen have been in theirs; it is that which can make an Indian feel that there is a day when he can be a Gladstone, when he can be a Wellington, when he can be a Lord Reading in his own country. Until and unless you can put education in such a form as to lead *man* to think that the highest is attainable by him you are stifling the essential object of education. It is that what I mean by "nationalism". It is the substratum, it is the basis on which all that is good, all that is desirable grows, has its being and is bred."

Great Social Servant

In Kashipur, while practising law, Govind Ballabh established several societies to promote social reform, literacy and political awakening. One such society, called Prem Sabha, was formed in 1914, for social reforms. In 1916, he was nominated to Notified Area Committee, and later became the Chairman of the Education Society of the Committee. During this period, he pushed through the plan for a free and compulsory elementary education for the children of Kumaon.

In 1916, he moved over to Nainital and established the Kumaon Parishad. The main purpose of the Parishad was to create political awakening against old social customs and injustice to which they were subjected.

One such custom was *coolie-begar,* according to which the villagers were forced to offer free labour to the British officers and other members of the administration like Commissioner, tahsildars, and police personnel, while they went on tour. Each village was expected to provide several labourers to carry the baggage and other touring kits of the officers for which they were paid nothing. This was a feudal practice, which was opposed by Govind Ballabh tooth and nail and he organised a movement against it. In 1921, during the Non-cooperation movement, nearly 15,000 persons assembled at Bageshwar, where he and other leaders asked the people not to offer free labour to the British or any officer of the government. The entire gathering took a solemn vow not to offer *coolie-begar.* In 1923, some villagers from Almora district moved the Allahabad High Court, praying that free *coolie-begar* should be stopped, and they won the case. Yet, the practice continued though some payment was made by officers to the labour. It was Govind Ballabh Pant, who as Chief Minister of Uttar Pradesh, finally stopped the practice by law.

Another problem which the people of Kumaon faced related to the use of wood from forests. Most of the hills provided plenty of wood for construction of houses as well as for fuel. During the period, we must remember, electricity was not available in villages. Even coal supply was limited. It had to be transported from the plains. The entire region was very cold during winter. Wood was used extensively in these areas as fuel for cooking and keeping the house warm. With the coming of the British, most of the forests of Kumaon were declared as reserved forests, so that cutting of wood, grazing of cattle was banned. The people as a consequence suffered. Govind Ballabh prepared an informative document on the "Forest Problems of Kumaon" and advocated that, while protection of the forest areas should be the duty of all concerned, the people of Kumaon should be permitted to collect:

- dry wood and grass from the forest adjoining the boundaries of the villages;
- that there should be no ban on hunting;
- and the government should permit the people to obtain weapons for protection of their crops and their life.

While advocating the above demands Govind Ballabh argued that unless some alternative source of energy for lighting, cooking and for warming homes was found, it was unreasonable to entirely ban the cutting of wood and collection of dry wood from the forest areas. By espousing these causes, he enhanced his reputation as a leader of vision and a man of action, and he became the undisputed leader of the Kumaon people. In 1920, when he fought an election to the U.P. Legislative Council, he was defeated by the rival candidate only by 33 votes, but in 1924, when he sought an election to the same Legislative Council as a Swaraj Party candidate, he was elected by an overwhelming majority, scoring more than 96 per cent of the total votes cast.

Let us not shirk from the path of non-violence, which has worked wonders. Do not forget the splendid awakening and supreme sacrifice which this weapon of non-violence has set before the world.... Have faith in its potency and do not betray any weakness in a moment of anger.

Weaknesses and Failings

If one want to make a picture complete, one must depict weaknesses and failings also. However big one might be there was no one who has no weaknesses. These were human qualities. He could be an exception. He had erred. But the most certain lesson which he learnt from history was to avoid old errors. He thought and pondered; and acted as Federick the Great once asked his generals "what good was their experience if they had not reflected on it." Sometimes what appeared to be his fault became his quality. His faults sprang from an excess of his good qualities.

He was too much disposed to fall back upon patience and delay—too much readiness to put a good thing into cold storage. He was never in a hurry. His indecisiveness till the last was his greatest defect. His reticence was carried too far. By his taciturnity he would permit the other person to go wrong. He would give a long rope to hang himself. There was too much balance and too much adjustment. He was too much cautious. He was likened to an old elephant, slow at times, even irritatingly undecided, but in the end sure. He weigh too much.

He was unpredictable. No one could be sure of his attitude. He could make a change at the last moment. It was difficult to fathom him. One was liable to make mistakes. He tried to do much himself. He wanted to keep everything close in his hands. He loved details. He judged from his own standards. It was very difficult to win his esteem.

His greatest defect, which was so widely known, was his unpunctuality. He was never punctual in his life. When he practised he reached courts late. He often missed trains, and was late for an engagement or meeting. Gandhiji sometimes complained to him about this but he could not be so punctual. Punctuality was never an obsession to him. He did not like to disturb him by this strict regard for punctuality. But, he had the sense of time.

One distinguished journalist of India once wrote about him:

> "One of the most astonishing qualities in the character of a man of that stature is his intolerance of criticism, including press comments, which he rarely forgets (or forgives),"

He would never show his dislike of any one however personally distasteful or irksome may be. He would not give an opportunity to the person to explain what he felt about him or her. He kept that to himself. He was very hard to those who were near him.

He tolerated too much. In the crowded days of his public life he had learnt in the phrase of Burke, "how much of an evil it is necessary to tolerate."

8

Significant Speeches

Imposing a Constitution

[Speech during discussion on a resolution regarding Simon Commission, U.P. Legislative Council Debates, 25 February, 1928]

The history of the growth of self-governing institutions within the British Empire has demonstrated that there is only one way for the solution of constitutional difficulties, and that can be found only in the country for which the Constitution has to be devised and only by those people who are to be affected by that Constitution. This principle had been discovered by actual experience before the sacred doctrine of self-determination was formally proclaimed from the housetops by self-seeking egoists, at an hour of crisis, to save their own *skins*. That is a principle which history has vindicated as being the only sound principle on which a lasting Constitution can be based. Do you not know what happened in the various dominions that are comprised in what is grandiloquently called the British Commonwealth? Sir, in South Africa, certain Constitutions were imposed by British Parliament *in* 1876 and 1877, but they came to naught, because they had not been framed by the citizens of the countries affected. They were thrust on an unwilling people; and what was the sequel? There was a lot of strife and bloodshed and Parliament had to give way. After the Boer War, in 1906, a Constitution was embodied in a statute by Parliament which to the very letter gave effect to the wishes of the people of South Africa. What happened *in* Canada? There too, the British Parliament imposed certain Constitutions at a certain stage which proved equally disastrous. In the end Parliament was forced to adopt the same expedient which it later followed in the case of South Africa, and a Constitution framed by the people of Canada had to be accepted. Only home-made Constitutions put an end to the fierce bitterness, hostility, and misery in these countries and secured peace and progress. Exactly the same thing happened in Ireland. The British people had a scheme of Irish Home Rule before them in 1884. The Parliament framed a certain Act in 1914. They followed it up by another in 1920, but still there was no peace in sight, and it was only when in 1921 the Parliament accepted the Constitution that had been framed by the representatives of Ireland itself that chaos and suffering ceased in Ireland. So, Sir, history has established two or three principles indubitably and they are indisputable. It has been repeatedly proved that unless and until a Constitution framed and formulated by the representatives of the people of the country for which the Constitution is intended is introduced, makeshift contrivances cannot put an end to the struggle for liberty nor can they secure satisfaction or stability. It is equally clear that whenever efforts have been made to superimpose something from without, it has only added to complications and bitterness and has made things worse.

Indian Constitutional Reforms

[Speech an Report of Joint Parliamentary Committee on Indian Constitutional Reforms, Central Legislative Assembly Debates, 7 February, 1935]

Sir, to us in particular the question is of more than academic interest. We, Sir, have concentrated upon this question for several years to the exclusion of everything else, and some at least of my friends here, and many of those outside, have sacrificed their all for the attainment of that object which is supposed to be covered by the Joint Parliamentary Committee's scheme. There are people, Sir, who are thriving under the present order, but for us the prolongation of the struggle means the prolongation of our trials, - and greater austerity in life. We would, human nature being what it is, be prompted by the self-regarding instinct to accept any proposal or scheme that could serve the purpose we have in view. Sir, it is painful to *us* that we have to reject this scheme. We feel that nothing else is possible in the circumstances, and we have to carry on the struggle. We are conscious of our responsibility, as I just observed. Sir, we do not know how far our vote will influence the decision of Government here or of Parliament in England, but we do know that our decision will have repercussions in the remotest hamlets in this country. We are certain that it will influence the course of events and the course of history for some years. Sir, even now, how very painful it is to *us* that our colleagues, our respected leaders like Pandit Jawaharlal Nehra, should be confined in jail while his wife is in the grips of tuberculosis and his old mother is suffering from paralysis! Would we not like to secure for them the healing balm of his presence? Sir, we know *the* continuance of this straggle involves all these sacrifices; but our self-respect, the requirements of the country and the requirements of the world situation today do not leave any other alternative to us.

Constituent Assembly - Advisory Committee

[Speech on the resolution the Aims and Objects, Constituent Assembly Debates, 24 January, 1947]

I hope this Advisory Committee will place before itself the ideals for which humanity has worked. It will try to forge such sanctions and such rights as will enable this Assembly not only to frame a Constitution but to achieve the independence of India. We are here not only for a formal task but for a real one and that has to be fulfilled. Let us hope that this Advisory Committee will bring concord and amity, goodwill and trust, in place of mutual strife, that occupies the political stage today and that as a result of the deliberations of this Committee we will have prepared the ground for Independent India for which we live, for which many have died and for which alone, life is worth living. *(Loud Cheers.)*

Minorities and the Constitution: The question of minorities everywhere looms large in constitutional discussions. Many a Constitution has foundered on this rock. A satisfactory solution of questions pertaining to minorities will ensure the health, vitality and strength of the free State of India that will come into existence as a result of our discussions here. The question of minorities cannot possibly be overrated. It has been used so far for creating strife, distrust and cleavage between the different sections of the Indian nation. Imperialism thrives on such strife. It is interested in fomenting such tendencies. So far, the minorities have been incited and have been influenced in a manner which has hampered the growth of cohesion and unity. But now it is necessary that a new chapter should start and we should all realise our responsibility. Unless the minorities are fully satisfied, we cannot make any progress; we cannot even maintain peace in an undisturbed manner....

Let not the minorities look to any outside power for the protection of their rights. This will never help them. Let not the lesson of history be lost. It is a lesson which should be burnt deep in the hearts and minds of all minorities that they can find their protection only from the people in whose midst they live and it is on the establishment of mutual goodwill, mutual trust, cordiality and amity that the rights and interests not only of the majorities but also of the minorities depend, This lesson of history, I hope, will not be forgotten.

It is not for me to attempt any dissertation on the various aspects of minorities or fundamental rights. I cannot however refrain from referring to a morbid tendency which has gripped this country for the last many years. The individual citizen who is really the backbone of the State, the pivot, the cardinal centre of all social activity, and whose happiness and satisfaction should be the goal of every social mechanism has been lost here in that indiscriminate body known as the community. We have even forgotten that a citizen exists as such. There is the unwholesome, and to some extent a degrading habit of thinking always in terms of communities and *never* in terms of citizens. *(Cheers.)* But it is after all citizens that form communities and the individual as such is essentially the core of all mechanisms and means and devices that are adopted for securing progress and advancement. It is the welfare and happiness of the individual citizen which is the object of every sound administrator and statesman. So let us remember that it is the citizen that must count. It is the citizen that forms the base as well as the summit of the social pyramid and his importance, his dignity and his sanctity, should always be remembered. If you bear this in mind, I think we shall understand and appreciate the importance of the fundamental rights- Because, on the proper appreciation of these rights has depended the progress of humanity. The Atlantic Charter with its Four Freedoms, the Charter of rights of men from the time of Paine and Wells to that of the Declaration made last year represent the noble advance in the history of human race. After all we must remember that the goal and objective of all human activity is a World State in which all citizens would possess the cosmopolitan outlook, would be equal in the eye of the law and would have full and ample opportunity for economic, social and political self-fulfilment.

Separate Electorates

[Constituent Assembly Debates, 27 August, 1947]

I am one of those who feel that the success of democracy is to be measured by the amount of confidence that it generates in different sections of the community. I believe that every citizen in a free State should be treated in such a manner that not only his material wants but also his spiritual sense of self-respect may be fully satisfied. I also believe that the majority community should, while considering these questions, not only try to do justice, but throughout it should be informed and inspired by genuine feelings of regard for the minorities and all its decisions should be actuated by a real sense of understanding and sympathy.

So when I am opposing this motion, it is because I am convinced that it would be suicidal for the minorities themselves if the system of separate electorates were countenanced and upheld now. In fact, we *seem* to forget the great change, as I said, which has come over the political slates of our country. In the olden days, whatever be the name under which our Legislatures functioned, in reality they were no more than advisory bodies. The ultimate power was vested in the British and the British Parliament was the ultimate arbiter of our destiny. So long as the power was vested in the foreigners, I could understand the utility of separate electorates. Then perhaps the representatives of different communities could pose as the full-fledged advocates of their respective communities, and as the decision did not rest with the people of the country they could satisfy themselves with that position. But it is not merely a question of advocacy now. It is a question of having an effective and decisive voice in the affairs and in the deliberations of the Legislatures and the Parliament of this free country. Even if in an advisory capacity one were a very good advocate, he could not be absolutely of any use - whether to his clients or to himself - if the judge whom he had to address did not appreciate his arguments, sentiments or feelings, and there was no possibility of the advocate ever becoming the judge. I want the advocate to have also before him the prospect of becoming a judge.

In the new status that we have now secured every citizen in this country should, in my opinion, be able to rise to the fullest stature *and* always have the opportunity of influencing the decisions effectively. So I believe separate electorates will be suicidal to the minorities and will do them tremendous harm. If they are isolated for ever, they can never convert themselves into a majority and the feeling of frustration will cripple them even from the very beginning.

The minorities, if they are returned by separate electorates, can never have any effective voice. And what has Mr. Jinnah and other leaders of *the* Muslim League Party repeatedly declared? They had separate electorates and separate electorates with weightage and it was their definite pronouncement, after the experience that they had for the last three decades of separate electorate combined with weightage, that it was an illusory safeguard and that it did not secure their rights and their interests.

In spite of separate electorates and weightage which the Muslims and the Hindus enjoyed in the provinces of Bengal, Bihar and the North-West Frontier what have we not been hearing all these days during the last many months? Has the system of separate electorates helped them? Have separate electorates even with weightage been of any real assistance to them in this pitiable predicament? It is really unfortunate that in spite of all this experience there should still be a demand for separate electorates today.

Then again, what do the minorities desire? Do they want to have any share in the Government of the country and in its administration? I tell you, you cannot have a genuine seat in the Cabinet if you segregate yourself from the rest of the community, for the Cabinet acts as a team in a harmonious manner and unless every member of the Cabinet is answerable to a common electorate the Cabinet cannot function in a fruitful manner. Are you prepared to give up your right of representation in the Government? And will you be satisfied with the pitiable position of being no more than advocates - if advocates alone you wish to be? Your advocacy will be treated, if not with scorn and ridicule, in any case with utter disregard and unconcern, which is bound to be the case. Those who are judges are not in any way answerable to your electorate? Your safety lies in making yourselves an integral part of the whole which forms the real genuine State.

Further, what is your ultimate ideal? Do you want a real national secular State, theocratic State? If the latter, then in this Union of India a thous State can be only a Hindu State. Will it be to your interest to isolate yourself in such a manner? Will this State care for those who have no share or voice in the election of the representatives who will have real control of the affairs of the State? Will anything be more dangerous than that? Then you have also to consider, if such a system is introduced, how it will react on you now and hereafter. If you have separate electorates for the minorities, the inevitable result is that the majority becomes isolated from the minorities, and being thus cut off from the minorities it can ride roughshod upon them. So I ask you whether you want the majority to be cut off in such a way that it will not be answerable to anybody belonging to your community and no one in the majority will have to care for your sentiments or for the reactions of his acts on you and your associates? Nothing will be more harmful than that. And don't you see the signs today? Don't you see that upsurge of communal passions even in quarters which had remained uncontaminated in the past?

I have no doubt that from whichever point of view you may look at it, it will be extremely detrimental to your interests if you now clamour for separate electorates. Apart from others things it is an absolute anachronism today. In a free country nobody has ever heard of separate electorates. After all what is the essence of democracy. For the success of democracy one must train himself in the art of self-discipline.

In democracies one should care less for himself and more for others. There cannot be any divided loyalty. All loyalties must exclusively be centred round the State. If in a democracy you create rival loyalties, or if in a democracy you create a system in which any individual or group, instead of suppressing his extravagance, cares nought for larger or other interests, then democracy is doomed.

So, separate electorates are not only dangerous to the State and to society as a whole but they are particularly harmful to the minorities. We all have had enough of this experience, and it is somewhat tragic to find that all that experience should be lost and still people should hug the exploded shibboleths and slogans. In the olden days one could have shouted like that; but now, especially these days, when we are seeing all the orgies of violence before our very eyes, when we are every hour hearing harrowing tales of massacres, of rapine, of plunder, of rape and what not which make everyone of us hang his head in shame, if not hang himself by the neck, I say, does it occur to you that we have paid amply for this abominable cult of separation and we must grow wise?

Democracy, Discipline and Tolerance

[Lok Sabha Debates, 20 August, 1954]

So my submission would be, let us, not only on this occasion but also generally accept that we have a democratic system in this country. Democracy cannot function unless we exercise tolerance and discipline. Without these, no democracy howsoever wise the people be can produce adequate results.

So, let there be tolerance. Tolerance implies the acceptance of views with which one does not agree when the vast majority accepts them. And, discipline in a community requires that the majority decisions should be accepted at least for the time being without any sort of resistance. It is only thus that we can carry on the democratic government in this country in a constitutional way.

Democracy vis-a-vis-Casteism and Communalism

[Rajya Sabha Debates, 14 February, 1958]

Democracy on the one hand and casteism and communalism on the other are incompatible. They cannot go together. Especially when we want to establish a society on a socialistic pattern, it is obvious that there should be complete equality in the social sphere, and so far as possible economic conditions should be so adjusted that every man can stand on his own legs with confidence in himself; with that degree of self-respect which a citizen of a country like India should enjoy and with the readiness to treat everyone else as a brother, as an equal, and as one who is entitled not only to consideration but also to respect. That is the atmosphere which we have to create and it is only thus that we will be able to get rid of these long standing ills from which our country has been suffering.

Leakage of Budget Proposals

[Lok Sabha Debates, 20 March, 1956]

The leakage of the budget proposals is a serious affair. I quite appreciate the interest taken by this House in the subject They are the custodians of the finances of the country, and the Members have to see to it that everything with which the administration is concerned is done in a straight-forward manner, maintaining the highest standards of integrity.

This anxiety shown by the House is wholesome in every way. And we have to admit that Government stand in need of correctives; sometimes, we might slur over things which call for special attention, and we could perhaps miss the opportunity of revising our ways and correcting our errors, if the Members were not vigilant. So, I am in a way thankful to the Hon. Members who have drawn attention to this matter.

But I feel that to some extent there has been unnecessary excitement over certain parts to which the criticisms have been directed. Nobody here denies that there has been a leakage, and everyone of us regrets that such a leakage should have occurred. It is also our desire that we should seek the assistance and the cooperation of the Members in administering the affairs in an efficient and appropriate manner.

Rules of Procedure

[Lok Sabha Debates, 23 April, 1956]

Members' - *includes* 'Minister': I have not much to say. I accept that I do not enjoy the proud privilege of being an equal member with other Hon. Members of this House. I am here by their sufferance. So, I am often grateful to them for their mercy.

But, I do not think that the word 'Member' has been used in Rule 402 in a very strict sense. If you look at other provisions in these Roles, for example, Role 196 which says that after a Resolution has been moved, any Member, may, subject to the rules relating to Resolutions, move an amendment to the Resolution. I do not think that anybody has, so far, contested the right of any Minister, who is a Member of the other House, to move an amendment to any Resolution. We have been doing so and we have been allowed to do so. But, if this word 'Member' were to be interpreted very strictly, then, those of us who are Members of the other House, would not be, in any way, allowed to move any amendment to any Resolution. Similarly, there are other Rules in which the word 'Member' has been used. They have all been interpreted always as including a Minister even if he be not strictly a Member of this House, for purposes specified in those particular Rules, So, I submit that that Rule does not really mean that a Minister cannot move for suspension but he has *to* whisper into another man's ear to make such a motion on his behalf. Anyway, if such be the meaning, then, two of my Hon. friends have already come forward to oblige the House and also to take the obligation on themselves.

In this case, I may also submit that the Business Advisory Committee has really agreed and it is not particularly edifying to see long debates carried on points which have been accepted unanimously by Members of the Business Advisory Committee. And, when they have once extended their indulgence in a matter, then, other Members belonging to the parties to which the Members of the Advisory Committee belong can also be expected to be a little more generous than sometimes they actually happen to be. In fact, I have made this motion just because I wanted to observe more than ordinary caution. If you will be pleased to refer to article 110, a Money Bill or a Financial Bill can only be described as a Bill which contains only provisions dealing with all or any of the following matters. Really the bill contains provisions relating to other matters, but I thought that it provided for some expenditure to be incurred on Zonal Councils and also for certain liabilities to be undertaken by the Central Government with regard to the debts owed by certain Stales and that it would be better to give the Members here the authority, even for having them *in* this matter. I was trying to enlarge their powers more than they seem to possess under the law. If they grudge it, well I, being a Member of the other House, would only ask them to look at things in a more generous way. But what is the whole proposal? It is only this, that this House orders the Bill to go to a Joint Committee, If the other House were to exercise such a power, one would have said that it is an encroachment of the power of this House. Bet when this House is being requested to allow the Members of the other House to join a Joint Committee this House is exercising its powers and it is to its advantage that it should have an option to refer a matter either to a Select Committee consisting of its own Members or a Joint Committee consisting of the Members of this House and also of the other House. Why should it like to restrict its power? Why should it say that it is not empowered or authorised to do so?

Bicameral Legislatures

[Speech while replying to the discussion on the Constitution (Ninth Amendment) Bill, Lok Sabha Debates, 27 April, 1956]

Something has also been said about bicameral legislatures. Some friends here feel that we should have only one chamber in each State and there should be no Upper House. Well, the States are free to make their choice. The essence of democracy lies in giving the maximum freedom to every section that is consistent with the unity, integrity and progress of the country for its own development and for the satisfaction of all its aspirations and sometimes even its vagaries. So, if some people want to have this second chamber, we do not want to come in their way. As Hon. Members are aware, under our Constitution, it is open to the Lok Sabha at any time to propose that the second chamber be abolished. It is also open to the Assembly in the States to suggest the abolition of the second chamber, if it happens to be there, in that particular State. So, even if the Council or the Upper House is established in any State, it is an arrangement which will last only so long as the representatives of the popular House wish to retain it. It is there more or less at their mercy but on my part, I will say that sometimes the Upper House does serve a useful purpose. When legislation has to be examined, it is often desirable that the Bills framed might be examined not only by the House in which they originate, but also in another chamber. Sometimes when you add up the figures, you go on making the same mistake again and again, though the mistake may be almost a patent one. Sometimes you put down 100 plus 10 as 120: you go on adding and checking again and again but you always obtain the figure 120. But, if another man does it, he immediately spots if out and says, it is not 120 but 110. So, it is sometimes useful loo, but all the same, the choice lies with the States concerned.

Parliamentary Rhetoric and Decency

[Lok Sabha Debates, 28 November, 1957]

I listened to the speech of Shri Mukerjee yesterday. I need not say that I was surprised. He used, I think, the expression "rhetorical flourish" in the course of his speech. He flourishes on rhetoric and his speech had hardly much more than that character and that characteristic. But I was really taken aback, some what like a feeling of consternation overwhelming me, as I listened to some of the remarks made by Acharya Kripalani. He is a respected leader. We all have looked to him for guidance and he has been with us for a long time. His presence here is due as much to the support of others as to our own. So, in a way he indirectly also represents us.

So, when he made certain remarks, we were really somewhat confounded. He is an apostle and an exponent of Gandhian philosophy. Would Gandhiji have ever used such words even for the worst of his enemies? We expect from Kripalaniji not only the normal standard of decency but something more. We expect him to set a standard of sublime dignity in this House, When he speaks in a way which is, to say the least, vulgar, one becomes sad. The pathos and the anti-climax are both equally unthinkable, but when they actually occur, then ones faith in human nature is shaken. One's hope and trust that decency will mark the behaviour of decent people whatever be the provocation fades away. So, I was greatly distressed.

Indian Statutory Commission

[Remarks before a motion on the Indian Statutory Commission moved by the Finance Minister, U.P. Legislative Council Debates, 18 September, 1928]

The Assembly is now being coerced to send some of its representatives to this Commission. They stoutly declined to do so, but the Government comes to their aid and says they will nominate members if the Assembly does not elect them. If the wishes of the highest House in this country representing the most enlightened of our leaders are going to be flouted like that, what is the use in carrying on a sham controversy inside the four walls of this House when we know full well that ultimately our verdict is to be disregarded most unceremoniously? If the Government is determined to nominate people even if we throw out the resolution, why should we waste our time over this discussion? So we leave it to them to do what they like.

Besides, I feel that there can be a duel only when we stand on common ground. Our valuation of vital matters and eternal varieties of life, our opinions about moral factors, differ fundamentally. What the Government are after is entirely different from what we can conceive to be the normal rule of life for a normally moral course and under these circumstances we cannot even meet to part. We decline even to stand face to face so far as this particular proceeding goes, for in their activities, regarding this matter in particular, they have demonstrated it in an unmistakable way that they are after purchasing every one among us, they are after compromising our honour, and after reducing us to impotent figure heads and then to press all these matters into service against us in order to demonstrate the weakness of Indian character and Indian courage and Indian intrepidity. The Government's attitude has never been anything if not hypocritical. They bemoan the differences between us and they foment those differences day in and day out. They think that we not being fit for the defence of our country cannot have self-government, and they lake every step for the emasculation of our people. They on the one hand, make a false pretence of respecting public opinion; and, on the other hand, they throw over board those people who show any deference for the recorded wishes of this House and instal in most responsible offices those who have shamelessly swallowed their solemn declarations. In these circumstances it is not worthwhile to waste the time of this House...

There are those in whose scheme of things the central figure is the starving skeleton in the field, and there are those in whose scheme of things there is the pampered fat man on the pedestal to whom everything and everybody must bend and submit Between these two classes there is little chance of agreement There are those who want the people to rise; there are those who want the economic uplift of the masses; there are those, on the other hand, who would only desire to have more of the loaves and fishes, who would care more for high posts and for high salaries than for the service of those for whom these services are meant If there are people who want to whine before the Commission let them have unrestricted scope. If there are people who want to make a demonstration of their petty wranglings before the Commission let them do so- We need not stand in their way. Let those who desire dance to the tune of their masters and have the joy of it. But we, on the other hand, Sir, have only one goal before us, that is, the goal of liberty, of freedom for the country. We feel that in the present circumstances, when all constitutional methods, when everything that savours of constitutional, has been thrown to the winds, has been trampled upon, there can be only one goal, that noble goal, that glorious goal of Independence for this great country. We cannot think of anything else. We have to live and to die for that, and for us these little juggleries in the form of commissions and committees, these little devices in one name or another have little meaning. We must steer clear of them all. We refuse to be deluded, to be misguided, to be misled by these things. We see the vision of the glorious mother installed above all these bickerings, above all these little handicaps, high up in the clouds, and we want to seek that road which will lead to that, road which is not to be found inside the nets of this House, that road which is not to be found inside the machinations of the bureaucratic nets, but which is to be found apart and away from that; that road which, however long it may be, is sure to lead us to our goal. We depend on ourselves to carve our future. We know that nations by themselves are made. We care not for your commissions, we care not for your manipulated, manoeuvred factious intrigues. We are after something better. We know that it is only through self-sacrifice, through self-abnegation, that object can be attained.

No-Confidence Motion

[Speech on a no-confidence motion moved against Raja Jagannath Bakhsh Singh, U.P. Legislative Council Debates, 22 September, 1928]

It is, Sir, painful to me, it is unpalatable to me, it is something which creates sentiments bordering on agony to have to deal with anything vulgar, even if it be for the purpose of exposing the miscreant and getting him convicted before a competent tribunal. Though I stand for decency in manners and decency in morals I would have very much liked to keep out of this affair this day. So far as my honourable colleagues opposite are concerned they can afford to chuckle over the sorry spectacle of the demoralisation of one of us. So far as foreign governments are concerned they feed on the weaknesses of character of the people over whom they desire to dominate. So far as alien rulers are concerned they are interested in our moral degradation. For them there is no solemnity on this occasion - for they are out to profit by it. For us the question is of a very grave character. It is more grave than anybody can imagine.

Sir, we are told that public opinion is a vacillating factor, that it is never rigid. I am prepared *to admit that there is some substance in* this statement. There was a time when His Excellency the Viceroy was prepared to come down from his pedestal and even bend down on his knee asking Mahatma Gandhi to enter into a round-table conference with him. I know there was a time during Mr. Montague's Secretary of Stateship when every person who entered the Council was regarded by Government as its staunch friend. I know there was a time when there was a sincere desire to help the course of what are called Reforms in these provinces and in other parts of the country. I know there was a time when there was apparent enthusiasm for the promotion of Indian interests in every way. But today what change do we notice? We have passed through all these stages of public opinion and its repercussion and reaction in the opinions of my friends opposite. We have passed through all these of public opinion and we find today that they cannot even tolerate the idea of Indians sitting on equal terms with themselves. We have passed through all these reactions *in* English public opinion, and we know that all these were due to the vicissitudes of Indian public opinion. I also know, Sir, that public opinion has changed very often in other countries. There was a time in England when the question of granting Home Rule to Ireland was looked upon as most dangerous, wild and irresponsible heresy. There was a time when Gladstone came in for abuse for having espoused that cause but ultimately England had to make Ireland a Free State. I know the time Sir, when South Africa could not get any sort of internal autonomy; yet they had to grant South Africa dominion status. I know many things about the vicissitudes of public opinion in many countries and in many Parliaments. I have some acquaintance with the history of England. I am prepared to admit that public opinion has been nowhere cast on an iron mould. This is, however, beside the point. We are concerned here with the conduct of an individual. The question is this, whether you can regard a man as decent, reliable dependable and fit to be a trustee of the interests of the public when he has been swayed by personal considerations. The one characteristic feature of all citizens and especially of those who rise to important positions in all democratic bodies is their readiness to subordinate personal interests to the public weal. When a man has demonstrated that he subordinates public weal to his personal interest, is he the right man to be appointed the trustee of the people?

When did the Government care for any moral factors? They have managed to get votes not by honest means, but by various devices. The Government's ways are in keeping with their innate corrupt nature, and this one case is only an illustration of the ways of a foreign government in a foreign country. They know that it is only by demoralising the Indian people, particularly by discrediting the most valuable asset of their character, that they can carry on the administration and prolong their rule. They will carry on these things until Nemesis overtakes them. I appeal to this House to look at the issue dispassionately, to sever it from political juggleries and technical manoeuvres, to keep away from the net which has been cast for them by the astute Chief Secretary in his usual mischievous style. If it is not a mischievous style, at least it is a style which is far from truth. Why should he bring in the question of landlord interests in connection with this motion? I do not think that the landlords will suffer in any way. The Government will not appoint as Minister any person who does not agree to cooperate with the Simon Commission. None of the Nationalist Party will be so mean, so devoid of honour, so unscrupulous as to accept that condition. Fortunately for me nobody suspects the Swarajists of such base design. I can say this much that from these two parties there is no danger to the interests of the landlords, even if the landlords interests are concentrated in that Chair. I ask how will they preserve their position? How will they perpetuate their hold on their constituents? How will they prove their moral worth in the eyes of the people? Are they not the representatives of that order which has been always respected for its fine sense of honour? Are they not the descendants of the ancient aristocracy which was famous for its moral hold in this country? I am one of the admirers of the old aristocracy.

Our aristocrats were men of character. If they once took up a cause they would die for it. So I ask my landlord friends how are they going to consider this question? How are they going to prove their fitness for furthering the interests of the peoples in this country? Is it by handing over their powers to those who do not possess their cherished qualities? Would that lead to the consummation of their desires? Should not the representative of their class be the best of their men? Men belonging to the aristocracy have shed their blood, have lost their lives to keep up their word. I can only ask them to give precedence and priority to their best men, to elect as their representatives those who represent the best in them and not those who will expose them to contempt and ridicule.

Democracy, Constitution and Communism

[Lok Sabha Debates, 20 August, 1959]

I came across an article by Dr. Mukerjee recently published in a magazine—"Pushpanjali" or some thing I do not exactly remember - in which he has stated that while working for socialism no opposition need be allowed to function; and that it would be better to have only those who would subscribe to those views to enter the legislatures and occupy the places within the legislatures, I think I am not summarising wrongly what he has said in that article. Our Constitution, however, is of a different type. It allows all citizens an equal share in the affairs of the State. The noble preamble enshrines the objectives for which we stand, that is, *justice*, equality, liberty, and fraternity along with the dignity of the individual. So, harmony is to be one of the main objectives. We do not want any sort of class conflict in our country. But, all the same, there are special provisions in the Constitution for giving assistance to the backward people and to those who need some special aid, but so far as the law is concerned, so far as the fundamental rights are concerned, they are equally meant for the protection of every citizen, to whichever class he may belong, and whatever be his profession or calling. So, we have to keep that basic principle of democracy and of our own Constitution in view. I am not sure if that quite agrees with the outlook of those who have sworn by communism. I have no quarrel with communism myself. I may not quite agree with it. I am a very humble person—my agreement or disagreement does not matter, but their approach to these problems is different, and they stand essentially for the dictatorship of the proletariat. The communist countries themselves are perhaps getting out of the old groove, but in other places, there is a tendency to follow outmoded policies and principles. *(Interruptions).*

By communist countries, I meant those countries which are showing signs of progress and readiness to negotiate and to find a common ground, so that the differences may be minimised and tension may be relaxed.

I submit that our own guiding principles are there in our Constitution. So, we have to follow them not only here in Parliament at the Centre, but also in the States. We are as much bound by the Constitution as any State or any local body. If we make any departure from it, we would be doing something which would be extremely, I would say, not only undesirable, but also dangerous because we have not only to work for the present, but we happen to be in a position also to influence the future course of events. In the circumstances, we have to take good care before we take this step. So, in this particular case too, we did do our very best to avoid what might possibly be abused in future by those who want to abuse or to make a misuse of the Constitution.

Additional Representation to Zamindars

[Speech during discussion on a resolution seeking additional representation to Zamindars in the Legislative Council, U.P. Legislative Council Debates, 19 December, 1924]

So far as our regard for the zamindars is concerned it is unstinted and unreserved. Their name has always been associated with benevolent, educational and other activities and they have done much for the good of the province. On the other hand we do not want the zamindars to remain away from us; we want them to be part and parcel of ourselves; we want to remove any line of distinction that may have existed so far. They are advanced enough; their nationalistic ideas are as good as those of many others, though, owing to the situation which they occupy the attitude which they have to adopt towards those with whom they have to deal more closely perhaps than many of us may impose certain restraints upon them, but so far as the good of the country is concerned, I should think that they have as large a heart as any of us.... I am concerned with a question and a principle of a more comprehensive character.

What and from whom do the interests of the zamindars differ? Is it from the tenants or is it from the urban class? If they differ from those of the urban class then the representatives of the latter class on the Council are much less in number than those of the rural parts. If it asserted that there is a conflict of interests between zamindars and tenants, then you are setting up a principle which will bring nemesis in its wake and that of a disastrous character.

Why should you encourage a sentiment in the tenants that zamindars are so situated that they want to be safeguarded against them? Why should not the tenants feel that zamindars are one with them and that their interests are identical with them? I have just heard that the progress of the country depends on agriculture. I have just heard that the agricultural interests deserve the greatest consideration. I hope the honourable members on the other side will pardon me for saying that we realise the importance of that statement. We realise the vitality of that subject.

We feel that it is the agricultural interests, it is the agricultural classes, it is the peasantry and the zamindars on whom the future of this province depends. It is because of the realisation of that fact that we do not want to widen the gulf or broaden the differences, if any have been introduced, between the zamindars and tenants by means of special electorates.

After all who are here in larger numbers? Is it the tenants or is it the zamindars or the urban classes? Whom are you going to protect by adding to the numbers? If I had asked for protection for tenants because of the present state of things, it would have been right, because so far as I know there are very few here who can claim to belong to that honourable class. Perhaps there might have been some plausibility about my argument taking the present alone into consideration.

But when I see the zamindars of the province arrayed before us here, and that in such fine order, it does not look very generous on their part to come forward with further claims. Well, times many change, they say. Let us assume for the moment that times will change. What will it come to then? If the interests of the zamindars and tenants are identical, the times can change only in bringing a larger number of tenants. So far as the agricultural interests are concerned, they will be as strongly and is soundly looked after then as they arc today. On the other hand the zamindars profess that their interests do not differ from those of the tenants. Such being the case I submit that their plea for more representation on the Council becomes much weaker. For whom do you seek the protect? For those who are in large numbers here or for those who are practically not represented at all? I accordingly submit that it is because I hold that the tenants and the zamindars should form one body, because I hold that every one who has a vote must be entitled to use it not for any particular individual but for the good of the country, for the promotion of progress, order, liberty and emancipation of the land that I think it is not proper to encourage any sort of differences which may have accidentally crept into the system.

Preventive Detention and Constitution

[Speech during discussion on the Preventive Detention (Continuance) Bill, Lok Sabha Debates, 5 December, 1960]

This Bill, as I said, was first introduced in about 1950, just after the Constitution had come into force. The Bill is intended to deal with such persons as cannot be otherwise produced before courts, and whose detention becomes essential for the protection of the civil liberties of millions of people. It may be an evil, but all criminal laws are, I think, in a way undesirable from the Sarvodaya point of view. Acharya Kripalani expressed that view the other day. He saw the dangers ahead. He also saw, the omens of the coming times, on account of the growing fanaticism connected with languages, with regionalism and other things, of which we see examples even within this House, more frequently now than we even did before. But he wanted us to rely on moral force for all that. I wish we could do that. I wish we could abolish the Penal Code. I wish we could at least carry on a sort of campaign for the removal of social evils, which can perhaps be tackled more effectively through moral means than other things, but we have found it difficult to achieve any results even in that field by purely moral suasion. So, we have to reconcile ourselves to methods that may not be ideal - and man being imperfect, few things can be ideal—but which can yield results that are considered essential for the orderly existence of society and for the progress and development of the country.

Very eulogistic references were made, and quite rightly and appropriately too, to a remark that Sardar Patel had made when the Bill was introduced by him. I wonder if Hon. Members had read the whole of his speech. I would just refer to one or two sentences from what he said. In fact, he began by saying:

The House or at least a majority of the Members of this House were members of the Constituent Assembly are aware of the discussions which we had on article 22. I can say straightway that unfortunately owing to my ill-health I could not be present when the discussions were going on, but I was very apprehensive that certain aspects regarding the security of the State were not properly emphasised before the House at that time, and with all respect to that body, I felt that due weight was not given to those considerations.

When we think of civil liberties of the extremely small number of persons concerned, let the House also think of the liberties of the millions of people, threatened by the activities of individuals whose civil liberties we have curtailed.

Democratic Set up for Delhi

[Lok Sabha Debates, 26 November, 1957]

By denying democratic administration, I do not mean that the people of Delhi are not associated with the Government machinery in any way. It is a fact that representatives of Delhi are there in the Lok Sabha, and they take part in the deliberations of this House which formulates and shapes the policy of the Government But at the same time, we have to take into account that larger sections of the people will have no opportunity to express their views on smaller matters of administration which they generally get in other States. There are so many avenues besides the State Administration. There are village panchayats and there are other regional administrative spheres where the people are represented to voice their grievances. Here they have no such opportunity.

So, it was all the more necessary that we should have followed the recommendations of the States Reorganisation Commission which categorically stated that Delhi being the metropolis should have a Corporation which would have larger powers than those ordinarily enjoyed by other corporations. They also stated in their report that municipal autonomy in the form of a Corporation which will provide greater local autonomy than is the case in some of the important federal capitals is the right and, in fact, the only solution of the problem of Delhi State. Viewed in that aspect I feel that this measure will not satisfy the demands of Delhi. The people will be rather disappointed. They may congratulate the Home Minister because of the voluminous nature of the Bill, and probably because he has taken care to see that the Bill has as many clauses as the number of square miles under the jurisdiction of the Delhi Corporation. But there, it will be seen that so far as the representation of the people or their association with the administration is concerned, there is nothing very much different from what is prevalent in other Corporations.

I do not want to stress this argument that the elected representative's right is being taken away by the introduction of the Commissioner. I think this is a salutary policy and from the experience that we have in the local self-governing bodies, it is proper that the executive functions should be discharged by persons who are permanent officials and who can devote their entire attention to the administrative side of it, although I would have liked some more powers having been given to the Mayor, considering the position and presage that he occupies in this Corporation. But still, I do not want to quarrel on this point because it has been found, especially in Bombay or which model this bill is formulated here, that that system has worked very efficiently.

9

Selected Letters

To Shyam Sunder

Almora,
12 February, 1952

My dear Shyam Sunder,

I managed to find a few minutes to dictate two or three letters to some of the leading workers at Bareilly yesterday at Ranikhet. I am constantly moving from place to place and the programme is sufficiently tight. It leaves little time for any other work. I am, however, somewhat impatient to offer thanks to those to whom thanks are due. Even if I were to omit you for the present I cannot forget your wife, but you would not like to be left out in the cold if I were to single out your better half alone. So I should express my appreciation for the excellent work done by your wife and yourself in the midst of adverse forces and numerous other difficulties with which you were faced at Bareilly. You had many sleepless nights and restless days. I wonder if you had occasion to work equally hard even before. It is difficult to say which of you two had the better of the other. Please convey my grateful thanks to all who contributed towards your success and let your wife help you in this equally heave though pleasant task.

With good wishes for both,

Yours sincerely,
G. B. Pant

II

Minister for Home Affairs,
India, New Delhi,
3 September, 1955

My dear Shyam Sunder,

I have your letters of August 31 and 1st September. I am glad that Savitri will now have the opportunity of serving in a wider field and I am confident that she will acquit herself well. She has always taken a keen interest in public affairs and with your collaboration she will be able to handle even difficult problems with ability and competence. She was chosen for this place because of her merits. I hope you both appreciate the consideration shown by Dr. Sampurnanand and other members of the Board and I am not entitled to any credit for this.

Please accept and convey to her my heartiest congratulations.

Yours sincerely
G. B. Pant

III

New Delhi,
1 Aprl, 1942

My dear Shyam Sunder,

It our work is finished I should be leaving this place tomorrow so as to reach Bareilly on my way to Nainital on Friday morning. If detained I shall arrive a day later. I do not know whether Dwarka Prasad has returned to Bareilly or not. Trust his son is better now. Remember me to local friends there.

Yours sincerely,
G. B. Pant

IV

Nainital,

7 March, 1942

My dear Shyam Sunder,

I was glad to receive yours of 2nd inst. I too share your regret on your inability to join any of the conferences I attended in your division last month. In view of the fresh declaration on India expected early next week. I need not refer to the points raised by you in your letter.

I am particularly concerned about the political prisoners' hunger-strike in District Jail Bareilly. Their condition must be progressively deteriorating and it is giving me cause for concern. I sympathise with their demands. The question of the treatment of C class prisoners, as they are called, has already attracted considerable public attention of prominent leaders and even Mahatma Gandhi have been taking an active interest in the matter. No relief will be available so long as the hunger-strike continues. So no useful purpose will be served by prolonging it. The question is already before the public and they have brought it still more prominently to the forefront by their strike.

So kindly do all you can to persuade them to break their fast. The whole world is in a fluid state today and the political conditions in our own country are bound to change enormously before long. In the circumstances they should not undergo any further hardship and suffering. Hope you will do the needful and succeed. I may pass through Bareilly on 15th March.

Yours sincerely,
G. B. Pant

V

Nainital,
18 April, 1942

My dear Shyam Sunder,

Thanks for your letter received about a fortnight ago. Owing to the abscess in my leg I have not been able to handle the pen with ease and this has interfered with my correspondence. That accounts for this delay in acknowledging four letter. I am better now and hope to befit to move about in about another week. I have been confined to bed since my return from Badaun. I do not think it had any thing to do with my trip to that place. But owing to the chronological sequence such misconception is possible.

I am sorry for the trouble you were unnecessarily put to on 29th. I had sent you,' I think, a note on 28th informing you about my inability to leave for Lucknow. It does not seem to have reached you. Hope this finds you well.

Yours sincerely,

G.B. Pant

VI

Nainital,
25 April, 1942

My dear Shyam Sunder,

I shall be reaching Bareilly on my way to Allahabad tomorrow evening at about. If convenient please meet me at Bhojipura. In every case I hope to see you at the junction.

Yours sincerely,

G. B. Pant

VII

My dear Shyam Sunder,

As you may be aware I have to attend the District Political Conference at Ujhiani on 24th. It must be dreadfully hot and I do not want to spend there more time than may be absolutely necessary. I expect to reach Bareilly city at about 4.30 P.M. The train for Badaun leaves, I think at about 7 P.M. If I could get a car to take me to Badaun or Ujhiani on my arrival at Bareilly I would be saving about three hours. I am reluctant to worry friends in this regard on account of the scarcity of petrol. Dr. Pant and Dwarka Prasad have, I believe, both their cars but unfortunately even best cars cannot run without petrol. You might sec if there is any way out of this difficulty. I have already informed Raghubir Sahai about the likely time of my arrival at Bareilly but with their limited resources Badaun friends cannot be expected to arrange for a car.

Trust this finds you well.

Yours sincerely,

G.B. Pant

VIII

Nainital,
30 July, 1942

My dear Shyam Sander,

I shall be leaving for Bombay via Bareilly and Muttra on 2nd. When I was with you last I was thinking of taking the other route. But this seems more suitable. The train reaches Bareilly at about 9-30 and leaves for Badaun about an hour later.

Trust this finds you all well.

Yours sincerely,
G. B. Pant.

IX

Nainital,
May 1, 1945

My dear Shyam Sunder,

Thanks for your letter of 19th. Govind Sahai may have conveyed to you my message. I regret really that I could not see your wife during my short stay in Bareilly, mainly because you were then out of the station. We arc having splendid weather here now and I should suggest that you both should come up for a change for a few days.

I do not yet know when I shall be able to leave this place for the plains. I have no intention of doing so at least for the present. If I can manage it, I may go to Almora sometime about the end of this month, but not earlier.

I am anxious to know all about the life of Jawaharlalji in the Bareilly Central Prison. Have you any information as to the facilities accorded to him there? How is Narendra Dev? Let me hope that he has had no attack of asthma since his arrival there. It must be getting warm and even hot round about you now. Formerly, on more than one occasion Jawaharlalji was removed to Dehra Dun on the approach of the summer. Bareilly's climate may not agree with Acharya either.

Remember me to all. I trust this finds you both well.

Yours sincerely,
G.B. Pant

X

Nainital

My dear Shyam Sunder,

I regret that in the course of the few hours I have had at Bareilly the other day I could not manage to find a few minutes for a personal talk with you. There was nothing of any special importance to be communicated. I wanted only to offer you my heartfelt sympathy for the series of misfortunes and bereavements you had to face in recent months. I was deeply moved when I got your letter just before my leaving for Lucknow. I had the subject in mind when I saw you but it would have been incongruous to broach it in public; and I had hardly any breathing space or private moments during my short stay. I may have occasion to meet you soon. I shall be going to Lucknow on the 20th but not via Bareilly proper.

Yours sincerely,
G.B. Pant.

To Governor of U.P.

Pandit Pant wrote to the Governor of U.P. on 15th February, 1938 thus:

As Your Excellency has now intimated to me and my colleagues that in compliance with the orders issued to you by the Governor-General under section 126(5) of the Government of India Act, you are bound to reject the advice which we thought it our duty to tender to you in regard to the release of political prisoners, we think that the only course open to us is to tender our resignation, which we hereby do. The issue now raised is of the widest importance both from the constitutional and administrative point of view.

G.B. Pant

To Dr. Rajendra Prasad

Lucknow, August 3, 1948

My dear Rajendra Babu,

Will you kindly refer to your letter dated June 23, 1948, together with a copy of a letter from Maulana Abul Kalam Azad on the position of Urdu in our schemes of educational reorganisation? I enclose a note in regard to the matter from which, I trust, you will see that the allegation that Urdu has been given no place in our educational system and that we are forcing Hindi on the minority community is baseless. Provision has been made for the teaching of Urdu in all types of educational institutions of the Province. At the same time the importance of Hindi has naturally been greatly increased and in this probably lies the explanation of the fact why it is being alleged in certain quarters that Urdu is being driven out of the United Provinces.

2. A copy of the reply to Shri Lari's letter who is not satisfied with the position of Urdu in the new educational syllabuses and has raised the question is also being sent for your perusal.

Yours sincerely,
G.B. Pant

Dr. Rajendra Prasad
Congress President
1 Queen Victoria Road,
New Delhi.

II

Camp: Nainital
August 7, 1948

My dear Rajendra Babu,

I have just learnt from the papers that you have shifted to Pilani for a short rest. Trust you are feeling better.

I am sorry to have to bother you. This is in connection with the letter you sent me on the 26th of June regarding certain complaints about the way money was being collected for the Gandhi National Memorial Fund. The complaint enclosed therewith did not give any particulars about the place where the excesses were said to have been committed. It referred to a report which had been published in the Netaji of 20th June 1948. It took me some time to get a copy of this paper. I was not aware of its existence and do not yet know what circulation it commands.

I have had enquiries made about the alleged compulsion. I enclose herewith the report of the District Magistrate. He has characterised the complaint as quite false and baseless. The paper stated that a villager attacked a Tahsildar with a weapon as the latter was compelling another villager to pay for the Fund. No collections are being made by any official of the district and so no occasion for such treatment could possibly have arisen. Collections are being made only through non-official agencies and the officials, as I have already informed you, are not taking any part in making these collections. The story that a chaprasi was found weeping because Rs. 10 had been deducted from his salary is equally unfounded. Some Civil Court and Colkctorate officials voluntarily agreed to contribute ten days pay in seven instalments. Only they are making this contribution. No pressure was exercised on anyone and those who did not like have not made any contribution whatsoever.

I shall be going back to Lucknow in three or four days. With kind regards.

Yours sincerely,
G.B. Pant

III

Lucknow
March 1, 1948

My dear Rajendra Babu,

I have been reading disquieting news in the papers about your continued indisposition. I am somewhat concerned. You have been continuously unwell for several weeks. Hope you are taking proper care. I shall feel grateful if you will kindly ask Chakradhar to drop a line occasionally to inform me about your progress.

I have to apologise to you for my unavoidable absence from the last meeting of the A.I.C.C. I had every hope of being there on the 19th but suddenly I got a bad boil on my back which did not allow me to move out for several days. I was very sorry to miss the Working Committee and specially the A.I.C.C. which I have been regularly attending for the last many years.

I have just seen in today's papers that you have fixed the personnel of the Provincial Branch of the National Memorial

Committee. I had been informed by friends who had seen you that the list which had been prepared by us here in consultation with the Provincial Congress Committee had been approved by you. I am, however, awaiting formal communication on the subject. The matter is somewhat urgent and calls for immediate action. People have been unable to make their contributions for want of definite directions and during the interval many local schemes have been put forward by stray individuals here and there. Such frittering of energy and resources has to be discouraged. I think it is time that a vigorous drive were launched. The sooner we do so the better.

Hope this finds you well.

Yours sincerely,
G.B. Pant

IV

Camp: Nainital

May 19, 1948

My dear Rajendra Babu,

I write to acknowledge with thanks receipt of your circular D.O. No. 2/20 dated May 4. 1948, regarding collections for the Gandhi National Memorial Fund.

We have in this Province already taken necessary action for the setting up of an internal machinery to look after collections of voluntary contributions from Government servants. This has been done with the concurrence of the Provincial Committee for the Fund. I enclose copies of an appeal issued by me (D.O. No. 2285/111-311(2)/ 48, dated April 7, 1948) and supplementary directions issued by the Chief Secretary (D.O. No. 2285(2)/111-34-2-48 dated April 8, 1948). The matter was also fully discussed at a recent Conference of Administrative Officers and it was decided to make departmental officers responsible for collections from their subordinates. The unit for collections is, in any case, the district and it is felt that this will give greater satisfaction to the people in general, as a substantial portion of the amount collected will be utilised in the district itself. For this reason it is not considered necessary to prepare separate reports of amounts collected from employees of different departments in the various districts. Reports of collections will, of course, be prepared districtwise.

We do not anticipate any difficulty in collecting voluntary donations from Government servants. When for the sake of facility anyone of them prefers to make payments by deductions from his salary, this has also been allowed as a special case. A copy of these orders is also enclosed for your information (G.O. No. A-3241/X dated April 24, 1948. and No. A-3370/X-628-1948 dated May 1, 1948).

We have also, in consultation with the Secretary, Provincial Fund Committee, allowed contributions to be made until January 1949. This has been done to provide all reasonable facilities to Government servants as the Fund will remain open until the first death anniversary of Mahatma Gandhi. A copy of instructions issued regarding this is also enclosed (D.O. No. 2947/111-311(2)/1948 dated May 6, 1948). Departmental orders implementing this decision are being issued in continuation of CO. No. A-3241 / X dated April 24, 1948, referred to in paragraph above.

Departments of Government of India who are making collections from their employees continue to do so as in our circular DO No. 2822/111-311(2)-1948 dated April 26, 1948.

Yours sincerely,
G.B. Pant
Premier, United Provinces

Dr. Rajendra Prasad
President, Indian National Congress
New Delhi.

V

Subject: Mahatma Gandhi Memorial Fund

Dear Rajendra Babu

I write this letter to you about collections for the Mahatma Gandhi Memorial Fund.

You are undoubtedly aware that a Provincial Branch of the Mahatma Gandhi Memorial Fund has already been established at Lucknow. It has a regular office at the Wataqadar Road. Lucknow. Her Excellency the Governor is the President of the Provincial Branch and I am one of the Vice-Presidents.

It is impossible for us to discharge the debt we all owe to Mahatmaji for his services to the nation. But as a token of our affection and deration for him it is incumbent on us to make our due contribution to the Gandhi Memorial Fund which has been started with the object of furthering the ideals which Mahatmaji had set before us. The President of the Congress and the Working Committee have suggested that every individual should contribute at least his ten day's' income to this Fund. On that basis it has been calculated that about Rs. 100 crores would be collected in the whole of India. The quota of our own Province on that basis would come to a minimum of about Rs. 10 crores. You may make your own estimates for the towns in your district and the total for the whole district in consultation with your district committee. In meeting this estimate the factors of population and the contributing capacity of the people will no doubt be taken into account. You will agree that success in collecting the estimated figure can be assured only if approach is made to each individual. Persons engaged in trade, commerce, professions and services as also the kisans have all to be approached. Perhaps the work may be facilitated by enlisting the aid of recognised institutions, social and other, such as unions, associations and clubs.

There is no compulsion but when everyone it expected to contribute at lean 10 days' income, much more is expected from those who can afford to do so. Wherever necessary, payment can be made by instalments.

It is proposed to form a committee for each district forthwith. It is to be commuted initially as follows The District Magistrate of each district will kindly convene the first meeting. If he or the President, District Congress Committee or City Congress Committee, or preferably both, after consultation between them, feel that some other persons should also be invited to the very first meeting, it is open to them to do so. The district committees art empowered to co-opt others, to elect their office-bearers and alto to form executive and local committees. Similarly, it will be desirable to form separate committees for each urban urea in the district.

You should call in a meeting of the Presidents and Secretaries of the District and City or Town Congress Committees, all the members of the Legislature in the district as well as the President of the Development Association, or Chamber of Commerce, if one exists in your district. You may also nominate two or three persons who may be specially helpful. This committee may co-opt other important workers and persons.

The Provincial Committee are sending printed receipt books to District Officers. These an provisional receipt books. It will be essential to record the names and the full addresses of the donors so that when the regular receipts are received from the Central Office, there may be no difficulty in distributing them to the donors. It is important to remember that proper account of the receipt books themselves should be maintained. They should be entrusted only to fully responsible individuals. No person whose integrity is not absolutely above suspicion should be put on in this work. The signatures of persons receiving the receipt books should be obtained on a register in which the number of receipt books issued and other particulars should be recorded. It will be the duty of every person making collections to return the counterfoils of the receipt books along with the sums collected. Persons entrusted with collection work should deposit every week the amounts collected. But for those making collections in distant places, a period of a fortnight may be allowed. The collections made and deposited by them should be checked with the aid of the counterfoils of the receipt books when deposits arc made. The amounts, as they are collected, and the counterfoils of the receipt books thereof should be despatched to the Provincial Office as soon as the amounts are received at the headquarters.

Pending despatch of the amounts collected to the Provincial Office, the moneys should not be kept with you. They should be deposited in a bank and periodically transferred to the Provincial Office by means of cheques. It is essential that all necessary cart is exercised in this matter of collecting, handling and transfer of money's.

I should explain that the amounts collected for the fund will be utilised on those projects of national services and well-being which were specially dear to Mahatmaji. But it would be open to a subscriber to earmark the whole or a portion of his contribution for a specified item of expenditure in which he may be specially interested. The option to earmark the contribution will, however, be subject to the limitation that the Provincial Committee do not think that the Fund should be expended on memorial pillars or costly buildings. This could be explained to the donors in appropriate terms, if necessary.

The Central Committee and the Congress President have stated that endeavours would be made to utilise 75 per cent of the amount collected in a district in that very district This should be explained to the public.

It is hoped that you would not need to incur any expenditure for the purpose of making collections. If any such amount is required, then it may perhaps be possible to collect it separately. But if you haw any difficulty, please send details to the Provincial Committee which will then consider the matter and write to you. But the work should start at once and if any expenditure has to be incurred initially, you may sanction it and inform the Provincial Committee.

The donations should be free and voluntary. The methods adopted for the collection of War Funds should be eschewed. Police dangals and similar shows under official auspices need not be encouraged. Inferior and subordinate staff should not be employed for collecting subscriptions. Amongst officials no agency which might even have any semblance of compulsion should be employed, e.g. policemen and patwaris should not be burdened with this work. It is hoped that trustworthy and energetic non-official workers will be forthcoming in sufficient numbers so that every inhabitant in every pan of the district may receive the message and get the opportunity of making his sacrificial offering to this sacred fund.

It is hardly necessary to emphasise that the time and attention devoted to this work will have been spent on a cause of inestimable value to the nation.

Yours sincerely.
G.B. Pant
Premier, United Provinces

Letters from Prison

Govind Ballabh Pant was lodged in Ahmednagar Fort jail for nearly three years, between 1942 and 1945. He wrote from the prison loving letters to his children, who were quite young and were then studying in schools. Lakshmi, the eldest of Pant's children, was born in July 1928. Krishna Chandra was born in August 1931, and Pushpa in December 1934. In 1942, they were 14 years, 11 years and eight years in age, respectively. The children missed their father. So did Govind Ballabh Pant his children. The only way of communication between them was through letters. As a rule, the children wrote to the father on the 15th and the 30th of every month, and father did so soon after receiving the letters from his children.

These letters are extremely interesting and display great love of the father for them, his deep concern for their education and their health, Govind Ballabh Pant also wanted, through letters, to make them aware of the values which they should learn while in school. He wanted his children to be "healthy, proud, beautiful, clever, gentle, religious and patriotic". He wanted to make them conscious of the greatness of Indian culture, its arts, literature and great contributions that India had made to the world of thought and civilization in general.

At the same time, through his letters, he tried to give some practical guidance as to how to do home work, how to take the examination, how to occupy one's leisure hours and how to spend holidays.

He asked his children to maintain regular habits and balance their time between study and play. Above all, he asked them to maintain cheerfulness in all situations and develop a sense of humour. These qualities, he said, would make them become great in future and also make them friendly with everybody around.

While advising them in respect of examination, he asked his children not to worry too much about the examinations. He gave them confidence by saying:

> "You are sure to get through with credit, and as I have already written, your success in every undertaking is

> assured, if one faces the situation with undisturbed peace of mind and concentrated attention. You possess these qualities and will have their benefit in the present and also in the future". In another letter, he gave practical hints on how to solve the questions at the examination. It is interesting to read them. He wrote: "Do not be perturbed even if you find the question paper hard on your first reading. Nervousness has an upsetting influence. Calm composure is sure guarantee of success. So do not get confused or perplexed in any circumstances. Read the paper with undivided attention more than once, at least twice, before you start writing on your answer book. You need not begin till you have fully and precisely understood the questions. After you have made a careful scrutiny of the questions you will be able to make a rough estimate of the time that should be assigned to each. Divide the time accordingly and go ahead. Write your answers clearly in good, bold and in correct language. If necessary make rough notes before putting down final answers. See that everything is done neatly and no word or line has a shabby look".

He advised them to be active, buoyant and never to be depressed. He wrote:

> "Cultivate cheerfulness and be never downhearted. Nothing is gained by depression or gloom. He who keeps cheerful invariably does his work well and finds pleasure in doing it. His company is sought by others and he wins the esteem and confidence of his comrades. A ready smile is a great asset. Who goes about with a cheerful face introduces joy wherever he enters. Good humour and sound health are close companions, and if one acquires one, the other follows. So keep your spirit high and do good and be good. Bear this in mind when you prepare your programme for your holidays".

Similarly, in another letter, writing during the Christmas time, when normally the hills were covered with snow, he explained how beautiful was nature and how it was good to love nature and the environment. He also asked them to watch birds, recognise trees, flowers, which are grown during different seasons in the year and asked the children to devote some time to gardening. And he said:

> "Even if you have no land for gardens near your house and it is not convenient to do so at a different or distant place, you might, if you so choose, try some flower pots." He described the snowfall imagining the beauty of the lovely sight: "So you had the pleasure of witnessing a snowfall on the 16th. What a lovely sight! Snow flakes drop down gently like delicate petals from a celestial tree in the sky. The surface of the earth is wrapped up in a pure sheet of white. Nothing else is visible for miles round you. Even the trees put on a new garb. One does not feel the cold under the sleek freshness of this glorious feat of Nature....".
>
> Again he asked his children to develop interest in Nature: "Many educated people do not know even the names of the trees and the birds they see every morning and evening! It is not enough to have eyes or ears; one must know how to use them. Otherwise, as the proverb goes, there are those who have eyes but will not see, have ears but will not hear. We have laid out a sort of a flower garden here. Many and varied are the shapes and forms of the flowers. As to their colours one feels amazed by their richness and variety. Nature alone is capable of producing such marvellous crop. It is a fine, exhilarating pastime."

In addition to these friendly exchanges of information between the children and the father, in which father himself informed the children about the garden sin jail, the flower-beds, the birds and the trees he watched in Ahmednagar Fort, he also talked about the books their father read and the books which possibly the children could read. In this connection he suggested Lewis Carroll's book *Alice in the Wonderland*, Jules Verne's *Around the World in Eighty Days*. These books, he said, would be entertaining and would make you take interest in adventures. At the same time, he asked them to read the *Book of Knowledge*, the *Ramayana*, and *Glimpses of World History*, whieh Jawaharlal Nehru had written recently. The book, he explained, was an enlarged edition of Jawaharlal Nehru's *Letters to His Daughter* and was extremely interesting and instructive.

> "It gives a connected history of the world from the dawn of civilization to recent years. And if you will go through it you will be struck by the glorious past of our great country. Learned scholars and best thinkers of modern Europe and America have testified to the unique eminence of ancient India. And this supremacy was not confined to our marvellous acquisition in the domains of philosophy, religion, art, astronomy, literature and other branches of knowledge. Their advance in other directions were equally remarkable.... Our predecessors owned vast fleets and carried on commerce and trade with foreign lands in the East as well as in the West across the seas. They had their colonies not only in neighbouring countries in Asia but also in Pacific Islands. Many works of art, nearly 200 years old, of distinctly Indian origin and character are extant in Central Asia on the one side and in far off islands like the Philippines, Java, Sumatra in South-East Pacific and in comparatively nearer regions like Siam, Indo-China, Malaya, etc. And for nearly 1000 years all these were governed by Indians. The achievements of Sri Vijaya and other similar Hindu kingdoms form part of this history. In your schools you do not get any access to these, our magnificent treasures; but you have to find some means for getting over this deficiency so that you may draw befitting inspiration from the noble heritage which the sages, seers and statements of ancient Indians have left for their descendants. We

> are naturally proud of our past but we should not overlook our present with its numberless shortcomings. In any case, the future rests with us, and still more so with you and others rising and growing up like you; and, I look to it with confidence, certain in the belief that you will succeed in restoring new India to its rightful place of unsurpassed glory and unfailing nobility".

The main object in recapitulating in brief the greatness of India's past was to impress on the children that India was a great country with a rich culture, whereas under the British rule it had become culturally, politically, economically and socially weak and decadent. Similarly, on another occasion, he asked them to master not only the Hindi language but also Sanskrit. He said, "Sanskrit is our priceless heritage and has all our ancient treasures".

While writing about the benefit of exchanging letters he goes into the question of how the art of writing was developed:

> "Has it ever struck you that we would not have been able to exchange any letters between us, had we not been acquainted with this art of writing? It is a marvellous device and we owe a great deal of human progress and civilization to it. But for this method there would have been no record of the experiences, discoveries and achievements of the preceding generation. Only through this medium have the treasures built by innumerable men and women in different lands over thousands of years have been preserved and made available for our benefit".

And finally, he asked them to develop the quality of self-criticism and introspection also. That was the only way to improve oneself in life:

> "Do you feel stronger in body, mind and spirit than you did about this time last year? I am certain that you do, yet, on close scrutiny you may discover that in certain matters you might have achieved more and fared still better. Just recall the events from month to

month to see whether you had done something which you now feel you had better left undone, or whether you had at any time failed to do what you now think you ought to have attempted. We learn only by our mistakes even when we happen to do some wrong, by some such method. Only through self-examination and self-criticism can one avoid the pitfalls and keep to the right track. One may do just the proper thing in 99 cases out of 100, but unless he detects his error in the hundredth he will continue repeating it. And unless he applies his mind to examine his conduct he will not know where he had been found wanting.... I should also like you to recall all important things and events of the year. What was the best achievement of yours in the course of the year of which you are proud?"

10

Golden Words of Pantji

- Our citizenship is not related to political or other reasons. One can enjoy the rights only as citizen of India and all other divisions must be viewed in that light. They should not in any way impair that basic sense of citizenship.
- There should be some order, some arrangement, and we have to see that the best results are attained to enable us to do more and yet more with every passing day.
- We have to guard against disruptive tendencies, against linguistic fanaticism, against parochialism and other tendencies, which occasionally manifest themselves.
- In the formation of new States, language was an important factor to be kept in view. There were other considerations also which ought not to be overlooked and which deserved, a very correct appreciation and appraisement.
- We want to settle all problems and the more difficult they are the greater the challenge, and we are prepared to take any challenge with which we may be faced.
- We have to guard against fissiparous tendencies, against disruptive forces that are still at work.
- We realise the importance of maintaining the great prestige and reputation of our country..

- Let us join hands so that the different forms of culture that we see in our country complement and supplement each other and continue to give strength to this great composite, basic, fundamental product which is the characteristic of India and which gives a special mark to an Indian wherever he goes outside this country, in any part of the globe.
- Great countries and great people are not frightened by dangers. They have to face problems, to apply their minds in a positive way, to solve the problems in a dignified manner, to see them through and not run away from them.
- Linguism or linguistic fanaticism is a mischievous thing and we should steer clear of these linguistic rocks if we are to build a sound, integrated and united country.

11

Great Life at a Glance

1887, Aug. 30: Govind Ballabh Pant was born on August 30, 1887 in Shyahi Devi hills in Almora.

1897: After passing the High School examination, he was married to Chandramukhi Devi.

1914: Pant began his active movement against the British Raj, when he helped a local parishad, or village council, in its successful challenge to a law requiring locals to provide free transportation of the luggage of travelling British officials.

1921, Dec.: Pandit Govind Ballabh Pant tried to deal with the forest problems of Kumaon.

1923: Kumaon was then a part of United Provinces. In 1923, the first elections to the legislative assembly of U.P. were held. Govind Ballabh Pant was elected from Nainital.

1928, Nov. 29: While leading anti-Simon demonstration at Lucknow, Jawaharlal Nehru and Govind Ballabh Pant were beaten by the police.

1931: His son K.C. Pant was born. He was educated at St. Joseph's College, Nainital. Later, he did his M.Sc. from the University of Lucknow, and then joined politics and became a member of the Indian National Congress party.

1937, Jul.: In the United Provinces, the Congress Ministry under Govind Ballabh Pant assumed power.

1947: Birla Vidya Mandir, Nainital formally came into being. This School was the dream child of Pt. Govind Ballabh Pant. At the wake of the independence he was keen to have a public school for the new generation.

— Pt. Pant took charge as the Head of the Government in U.P.

1954, Dec. 27: Pt. Nehru called him to Delhi, the capital and seat of Central Government, to make him Home Minister of India.

1960, Nov. 17: Govind Ballabh Pant University of Agriculture and Technology was established with an aim to reach the remotest of the remote areas and to cater to the needs of Tarai region by the Government of India.

1961, Mar 7: His health had started deteriorating and he died after spending several days in coma.

Bibliography

Anil Chaturvedi: *Govind Ballabh Pant, Politician in India,* Calcutta, 2004.

B. R. Nanda: *Selected Works of Govind Ballabh Pant,* Oxford University Press, New York, 1998.

Bakshi, S. R.: *Indian Freedom Fighters: Struggle for Independence,* Hardcover, 2002.

Banerjee, S.N.: *A Nation in Makiing,* Calcutta, 1964.

Beasant, Annie: *How India Wrought for Freedom,* Madras, 1915.

Bhagwan Singh, M.C. Shah: *Pandit Govind Ballabh Pant: The Collosus Speaks,* New Delhi, 1987.

Bhagwan, V.: *Indian Freedom Movement and Constitutional Acts,* Atma Ram, 1999.

Bhattacharya, B. K.: *India's Freedom Movement: Legacy of Bipin Chandra Pal,* Deep and Deep, New Delhi, 2007.

Bose, N.S.: *India National Movement,* Calcutta, 1982.

Chakravarty, Shachi: *Quit India Movement: A Study,* New Century Publication, 2002.

Chandra, Bipan: *India's Struggle For Independence,* Penguin Books India (P) Ltd., New Delhi, 1989.

Chandra, Shailesh: *90 Years of India's Struggle for Independence: 1857-1947,* Alfa Pub, 2008.

Ganjoo, S.: *Muslim Freedom Fighters of India,* Anmol Publication, New Delhi, 2002.

Gaur, V.K.: *Pandit Govind Ballabh Pant Memorial Lecture VIII,* Almora, 1998.

Ghosh, Ratna: *Netaji Subhas Chandra Bose and Indian Freedom Struggle,* Deep and Deep, 2006.

Goyal, P. K.: *Battle of India's Freedom Movement,* Vista International, 2005.

Gupta, Shantinath: *Great Freedom Fighters of India,* Anmol, 2006.

Hari Hara Das: *The History of Freedom Movement in India (1857-1947),* National, 1998.

Indu Dave: *Indian Personality in Its Developmental Background,* Himanshu, 1991.

Iyengar, A. S.: *Role of Press and Indian Freedom Struggle: All through the Gandhian Era,* APH, 2001.

Joshi, S.K.: *Pandit Govind Ballabh Pant Memorial Lecture VI,* Almora, 1996.

Kailash Khanna: *History of Indian Freedom Struggle,* Commonwealth Publication, 2004.

Kaushik, A. S.: *Great Freedom Fighters of India,* Indian Publication, 2007.

Khairul Anam, Md.: *Indian Freedom Movement and Murshidabad District 1905-1947,* Bagchi, K. P., 2008.

Khoshoo, T.N.: *Pandit Govind Ballabh Pant Memorial Lecture,* Plant diversity in the Himalaya, Almora, 1992.

Krishan Mohan: *Encyclopaedic History of Indian Freedom Movement,* Book Enclave, 1999.

Kumar, Prafulla Pattanaik: *The First Indian War of Independence: Freedom Movement in Orissa,* APH, 2005.

Kumar, Raj: *Essays on Indian Freedom Movement,* History and Culture Series, Discovery, 2003.

Kumar, Ravindra: *Champaran to Quit India Movement,* Mittal, 2002.

Kumar, Sirisa Shadangi: *The Prisons of South Orissa and the Freedom Fighters in Incarceration*, Punthi Pustak, 2005.

Lion Agrawal, M. G.: *Freedom Fighters of India*, Isha Books, 2008.

M. Chalapathi Rau: *Pandit Govind Ballabh Pant: His Life and Times*, 1981.

Majumdar, R. C.: *History of the Freedom Movement in India*, Firma KLM, 1997.

Malhotra, Sumiti: *Thoughts of Great Personalities in 20 Century*, Raj Publishing, 2003.

Manju Verma: *The Role of Women in the Freedom Movement in Punjab (1919-1947)*, Abhijeet, 2003.

Maulana Syed Mohammad Mian: *The Prisoners of Malta (Asira'n-E-Malta): The Heart-Rending Tale of Muslim Freedom Fighters in British Period*, Manak, 2005.

Mazhar Kibriya: *Gandhi and Indian Freedom Struggle*, APH, 1999.

Mohan Ram, H.Y.: *Pandit Govind Ballabh Pant Memorial LectureIX*: Plant resources of the Indian Himalayan region, Almora, 2000.

Muthaiah, S.: *Women Freedom Fighters*, The Hindu, 2004.

Nanda, S. P.: *Freedom Movement and Constitutional Development in India*, Dominant, 2004.

Om Prakash: *Encyclopaedic History of Indian Freedom Movement*, Anmol, 2003.

Omesh Saigal: *Shaheed Bhagat Singh: Unique Martyr in Freedom Movement*, Gyan Publication, 2002.

Parashar, Parmanand: *Kashmir and the Freedom Movement*, Sarup, 2004.

Pradhan, K. B.: *Freedom Movement in India*, Arise Pub, 2007.

Qasim, S.Z.: *Pandit Govind Ballabh Pant Memorial Ledture*, Almora, 1995.

Rafiya, Nisar: *Shaikh-Ul-Hind Maulana Mahmud Hasan and Indian Freedom Movement*, Manak Pub, 2008.

Ram Sharma, S.: *Education of Women and Freedom Movement*, Discovery, 1996.

Ram, S. and Kumar, R.: *Quit India Movement: 1942-1945*, Commonwealth Pub, 2008.

Ramanathan, K. V.: *The Satyamurti Letters, Vol. II: The Indian Freedom Struggle Through the Eyes of a Parliamentarian*, Dorling Kindersley for Pearson Longman an Imprint of Pearson Education, 2008.

Ramu, P. S.: *Azad Hind Fauj (I.N.A.) and The Freedom Movement*, Freedom Movement Memorial Comm, 1998.

Rastogi, Mahendra Kumar: *Political biography of Govind Ballabh Pant*, Gyanodaya Prakashan, Nainital, 1987.

Rupa Kumar, K. K.: *Climate Change in India: Observations and Model Projections. In Climate Change and India: Issues, Concerns and Opportunities*, Tata McGraw-Hill Publishing Company Limited, New Delhi, 2002.

Sharma, S. K.: *Eminent Indian Freedom Fighters*, Anmol Publication, New Delhi, 2004.

Sundaram, V.: *Great Crusader for Women's Emancipation*, News Today, 2005.

Sundararaja, Saroja: *March to Freedom in Madras Presidency, 1916-1947*, Lalitha Publication, Chennai, 1989.

Taneja, Anup: *Gandhi, Women and the National Movement, 1920-47*, Har-Anand Publications, Delhi, 2005.

Valdiya, K.S.: *Pandit Govind Ballabh Pant Memorial Lecture: VII*, Almora, 1997.

Index